RUNNING
HOT & COLD

RUNNING
HOT & COLD
WHERE WILL YOUR JOURNEY TAKE YOU?

DOUG RICHARDS

First published by Pitch Publishing, 2016

Pitch Publishing
A2 Yeoman Gate
Yeoman Way
Worthing
Sussex
BN13 3QZ

www.pitchpublishing.co.uk

The quotation at the beginning of Chapter 16 is taken from 'Born Free' by Joy Adamson and is used by kind permission of Pan MacMillan: Copyright © Joy Adamson, 2000

Every effort has been made to trace the copyright, any oversight will be rectified in future editions at the earliest opportunity by the publisher.

A CIP catalogue record is available for this book from the British Library.

ISBN 978-1-78531-129-1

Typesetting and origination by Pitch Publishing
Printed by Bell & Bain, Glasgow, Scotland

Contents

1

The first step
is the hardest

THE noise from behind was deafening as I scrambled down the steep, rocky slope of the ravine, fighting for breath and praying I wouldn't stumble. Even above the trumpeting and the roaring, my heightened hearing could pick out the cracking sounds as tree branches were torn off and bushes were trampled beneath the feet of the enraged elephants. They were getting closer.

And then I was down, my foot sliding off the side of a rock, tipping me on to my left side. As I hurriedly regained my feet, I looked backwards for the first time since we had spotted the elephants coming towards us. Wide, flared ears, the trunk curling upwards with white tusks waving wildly: the lead elephant was now less than 20 yards behind. Adrenaline drove me on. I knew we were running for our lives, and, at that moment, I heard the rifle shot.

Until then it had been a routine bush walk in the African savannah, learning tracking techniques from our lead ranger, Sander. There were nine of us, all marathon runners in Africa for a race, walking in single file with Sander at the front, and Marco, his colleague, bringing up the rear. We had found signs of recent elephant activity in the area, but had failed to spot any from a rocky vantage point known locally as 'The Lookout'.

With time pressing we had decided to return to our lodge and began to climb out of the wooded ravine. I was immediately behind Sander when we spotted the elephants coming out of the trees ahead of us. We were immediately signalled to descend rapidly into the ravine as the elephants, six in total, lumbered towards us with obvious aggressive intent. This meant of course that I was now at the rear of our group, with only Sander behind me, and, being the oldest member by some distance, I was perhaps a little less fleet-footed than the others.

Now a golden rule of bush-walking is that you should never run away from an aggressive animal as this will only encourage the chase, and they will surely catch you. Sander stood his ground as best he could, urging the rest of us to descend, the steepness of the slope being in our favour as this terrain was more difficult for elephants to run on. Shouting and waving his arms, he tried his best to persuade the matriarch elephant to call off her pursuit but to no avail. When I stumbled, the gap between us and the stampeding elephants was closing rapidly, so it was Sander who fired the warning shot from his rifle into the air. Unfortunately, it served only to increase the rage and the volume of the bellowing behind.

A second warning shot rang out – and this time the elephants hesitated. We didn't but breathlessly continued our escape to the foot of the ravine and then to climb up the other side to a track from where we would all be rescued by jeep.

Had we not been a group of fit and fairly athletic marathon runners, would the outcome have been the same? Quite probably not. As we waited to be picked up, my heart still pounding in my chest, I said a little prayer of gratitude that all those years ago I had taken the decision to start on my running journey, although at the time I had no inkling of the fantastic journey I was about to embark on.

✻   ✻   ✻   ✻   ✻

Some people are born to run; not me.

The eldest of three siblings, followed by a sister, Lin, and brother, Dave, I was born in Brighton, Sussex about three years after the war ended. My father had served on a minesweeper and had survived being torpedoed, but had now returned to his true vocation as a steward on the Pullman car train, the 'Brighton Belle'. Mum was the traditional stay-at-home housewife of that era; we never had much money in the family but, as children, we also never really went without.

Although I was apparently quite a chubby baby, a three-month hospital stay with tuberculosis, which included my fourth birthday, left me rather skinny for the rest of my childhood and indeed for much of my adult life. In fact my lack of physicality led to a nickname that persisted through my secondary school years – Douggie Dust.

I went to a grammar school in Brighton where the aggressive style of PE teaching would not be tolerated in today's world. I remember being punched in the stomach for having a grass stain on my white plimsolls and being thrown into the deep end of a swimming pool to see if I could swim. I couldn't, and had to be fished out from the bottom, an experience that has left me with a fear of water near my airways, and as a lifelong non-swimmer. Being a fairly timid child this was not good for my self-confidence and PE became a subject to avoid wherever possible.

This didn't mean I didn't enjoy sport. I was an avid football and cricket fan, and would spend hours every week in the local park with my brother Dave who, although nearly six years junior to me, eventually played both sports at a higher level than I could ever manage.

At school, our outdoor sports year was split into three seasons: the football season, the cricket season and the athletics season. The first two I really enjoyed, although I always ended up in the matches for those who simply weren't good enough to represent their house at any level. At athletics I was a disaster.

Every year we were presented with A, B and C standards appropriate for our age for a variety of running, throwing and jumping events. I was one of a select group of pupils who never achieved even a single C standard in their whole school career, although it wasn't for the lack of trying. I was just not very good.

And then there were the runs during the winter PE lessons. The teachers would show us a route of two or three miles through the streets of Brighton, and then send us on our way. What they didn't know was that a small group of us (I wasn't the only one) would wait until we were out of sight of the school and then hop on a bus that covered most of the route. The bus conductors knew what we were up to and would helpfully turn a blind eye to our presence. We would then hop off a few stops later and hide behind trees until the lead runners went past, leave it a few minutes, and then run breathlessly back into school.

There was one school running ordeal that was almost impossible to avoid: the annual cross-country race on the Sussex Downs. It was compulsory for all pupils and this time there was no helpful bus service. Resourceful to the end, I found the only way out!

From the age of 13, I had joined the army section of the school's combined cadet force – again, this was compulsory rather than voluntary. Once I had completed my basic training, which was largely marching and rifle drill and learning to fire a .22 rifle, I could then specialise and I chose to join the signals section for one reason and one reason only. Members of the signals section were excused from the annual cross-country race as they were needed to provide communication out on the course in case any of the runners got into difficulties.

On the academic front, progress was as erratic as my sporting achievements. A career in science was always my goal with chemistry topping my list of favourite subjects. I would spend hours mischievously collaborating with my brother experimenting with a home chemistry set, often to the despair of my parents as foul smells permeated the house. Attempts to launch a mini-rocket housing a snail and to design an underwater chamber capable of sustaining insect life both ended in predictable failure.

At school I opted for A levels in maths, physics and chemistry with a longer-term aim of a university degree in applied chemistry. However, during the first term of my A Level studies I was rushed into hospital with acute appendicitis which in those days meant a ten-day hospital stay, and then several more weeks of recuperation at home.

Looking back at that time now, although I missed several weeks of crucial foundation studies in all of my A level subjects, I still had time on a two-year course to 'catch-up' if I really put my mind to it. I obviously didn't put my mind to it.

Although a very attainable offer for a place at Leeds University should easily have been within my reach, my A level results were an unmitigated disaster and it was time for a major rethink. I couldn't expect my parents to continue to support me on their modest income so, in the end, the plan was to find a full-time laboratory-based job for a year to gain some experience and earn some money, and then to attend evening classes to retake my A levels and have another go at getting to university.

On my very first visit to what was then called the labour exchange, I was offered a job in a hospital laboratory in Brighton. Not ideal – biology more than chemistry, and biology was my least favourite science subject and not one of my A levels. The money wasn't great either – certainly below the £10 per week my dad suggested should be the minimum I should consider. On the other hand it would give me valuable laboratory experience, and it would only be for a year while I retook my A levels. I took the job and, with that single decision, my whole life changed.

By the time I'd completed my first month's work, and collected the princely sum of £32 for my efforts, I knew I was in a job I would learn to love. I was still getting the buzz that being in a laboratory gave me but now, instead of producing nasty smells at home, I was doing something really valuable within the NHS and feeling a useful member of society. Suddenly three years at university was a less attractive option. I now had an opportunity to embark on a series of day-release professional examinations, and earn a salary at the same time.

To cut a long story short, my one-year temporary job at the hospital eventually became a career that occupied the next 21 years of my life. After completing all of my professional qualifications, I began to develop an interest in medical research, combining this with my routine health service commitments and, several years later, I was awarded a D. Phil. degree by the University of Sussex. From fluffing my A levels, and blowing my chances of going to university as an undergraduate, I had taken an unusual but nevertheless rewarding pathway to becoming Dr Doug Richards.

During the course of that journey, I had met and married Gill, who had joined our laboratory as a junior technician, and we were blessed with first a daughter, Angela, and then two and a half years later, a son, Chris. Sadly both Gill and I had lost our fathers to cancer in the earlier years of our marriage, but my mother proudly saw me through to the completion of my doctorate before she too succumbed to cancer a few years later.

* * * * *

However, I digress. This is a tale of running adventure, so how did my sporting aptitude advance from the evasive practices of my school days through to early adulthood, and eventually fatherhood?

There had always been an element of endurance in my make-up, just as long as it didn't involve moving at anything faster than walking pace. I enjoyed my time as an army cadet and the annual camps in Norfolk, Dartmoor and the Lake District, as the activities were invariably carried out in military boots and with weight on your back. Nobody expected anything more than a brisk march under those conditions.

As a young teenager I had dreamed of walking from London to Brighton but my parents wouldn't let me, arguing quite reasonably that there was a perfectly adequate train service. But I eventually broke free, dragging younger brother Dave the 80-odd miles from Southampton to Brighton in just three days. He has never quite got over the hike up Portsdown Hill above Portsmouth in blazing sunshine, singing 'Hey Jude' at the tops of our voices, and with only concentrated orange squash to slake our thirsts.

This adventure eventually sparked Dave and I into an annual camping trip around the UK during the summer holidays and, as by now I was the proud owner of a driving licence, the hiking boots that had dragged us along the south coast were now replaced by a car. We would engage in the occasional hike during these trips, but now the measure of enjoyment had become how much ale consumption we could record in the beer book!

Time passed, we both got married within a year of each other, and soon enough our families began to grow, and young children don't leave a lot of time for recreation, particularly as I was also doing a lot of on-call duties through the night at the hospital in addition to the day job. I wasn't entirely physically inactive once I started work. I joined a fledgling Brighton Hospitals football team that had just signed up to the local Sunday league and quite enjoyed the training sessions. However, I rarely got into the team on matchdays, largely due to the fact that I was pretty useless at football. I simply didn't possess enough skill to compensate for my lack of physicality and even a brief flirtation with weight-training had little impact on this.

There was a bit more success when I joined the well-established Brighton Hospitals cricket team. At the time they just played a series of friendly games and although I was never considered to be a first-choice batsman or bowler, I was once commended for my 'agility and anticipation' in the field.

There were two highlights of my cricketing career. The first was when I was involved in a century partnership, although my personal contribution was less than 20, and my partner at the other end was a recently-appointed doctor who happened to be a Cambridge Blue at cricket. My second high spot was taking a slip catch to win a match on the last ball of the game.

I knew very little about the catch but the ball hit me squarely in the chest, knocking me off my feet backwards. As I clutched at my ribs in pain, I was as surprised as anybody to feel the ball within my fingers. What made the victory even sweeter was that brother Dave was on the opposition.

While I enjoyed my cricket, the highlight of any game for me was always the visit to the pub afterwards which would often last longer than the match itself. Eventually, the club joined a local league and the cricket became rather more competitive: so competitive in fact that people actually became annoyed with you when you dropped a catch rather than falling about laughing. My cricketing limitations were now much more apparent, and another sporting avenue gradually faded for me.

And then along came badminton. This time it was my brother-in-law, Mike, who was the regular opposition and a couple of times a month we would head off to the local sports centre for an epic hour of combat. We weren't bad, although probably not up to club standard; the important thing was that we were very evenly matched and so the games were tight and competitive every week. After our exertions, we would adjourn for a post-match discussion in the sports centre bar – do you see a theme developing here?

Then, in early July 1981, a not uncommon and apparently insignificant incident was to change my sporting life forever. An evening television viewing session was suddenly interrupted by shrieks of panic from upstairs. It was another nightmare! I raced up the single flight of 13 stairs to pacify my four-year-old son, Chris. As I tried to calm him with words of reassurance, I was acutely aware that I was having a real struggle to force them out. Just 13 stairs, and a 33-year-old was out of breath! As Chris began to settle, I resolved there and then that this couldn't continue. I must get fitter. I needed to be fitter, not only for my own good, but also for the sake of my young family.

Already lodged in the back of my mind was the method I would use to effect this transformation. It just needed a trigger to bring it to the front, and Chris's nightmare was that very trigger. I was going to become a runner; not a medal-winning, tape-breasting athlete, but one of a new breed of runner who couldn't go particularly fast but who could just keep going and going and going.

Just three months earlier I had sat glued to the television as Dick Beardsley and Inge Simonsen crossed the finish line of the very first London Marathon, hand-in-hand. It was not so much this tremendous achievement that grabbed my attention, but the 6,000 or so brave souls who followed in their wake. All ages, all sizes, all shapes: these people were actually completing a marathon.

Until what was then being described as the 'running boom', the only people I was aware of who ran marathons were heroic figures on black-and-white newsreels who staggered and crawled across Olympic finish lines. Now, it seemed, anybody could run a marathon with some dedication and hard work, and, with my fascination for long distance and endurance events, I felt myself being drawn in.

I didn't hang around. I was a man of action, sort of. I went out and bought a book called *Challenge of the Marathon* and, over the course of the next few weeks, I read it from cover to cover, over and over again. I read every running-related magazine article I could get my hands on, diligently drew up training schedules, planned a new dietary regime and visualised myself crossing the finishing line, but I got no fitter. The one thing I didn't actually get round to doing was to start running. Eventually it dawned on me that sooner or later I was going to have to bite the bullet and take that first step. It just needed a spark to set the process in motion and now Chris's nightmare had provided exactly that.

I woke at 7am the following day, informed my disbelieving wife what I planned to do, donned an old T-shirt and some baggy shorts, put on my gym shoes that I used for badminton, and headed over the doorstep as quickly as I could before there was any chance of a change of heart. The route I'd chosen for my first run was around the block and it was one mile long, give or take a few yards. I'd checked the distance several times by driving the route in my car, and I'd also resorted to my cadet training by using a map and a piece of string to make sure; there was no satellite navigation in those days.

The front door slammed behind me and I was away. The first 300 yards were steadily uphill and, before I was halfway to the top, I desperately wanted to turn round and go home. My lungs were burning and gasping for air, my legs were like jelly and no longer obeying instructions and the urge to be sick was overwhelming. Quite how those legs made it to the brow of the hill I'll never know, but make it they did, and as the saying goes, it was all downhill from there.

The remainder of the run passed slowly but without incident, save for the early-morning birdsong being interrupted by the rasping, staccato bursts of my breathing. When I finally reached the haven of my front door, some ten minutes or so later, I fumbled for my front door key in my pocket but even my fingers had stopped working. I can honestly say that I didn't enjoy one second of that first run but, once it was over, there was just the hint of a warm glow of satisfaction within. I had run every step of the way and soon I was back in my bed, still gasping, retching and aching but a tiny bit proud of myself. My journey had begun.

2

From progress to catastrophe

I HAD a theory in those very early days of running which, to be honest, doesn't seem to apply these days now that I am over 30 years older. Quite simply, I found that it took the same degree of effort to double the length of a run, whether it was from one to two miles, or from eight to sixteen miles. How I wish my body still obeyed that principle these days.

My initial mile-long run soon became two, and then four, and, by the end of September, I was able to run five miles non-stop. I was joined on a couple of occasions by my badminton partner, Mike, but running turned out not to be his forté. A more resilient partner was to be my sister's husband, Bob, although he lived too far away to become a regular training partner. However we did eventually run many races together during those early days although, not for the first time in my life, I was the slower partner.

After a good September, I had an awful October. Anyone with young children will know that they bring home a host of bugs from school and nursery and I constantly seemed to be fighting these off. Maybe the sudden increase in my physical activity was just a little too much for my immune system to cope with. I also had repeated ankle problems but this was rectified by treating myself to my first pair of proper running shoes. I just couldn't believe the difference they made.

The mileage picked up again in November, stuttered again through the Christmas-dominated month of December, and struggled to re-ignite during a snowy and icy January. But I was on a mission – I had already entered my first marathon at the end of February.

Looking back now it was madness and I just would never entertain such a poor preparation these days but my desire to put a marathon on my CV overtook any logical decision-making. If there was a redeeming factor, it was that this was not a road marathon, but a trail race around the rolling hills and valleys of the Sussex Downs. If anything, this made it a much tougher proposition but, at the same time, nobody expected you to run it all, particularly during the winter months.

With nothing longer than a single 12-mile run in the training bank, I set off with brother-in-law Bob on an icy Saturday morning to Eastbourne where the Seven Sisters Marathon started.

We were lucky even to make the start line. As my battered old Morris Oxford struggled up the hills above Eastbourne, a red warning light glowed on the dashboard and steam began to pour out from under the bonnet. A quick inspection revealed a broken fan-belt; I didn't carry a spare and the nearest garage was miles away.

However, all was not lost. Bob was wearing a pair of women's tights as an extra layer of protection against the freezing temperatures, and after peeling these off we were able to fashion a temporary fan-belt that got us to the nearest garage where a proper repair was hurriedly carried out. We made it to the start with minutes to spare.

The race itself bore very little resemblance to the marathon I had envisaged in my mind. Stiles, gates, cattle, bagpipes and lots and lots of ice; I remember one particular section through a narrow icy-floored chalk gully where a bobsleigh would have come in useful, although we made do with sliding on our backsides.

Did someone mention bagpipes? Sure enough, at the summit of one hill, a brave lone piper played alongside a sign displaying 'Welcome to Scotland'. A joke; at least I hoped it was. Nevertheless, for every lung-busting climb, there were plenty of fast downhill sections and, in a little over five and a half hours, Bob and I crossed the finish line and, in theory at least, an ambitious target had been achieved within eight months or so of setting it. However, I wasn't satisfied. I knew that if I could maintain the pace I had set on my longest 12-mile training run for just over twice the distance, then a sub-four-hour marathon was within my grasp, but for that I would need to find a road marathon. Just as it had some years ago when I introduced a reluctant brother to long-haul hiking, Southampton beckoned again.

Once again, Bob joined me, but this time we drove in convoy with our wives and young families, and this time we arrived without any unexpected car malfunctions. If I had had then the marathon experience that I have now, I might have thought twice about choosing the Southampton Marathon as it was a two-lap course and, as any old-stager runner will tell you, they are mentally much more challenging than the single lap variety.

Just imagine. You are halfway through the race, your legs, body and mind are just beginning to show real signs of fatigue and suffering, and the route takes you within a few yards of the eventual finish line. Ahead of you lies another long lap, and every hill and difficult section is etched on your mind as you've only just been through it.

The temptation to call it a day there and then can be overwhelming but Bob and I, running together, soldiered on through the second lap. Of course there was one advantage of the two-lap format and that was that at least our supporting wives and children could yell some encouragement at the halfway point, and that certainly gave us a lift to get us through that difficult mental barrier.

Not surprisingly, with so few training miles in the locker, I began to struggle on the second lap and Bob started to move ahead of me. However, I was nothing if not determined and eventually crossed the finishing line in a little over three hours and 52 minutes. I was absolutely triumphant, and even a little tearful. From barely being able to run a mile after Chris's nightmare, I had achieved my goal of being a sub-four-hour marathon runner within just ten months. It is hard to put into words what that did for my self-confidence, but now I was hooked on my running and wanted more.

The next target was obvious: I wanted to run the London Marathon, the event that had ignited my interest in long-distance running after watching the first ever race. Entries for the 1982 race were long since closed, the race only being about a month away, and with interest among the new breed of runners growing rapidly I vowed to get a place in 1983.

In the meantime, I knuckled down to a much more regular pattern of training, often running the hilly six and a half miles between home and work, and then back again, so as not to impinge on family time too much. This run could be a real challenge in the mornings as it was along the cliff-tops to the east of Brighton and, with a prevailing south-westerly wind along the coast, it was sometimes hard to stay where you were on a windy day, let alone move forward. The upside, of course, was that I could be blown home from work.

Watching Briton Hugh Jones storm home in the 1982 London Marathon only whetted my appetite still further, but I wasn't the only one. Demand for places in the race far exceeded the number who could be safely accommodated so the race organisers announced that, for the 1983 race, a revised entry system would be in force. Quite simply, you filled in your entry form and took it along with your payment to one of a few selected post offices at 8am on a November Sunday where it would be time-stamped. First-come, first-served would be the order of the day across the country.

Bob and I would not be denied a place. Each armed with a rucksack full of sandwiches and cake, a large flask of hot coffee and a sleeping bag, we arrived at the main post office in Brighton at lunchtime on Saturday only to find a queue of 50 people already sat on the pavement outside. We took our place in the line on a chilly afternoon that soon turned into a cold and frosty night. By midnight, the queue was several hundred yards long with police patrolling up and down, although it remained good-natured. It was the coldest night ever; were the organisers trying to keep numbers down by freezing us to death?

Eventually at 8am on the dot, the heavy wooden doors of the post office swung open and the queue very slowly edged forward on numbed feet. It took so long to get to the window. How long does it take to receive a cheque and time-stamp a form?

At last we made it to the front. The solemn and humourless clerk methodically checked all the details on the form and then slammed the time-stamp down on to it. Relieved, Bob and I went back to our respective homes for a long, long sleep but a week later we both received a letter to say our applications had been unsuccessful.

It was enough to make a grown man cry. Predictably there was unrest among the running community; stories circulated that, at some post offices, staff had moved down the queues time-stamping forms before then processing the entry forms and payments at their leisure. Unsurprisingly, the organisers never used that selection procedure again.

London 1984 was the new target and I continued a steady training programme of evening runs at home when the children were in bed, the windswept runs to and from work, and occasional longer weekend runs with Bob. We both had another crack at the fearsome Seven Sisters Marathon on a snowy February day but failed to improve on our previous time, and we also ran the fairly flat Worthing Marathon where I again ran under four hours but missed my Southampton personal best time by an agonising ten seconds.

When the time came round for London Marathon entries again, it was announced that this time it would be a straight ballot. Tellingly perhaps, the form asked if you had tried and failed to get in the previous year, and perhaps this was taken into account, as both Bob and I were successful.

However, my training during the summer of 1983 was interrupted by a persistent cough. Not just the usual bug brought home from school, but this one really seemed to drag on and, if you'll pardon the detail, involved coughing up an awful lot of vile-tasting yellow phlegm from my chest. With my history of tuberculosis as a child, this needed to be eliminated and thankfully a simple blood test did exactly that. However, despite several courses of antibiotics, the cough only continued to worsen.

Now one of the perks of working in the NHS was the ability to be able to jump queues and to be able to seek advice from the consultants that we worked with every day. Another blood test was sufficiently abnormal for the physician to send me scurrying over to the X-ray department one working afternoon and, within minutes of him viewing the image of my chest, I was on my way home with a diagnosis of pneumonia.

However, the cause of the pneumonia remained a mystery for a few more days until I received a call at home from the Public Health department asking me if I kept parrots. I didn't, nor could I recollect any close contact with parrots, or indeed any other caged birds for that matter. However, my blood samples had shown high levels of antibody against the bacteria that causes psittacosis, more commonly known as parrot fever. The good news was that I could now be treated with more specific antibiotics and within a fortnight I was feeling much better.

Where did it come from? My chief suspect was an old pigeon's nest on a drainpipe outside my second-floor office window at the hospital that I had been complaining about for some time, and which, within days of my diagnosis, had mysteriously disappeared. Within a few weeks, I was given the go-ahead to resume running again, with the warning that the psittacosis might reoccur, although thankfully it never has to this day.

The 1984 London Marathon was every bit as memorable as I had expected it to be. We arrived the day before to collect our numbers from City Hall, had an overnight stay in a West End hotel with our wives, and were up at the crack of dawn on race day to take the train from Charing Cross to Blackheath. It was crammed full of nervous runners and must have smelt of liniment for months afterwards.

The weather was kind but any prospect of a fast time soon disappeared as thousands of runners were crammed into narrow streets. But time should never be the only measure of an epic run. Compared to the fairly quiet streets of Southampton and Worthing, the crowds were six deep on most of the pavements; live bands of all genres generated the rhythm of the run and fruit, cake and even home-baked sausage rolls were handed out by enthusiastic bystanders eager to play their part in aiding us across the finish line.

Landmarks that had become familiar over three years of watching the race on television were now being ticked off: Woolwich Barracks, Cutty Sark, Tower Bridge and then suddenly we were plunged into a near-desolate wilderness – the Isle of Dogs.

These were the days before the Canary Wharf redevelopment revitalised the area and the contrast between the exuberant crowds of the first half of the marathon and the now silent, vacant pavements was not only stark, but provided a considerable mental challenge. This was the very part of the marathon where the wheels traditionally start to come off, the dreaded 'wall', and, without enthusiastic support to haul us through it, the urge to call it a day began to grow.

But then Tower Bridge loomed again, then painful cobbles at the Tower of London, before the long haul along the crowd-lined Embankment, Trafalgar Square, Buckingham Palace, Big Ben and, finally, the ecstasy and relief of crossing the finish line on Westminster Bridge.

I had run the race in aid of the Muscular Dystrophy Campaign and was proud to be welcomed into their post-race reception by the late Harry Carpenter, the BBC sports commentator. Although my time was some 12 minutes slower than my best, I could offer the congestion at the start as an excuse for this and, once again, I felt the enormous pride of a marathon achievement. Less than four years earlier I had set the completion of a London Marathon as a future goal. Now that it had been achieved, the bar had to be raised still further.

There were two ways forward. One would be to improve my times; I was never going to be anything more than a mid-pack jogger at best on the speed front but, if you don't set yourself challenging targets, you will never move forward. In the notebook that I recorded all of my runs, I set what for me were ambitious goals of 45 minutes for ten kilometres, 70 minutes for ten miles, 100 minutes for a half-marathon, and three and a half hours for a full marathon. I knew that with a combination of more structured training, and entering more races at various distances to gauge my progress, I would hopefully move towards these targets.

The alternative way forward would be to consider running beyond the marathon distance and here, for the second time in my life, my mind wandered towards the 50-plus miles between

London and Brighton. There was an annual road race along this route but it was for true athletes rather than joe-joggers of my ilk. The time cut-off points were far too rigid for my pace, but then a chance conversation with a friend over a pint (yes, I still enjoyed the occasional pint) threw up another intriguing possibility.

The Long Distance Walkers' Association organised an annual event along the 80 miles of the South Downs Way from Petersfield in Hampshire to Eastbourne in Sussex. This was open to both walkers and runners and, with a relatively generous time limit of 33 hours, seemed a much more viable proposition, especially as I would have about a year to prepare for it. I spoke to Bob and, in no time at all, our entry forms were in.

The 12 months after the London Marathon was a period of steady progress except for the usual lackadaisical period through December and January. My ten-kilometre target was comfortably beaten with a time of just over 42 minutes on a fast and flat Brighton course and suddenly the prospect of sub-40 minutes seemed entirely achievable.

Personal best times for ten miles and half-marathon were also posted, although I was unable to improve on my best road marathon time when I took on the hilly Farnham Marathon. As the June date for the South Downs Way approached so the training mileage increased with long downland runs with Bob at the weekends, and a couple of trial night-time runs equipped with torches.

On the eve of the big race, we camped at the start in Queen Elizabeth Country Park, with Gill and the children joining us to see Bob and I on our way. The weather was kind: dry and not too warm and, on completing what was to be the first of three successive marathons, both Bob and I felt remarkably fresh.

The west-to-east route cut across successive river valleys and a pattern of a comfortable downhill jog, a nice flat section and then an arduous climb began to repeat itself. After we passed the halfway point and approached the part of Sussex where we lived, Bob began to tire and to lose the willpower to carry on. Knowing your bed is just a couple of miles away can have quite an impact on your psychology.

We eventually reached Devil's Dyke, just north of Brighton, which was a major goal on two counts. The first was that the organisers were providing us with a hot meal of mince and potato, and the second was that Gill and the children had arranged to meet us there.

On arrival, Bob announced his intention to quit but, after a hot meal and drink, not to mention a good deal of arm-twisting, he was persuaded to push on for a few more miles. I felt surprisingly good but then made the critical mistake of taking off my shoes to inspect my feet. There was a blister the size of Brazil (almost) on my right big toe and suddenly the prospect of even getting my shoe back on, let alone continuing to run, seemed an impossibility. Luckily St John Ambulance were at hand and after a brief but painful encounter with a scalpel blade, my toe was taped up and we were back on our way again for the final 30 or so miles.

As we struggled on, it was now me battling the mental demons and Bob doing the urging. As night fell, the pace of progress inevitably dropped. Head torches had either not been invented or were not widely available at that time so we had to make do with the hand-held variety. We stumbled through darkened woodlands and, as the night wore on, so fatigue and the desire to stop and sleep increased.

There we were high on the Sussex Downs on a starlit night and I could clearly hear the sound of tennis balls being struck. I could hear muted applause at the end of each point, and a distant umpire calling out the score. I knew it was a hallucination, a Wimbledon-inspired hallucination, but at the same time it seemed very, very real.

Fortunately the hours of real darkness are relatively short during June and soon the warm glow of dawn began to light the path ahead. We pressed on slowly, for that was all our battered feet were capable of by now, and then we were looking down from the top of the Downs to Eastbourne below us, and the finish line. The descent down steep chalky gullies was agony, much more painful than any of the steep hills we had climbed over the past day. Battered, bruised and bleeding toes were being pushed forward into the unyielding toe-box of our shoes. It was actually easier to walk down backwards but eventually the ground flattened out and we were able to jog very gently, and I really mean gently, the final couple of miles to the finish where Gill, Angela and Chris were waiting for us.

There were massive hugs all round, most notably between Bob and myself after the experience we had shared. We had started out as marathon runners: 26 hours later we were now ultramarathon runners.

The year following the South Downs Way run was full of running highlights, both for myself, but also for my growing family. On the personal front I dipped under the magic 70 minutes at a ten-mile road race in Worthing, and then completed the Barns Green Half Marathon in Sussex in an hour and 33 minutes, taking six minutes off my previous best. I even managed to chip a couple of minutes off my best marathon time when I took on the Worthing Marathon for the second time, but my goal of a sub-40 minute ten kilometres was to be denied as I agonisingly watched the clock tick over the magic mark when I was just seven seconds from the finishing line at Brighton Marina. I was certainly not going to win any prizes with these times but the improvement in my personal fitness was now there for all to see in hard, cold statistics.

And it was not only me who benefited. Bob and I joined an athletics club in Brighton, Arena 80, and were able to take our children along to the weekly track training sessions, where we could all benefit from the advice and knowledge of their qualified coaches. Chris, and Bob's eldest, Jason, were soon taking part in junior races themselves and showing more early promise than I ever did.

But what next for Bob and myself? We were both ecstatic to have completed our 80-mile ultramarathon, but learnt so many important lessons along the way. Pacing, fuelling, dealing with mental fatigue, equipment; we knew we could improve in all of these areas and run a faster time. There was only one way to put this to the test. We entered again for the following year.

Training was relentless. Even more runs to and from work along the cliff-tops, long weekend runs over the Downs, and our running club also held weekly evening training sessions along the seafronts of Brighton and Hove.

With less than a month to go to our rerun of the South Downs Way, it was after one of these club evening runs that I returned home and my world fell apart.

3

Hitting the wall, breaching the wall

THIS book is the story of a running journey, but running is but one strand of life, and each of these strands is inextricably linked. Forgive me then that the next few pages, which cover several years of my life, contain little mention of running but nevertheless these exercise-barren years laid the foundation for what was to follow.

Following the births of Angela and Chris, we had agreed that Gill would stay at home to bring the children up during the early years. The extra income from my night-time on-call work made this economically possible and, of course, we wouldn't have to pay nursery fees.

There was a reasonably large social network of local mums in a similar position, and this also gave the children the opportunity to build early friendships. However, Gill was an educated woman who missed the academic challenge of working in medical science and, once Angela was old enough to go to school, Gill was able to get some part-time work with a clinical project investigating cot-death. This involved examining clinical data and records at home, so again there was only rare interaction with others involved in the project.

Once Chris began school, Gill was at last free to return to work full-time and when she was offered a job back in the laboratory in which we had first met, it seemed a perfect outcome for the whole family. It turned out to be anything but.

It was great to see Gill back in an environment that was not only intellectually stimulating, but also making new friendships with her colleagues, several of whom had only started their jobs in the laboratory during the years that she had been at home with the children. One particular friendship with a male colleague of mine seemed particularly close, to the point where it even became a light-hearted talking point at coffee-breaks. However, I laughed this off. After all, we had been happily married for 12 years and had two wonderful children. The gentleman in question was also married and his wife had only recently given birth to a baby girl.

Nevertheless, as time passed, there was an underlying tension in our life at home that hadn't been there before, and nagging doubts began to build in my mind. When I returned home from that final training run with Bob, Gill seemed very ill at ease and uncommunicative so I asked her directly whether there was anything in her relationship with her friend at work that I should be worried about, and she said there was.

Even many years after the event, it is very hard to talk about something so devastating as a marriage breakdown. However, looking back now, there was at least one positive to emerge from all this turmoil. Throughout the time we fought to save the marriage, and even after the battle was eventually lost, the top priority for both of us remained the well-being of Angela and Chris.

Even after the eventual break-up, we still tried to work together in guiding our children through the inevitable ups and downs of their own lives. Indeed, although Gill eventually married the man she had left me for, we have managed to remain friends to this day.

Having said that, Gill's initial revelation that our marriage was in serious trouble had a devastating effect on my health. Any thought of Bob and I re-running our South Downs Way adventure was quickly dispelled. Indeed, running disappeared from my life altogether as I needed every ounce of energy I possessed for the battle to keep our little family together. 'Hitting the wall' is probably a concept that even those with no interest in marathon running are familiar with – that point in a marathon when your body has exhausted all of its usual energy supplies and starts to break down. I was now hitting the wall of life.

At work, I was having to face my adversary every day in a department with fewer than 20 staff. Before long the strain took its toll and I was being treated for depression by the very psychiatrists I had been undertaking research work with during my PhD studies just a few years earlier.

At this stage, Gill was genuinely torn as to which direction her life would take, and an opportunity loomed that would give us the breathing space to get away from it all, and for me to try and show Gill just what was at stake. We fairly hastily arranged a once-in-a-lifetime fly-drive family holiday in the western United States. We studied endless guidebooks, drew up a schedule and booked the flights, car and hotels.

The holiday was magical. San Francisco, Sacramento, Lake Tahoe, Yosemite, Death Valley, Las Vegas, Grand Canyon, Phoenix, Tijuana, San Diego with its zoo and Seaworld, Los Angeles, Hollywood, Disneyland and Universal Studios were just some of the place-names that transformed themselves from the pages of the guidebooks to a jaw-dropping reality. There was something for each of us and, although my physical and mental health was still a little on the fragile side, the relief of being away from all the turmoil at home and at work meant I felt stronger and more positive than I had done for weeks. So positive that I even dusted off my running shoes.

As we booked into a hotel in Zion National Park, Gill spotted a poster on the wooden panelling of the reception desk advertising a five-mile run the following morning around the rim of Bryce Canyon which we were planning to visit.

'Why don't you enter that?' she asked, knowing just how important my running had been for me in better days. I was unfit and ill-prepared, not having run a single step for over two months, we were 9,000 feet above sea level where the air was so thin, but I had packed my running kit 'just in case', and might never have got another chance to run in such a spectacular setting again. The temptation proved irresistible. I signed on the dotted line, paid my fee and collected my souvenir T-shirt.

On the morning of the race it was raining, the first wet day of our holiday, but by the time I had taken the first few tentative steps it had stopped and was pleasantly cool – ideal for running.

The pounding of hundreds of cushioned shoes on tarmac was reassuringly familiar, even if the American accents chattering around me were not. As we turned off the tarmac road and into the forest, the starter's warning echoed in my ears: 'Keep your ears and eyes open for running and watch where you are putting your feet – there are a lot of snakeholes on the course!' I followed the route marked by pieces of red ribbon tied to the trees, and soon realised that too much focus on your feet and snakeholes was not necessarily the best strategy, as low-hanging branches nearly took my scalp off.

In time, the trees opened out and we emerged into open countryside. Directly ahead I caught my first sight of the canyon, the shadowy figures of the leading runners ahead of me silhouetted against the sky behind. It was an image that was burned on my mind forever: the beauty of nature and the toiling of man.

Bryce Canyon is the result of erosive forces. For millions of years, wind, rain and frost have worked relentlessly on the multi-coloured limestone of this great amphitheatre. They have shaped countless columns, spires, walled windows and figures of every description in soft reds, pinks, yellows, oranges, greys and whites. Like a vast fairyland, these fantastic forms, some beautiful, some grotesque, filled a huge bowl 15 miles across. As I turned to run along the rim of the canyon, in awe of my surroundings, I chuckled to myself as I recalled the description of this magical place I'd read the night before, given by its first settler and namegiver, Ebeneezer Bryce, 'One hell of a place to lose a cow.'

As we turned again away from the canyon edge and back into the forest, I passed a small wooden sign hammered into the red soil. Three miles completed, only two to go. So engrossed had I been by the spectacular scenery, my body had forgotten to tell me how much it was hurting, but at the same time there was a warm glow of health and happiness that I hadn't felt for months. Twigs snapping beneath my feet, the fresh pine scents of the forest, I seemed to be gliding across the surface and even overtaking others. Up a steep grassy bank and then out of the trees and there was the finish line and the inevitable elation of crossing it.

As I sat on the grass with Gill, Angela and Chris once more around me, wasting not a scrap of the half a watermelon I had been given to quench my thirst, I reflected on the fact that despite all the trials and tribulations of the previous months, I had now completed my first international race. We all had smiles on our faces and, for a while at least, life felt good again.

The American holiday built renewed hope that our marriage could be saved but it was not to be. Almost a year after our return, Gill finally left and our marriage was formally ended. Having been awarded the custody of Angela and Chris, then aged 11 and eight, by the courts, I now had the greatest possible incentive to get on top of my health problems, but it was not easy. After initially trying to battle the debilitating depression with willpower alone, I had eventually relented to the wishes of my psychiatrist and started to take antidepressants. I suffered some most unpleasant side-effects but at least the tablets gave me the strength to keep my head above water and to meet the new challenges ahead.

Inevitably the split had had an impact on the children. Angela, who from a very early age had been identified as an academically gifted child, had recently won a scholarship that paid two-thirds of her fees at a local private school as a day student. Micklefield School was perfect for Angela's quiet personality and, on the surface, she seemed to be able to internalise her feelings about what had happened. Chris, on the other hand, wore his heart on his sleeve and was much more open about his feelings and did struggle initially, although regular contact with his mum certainly helped to alleviate this.

However, my depression was never going to lift unless the love triangle situation at work was going to be resolved. Neither Gill, nor her new partner, was prepared to leave their jobs and, in the end, my situation became so desperate that I felt forced to hand in my notice despite warnings that this might be a financially catastrophic move. My health had to come first and it had now deteriorated to the point where my ability to continue to look after Angela and Chris was being questioned. So I had now lost both my marriage and a 21-year career that I loved.

The relief at escaping from the work situation was immense but now the hunt was on for a new position. There were nearby hospital laboratories in both Worthing and Eastbourne but neither had vacancies at the level of seniority I was at, nor were they likely to do so in the foreseeable future. I circulated my CV through various scientific career outlets but the need for a regular income was pressing, particularly with Angela's school fees to pay. There was no way I could afford to bide my time and wait for another scientific job to crop up, so I decided on a complete change of course and joined an insurance company, General Portfolio, as a self-employed financial consultant. Even if it were only for a few months until something more suitable came up, it would ensure I could keep my family afloat.

There was no basic salary, no pension scheme or other benefits, so my financial survival depended entirely upon my own efforts to sell financial products, and to earn commission from these. After what was, in retrospect, an astonishingly short initial training period, I was out on my own trying to build my own personal client base.

Now to those who knew me, and my personality, I was absolutely not the typical salesman who could convince anyone to buy something that they really didn't need, and this, to be frank, was a disadvantage in a rewards-based industry. Where I did have an advantage perhaps was being able to use my title of Doctor that, in combination with my early middle age, gave me an air of credibility and respectability that perhaps the younger salespeople I worked alongside didn't have.

Starting with family and former work colleagues and contacts, I slowly built a client list and from this came referrals. Using a standard pro forma, I would interview each new customer to evaluate their needs, but used to drive my branch manager to distraction when I would return from an appointment with no new business, and hence no income for me. However I soon learned that if you were honest with people then they would be more likely to trust you, and refer you on to their friends who might actually need your help.

Not all appointments were straightforward. On one occasion I was selling a small savings plan to a lady who didn't want her husband to know about it when he returned unexpectedly from work. He exploded when he discovered what was happening and I left that house via the back garden gate followed by an angry man with a garden spade! I didn't return for the business.

Of course this was no nine-to-five job and evening appointments were commonplace as many people were at work during the day. Juggling school pick-ups, childminders, meals and any of Angela and Chris's evening activities all had to be factored into the planning process. Some referrals were as far away as London or Essex so I tried to arrange these for the weekend when Gill had the children for the day, and I was also heavily reliant on both grandmothers. In truth, I had absolutely no time for myself and the thought of going out for a run never even crossed my mind.

The variation in my monthly pay was also difficult to manage. Occasionally I would have a bumper month and everything would look rosy, but more often than not the monthly pay cheque was a major disappointment and I would have to scramble around to make ends meet. Although Gill was contributing each month, the drain of meeting Angela's albeit-reduced school fees was a major concern. At least I was being treated sympathetically by Angela's headmaster, who was himself going through his own marriage problems at the time, and could thus empathise with me when I was struggling to get funds together to appease his much-less-patient bursar.

However, after two or three consecutive bad months my financial situation reached tipping point. I had built up an unwise amount on credit cards that I was struggling to pay off so I took the decision to cash in my mortgage endowment policy early – never a wise move at the best of times. It did give me the short-term relief of paying off my debts, and I also benefited from the commission I earned from selling myself a new endowment policy. It was, however, a once-only solution.

Of course, throughout this period I was still being dad to two very special young people and dealing with the day-to-day problems of their growing up. My health oscillated. On a couple of occasions I had felt well enough to convince my GP that I was ready to wean myself gradually off the antidepressants but

I was still unduly vulnerable whenever life threw a new obstacle at me, and I was soon back on the medication. They were a crutch to lean on but one I couldn't do without, and then, as if life wasn't already complicated enough, it then ratcheted up another notch.

The General Portfolio office was a stone's throw from Brighton's railway station and one lunchtime I happened to be in the station when I picked up a leaflet advertising a local commuter group. One of those little flashes of inspiration that happen all too infrequently was ignited. Could I tap into this pool of rail commuters as a source of new clients? I could meet them off the train when they returned from work in the evening and walk them to the office, and people who worked in London were generally well paid, weren't they? I made a note of the secretary's telephone number.

To cut a long story short, I met with Shelley, the secretary, and a few months later we were romantically involved. We were chalk and cheese. I was a family man, Shelley a career girl. I was fairly introverted, Shelley outgoing and effusive. She had never been married or had children, although she had strong views on how she thought children should behave, which didn't always mirror mine. And when would we meet? Shelley worked in London as a legal secretary, travelled up and down from Brighton on the train every day, and seemed to devote every waking hour to the commuter club. I had a house and a family to run, and was out working all hours of the day and night. Yet somehow it worked and we made some time to be together.

However, once again the dreaded depression seemed to be tightening its grip on me despite the medication and there was just too much at stake to let it win. Something had to change and there was a growing realisation within me that I just had to get back to science. Although I was now highly thought of within General Portfolio, and had even been asked to manage a small team of junior consultants, the income was still too erratic to sustain my family, and this was emphasised when a large commercial mortgage deal fell through at the very last hurdle. I had already earmarked where the commission money would be spent, and then it was gone.

Each week I would pick up *New Scientist* and bombard pharmaceutical companies, hospitals, colleges and universities with my CV, and although I got a few expressions of interest, I always fell at the same hurdle: with a PhD, I was overqualified.

Eventually, and not for the first time, the strain became too much for me to cope with, and I quit my job. At least it would give me some more time with the children and some breathing space to sort out a few other problems that had been pressing on my mind.

Although things were generally fine between Angela, Chris and Shelley there had been one or two tensions of late. Nothing major, and nothing that I couldn't normally cope with, but in the depressed state molehills can soon become insurmountable mountains. Once again I had been written off sick by my GP and for the first and only time in my life was reliant on benefits to keep us afloat. It was very hard to see any way out but then two quite unrelated events were eventually to turn my life in a completely new direction.

The first related to my health. When issuing yet another repeat prescription for antidepressants, my GP asked whether I would consider visiting a neighbour of his who was a hypnotherapist. At first I was very sceptical. My PhD studies had engraved a very biochemical picture of depression on my mind and previous counselling sessions with psychiatrists had been unhelpful and had only reinforced my prejudices. But I had nothing to lose and agreed to give it a try.

The sessions were a revelation. Recognising that money, or a lack of it, was a major contributor to my current state, I was taken on at a ridiculously low cost and seen as a challenge rather than a client.

Weekly sessions took me right back to childhood and gradually, little by little, I began to rebuild my self-esteem and confidence.

For the first time in many years I began to feel I was gaining control of my life rather than life events controlling me. Several weeks into this gradual rebuilding process, Shelley announced that she could no longer deal with my mood swings and that it would be better if we ended our relationship. A few months previously this would have destroyed me but now, although deeply upset, I could rationalise the situation and move on. Shelley wanted to remain friends, and to this day we have done exactly that – seems to be the story of my life!

The second unexpected turnaround in my life related to work. Although I was still actively seeking a return to science, one of the conditions of receiving benefits was that I underwent retraining in some other area of potential employment. This was the dawn of the era of the personal computer so I enrolled at a local college and started to learn about word-processing, spreadsheets and databases. After a few weeks of learning the ropes, I was seconded to a software-writing small business in my home town of Peacehaven. Within a short time, I was contributing towards writing programmes for major companies like Virgin although not getting paid for it. The office was within walking distance of my house so occasionally I would go home for lunch.

On one occasion, as I returned to an empty house, a red light was flashing on the answerphone. That red light would send my life off into a new and completely unexpected direction and signalled the beginning of the long-awaited upturn. I listened to the message.

The caller was a Professor Gerald Curzon from the Institute of Neurology in London. Professor Gerald Curzon! I knew the name instantly as some of his earlier work had been a cornerstone of my PhD studies and I had read and cited many of his previous papers for my thesis.

The message went on to explain that he had come across my CV when he went to visit a colleague in another building and was interested in talking to me about a research project for which he had just got funding. It seemed that the techniques I had used for my PhD studies were just what he was looking for and he asked me to ring him back if I was interested.

I played the message again, scarcely believing my ears. This was not even one of the dozens of jobs I had applied for and yet fate had dictated that my CV was lying on top of a colleague's desk just as Professor Curzon was visiting. Someone was looking out for me!

I rang him immediately and an interview was arranged for a week later. There it was explained to me that the project, which would last for three years, would investigate biochemical changes that occur during a stroke with the long-term goal of improving treatment options. There would be some new techniques for me to learn but I already had the laboratory skills he was looking for, and so I was offered the job there and then. I accepted, and once again I was a scientist.

The knowledge that I would be earning a regular salary for the next three years was a huge weight off my shoulders but now different problems presented as I tackled the difficulties of my being away in London all day while the children were at school in Sussex.

By now, of course, Angela was 14 and showing a maturity beyond her years so with the help of neighbours, childminders, family and, of course, Gill, most bases were covered, although each working week had to be planned ahead with military precision.

Angela was now well established at Micklefield and loved the school. Far from inheriting scientific genes from either of her parents, she was a talented artist and seemed destined for a career that made maximum use of these skills. Chris, on the other hand, was single-minded from a very young age that he was going to join the Royal Air Force as a pilot. Many of our family outings had a military theme that reflected this; air shows, navy days and the annual Royal Tournament at Earls Court. Chris was a member of the local Scout group from the age of 11, but yearned for his 13th birthday when he could join the Air Training Corps.

And my own health was now definitely improving. For the first time for a number of years I felt in control of my destiny rather than it being dictated by events beyond my control. As my research programme developed, I once again found myself writing scientific papers just as I had done during my hospital days.

I was attending conferences both at home and abroad to present my research findings and having the confidence to do this in front of an audience of hundreds of gifted academics did wonders for my self-esteem, which had taken such a hammering in the preceding years.

There was one other benefit of working in Professor Curzon's laboratory; several of my colleagues were runners and, just occasionally when our work schedules permitted, we would squeeze in a lunchtime jog in Regent's Park. It felt good to be running again but the hectic schedule of work, commuting, cooking the evening meal and ferrying Angela and Chris to their evening activities left no time for a more substantive training schedule.

Time passed and I moved into the final year of my contract. Attempts to raise more funds to continue the stroke project had proven unsuccessful and, once again, I faced the prospect of being thrown on to the scientific scrap-heap. But I was in a stronger position this time, having built contacts within the research community in London.

A colleague tipped me off that there was one year's funding available at the nearby School of Pharmacy for a project on epilepsy and I made an appointment to see the head of the pharmacology department, Professor Norman Bowery. From the moment I walked into his office, I knew we had something in common.

On the wall was a mirror decorated with the logo of Brighton and Hove Albion Football Club, the team I had supported since going to my first game with my father at the age of seven. As a result of my disjointed and unique career pathway, I was considerably older than others who might be applying for such a position, and only a few years younger than Norman himself who had spent his whole working life in the pharmaceutical industry, and was a world renowned figure. There was immediately a good rapport between us, aided of course by our common football interest, and I was offered the post to begin as soon as my contract finished at the Institute of Neurology. Another 12-month stay of execution!

By now Angela and Chris were both teenagers and developing increasing maturity and independence. On one occasion they made their own way by train from Brighton to London to join me after work at a Pink Floyd concert in Earls Court, and we again visited the same venue for the Royal Tournament, only this time Chris was performing in the arena with his Air Training Corps band. It was an evening of great family pride and one of reflection that, despite the trials and tribulations of the past few years, they had both turned out to be well-rounded individuals of whom I was very proud.

In due course I moved to my new post at the School of Pharmacy and one of my first tasks was to write a research grant with Norman to extend the funding beyond the initial 12 months. On this occasion we were successful in obtaining a further two years of support, so once again I entered a period of relative stability.

Angela was by now approaching her A levels at Micklefield with a view to taking a year-long foundation course in art and then going on to university. Chris was not quite as academically gifted and, although he realised he would not obtain the qualifications necessary to train to become a military pilot, he was adamant that a career in the Royal Air Force was for him, despite his aspirations being constantly dampened by a pacifist headmaster.

In fact, Chris did fulfil his dream of piloting an aircraft when, as an Air Training Corps cadet, he took the controls of a twin-seater Chipmunk trainer as it flew over the English Channel.

During the summer of 1995, a full ten years after I had run the South Downs Way with Bob, I again tried to kick-start my running career. With the light summer evenings I could get home from London and still fit in a run before it got too dark. I also now had a new running buddy in Chris although I didn't so much run with him as behind him.

I was a shadow of my former self in terms of speed and Chris was a fit young man preparing his body for the exertions of the military career that he hoped lay ahead. We both entered a ten-kilometre road race in Eastbourne and, while I huffed and puffed towards the rear of the field, Chris came away with a trophy for the leading junior. My son obviously had far more natural running talent than I had ever had.

It was shortly after that race that my life once again took a dramatic and totally unexpected twist. As I came into work early one morning, Norman met me in the corridor and ushered me into his office, closing the door firmly behind him.

'I'm planning to resign,' he pronounced. 'I've been offered the post of head of department of pharmacology at the University of Birmingham, and I'm going to take it. It's too good an opportunity to turn down and I can't really take things any further here. I wanted you to know before I announce it formally because I'd like you to come with me.'

He went on to explain that if I didn't want to move, I could stay in London and see out the remaining year or so of my contract. If I did move to Birmingham with him, he would try and get me a more permanent position, but there could be no promises.

I was stunned and now had one of the biggest decisions of my life to make. I was born in Sussex and had lived within a few miles of Brighton for every one of my 47 years. Even working in London was stretching the limits of my comfort zone. There was no way I could expect Angela and Chris to move with me but then, if this was going to happen, there couldn't have been a more ideal time as they were both very close to leaving home. Angela was on her art foundation course and had gained a place at the University of Brighton the following year, and Chris would soon be old enough to live his dream and join the RAF.

There was of course the risk that I might only have a job in Birmingham for a few months until the funding ran out, but Norman seemed pretty confident that he could negotiate me a permanent position and that, in the scientific research community, was the holy grail. I agreed to the move. Over the winter months I made several trips to the Midlands and eventually found a lovely two-bedroomed house in Redditch. We found a buyer for our house in Peacehaven, Gill was delighted to house Angela and Chris until they were ready to leave home, and I even eked out a few final miles of running with Chris along the Sussex coastline.

On our last Sussex night together in May 1996, with the furniture having already been taken by the removal company, I sat with Angela and Chris on the carpeted floor of our home and we shared a drink or two. It had been a tough few years, but we had all come though it in one piece, and now each of us was embarking on an entirely separate life journey. We laughed, joked and dozed in sleeping bags that night and, when morning came, Gill arrived to collect Angela and Chris, and I set off alone in the car to the Midlands. Well, not entirely alone: I did have our three cats with me.

4

The road to Morocco

THE transition from a family life in Sussex to a single person's life in the Midlands proved far easier than I had envisaged. My new neighbours were immediately welcoming and friendly, and in those first few months I had a constant stream of visitors, family and friends, to see my new house and to visit the local attractions and, of course, public houses.

At the university it hadn't only been Norman and myself who had made the move from London. Norman had several PhD students under his supervision and they also had moved, sharing a large house in nearby Edgbaston. Of course the pharmacology department already had its own resident staff of all ages, so there was a determined effort all round to avoid any Birmingham/London split and to integrate us all, with a succession of social events. In truth, I hadn't had so much fun for many years.

Weekend parties at the Edgbaston house, and nights out on Birmingham's Broad Street, all became part of my social life and we were occasionally joined by both Angela and Chris if they happened to be visiting at the time. Although I was probably a generation older than most of the students I was socialising with, they were very happy to accept me as one of them, not least because I could probably outrun most of them.

And yes, running was now becoming a key part of my life again now that I had the time to devote to it. The university boasted a superb sports centre and outdoor track, and Birmingham itself is at the centre of the British canal network and possesses more miles of these waterways than Venice itself. The towpath ran right through the university campus, providing a seemingly endless variety of traffic-free running routes in all directions. To cap it all, my new home, which lay on the Warwickshire/Worcestershire border, was surrounded by country lanes and footpaths within yards of my front door. I had landed in a runner's paradise.

I also had a host of new youthful running buddies who, as I have already suggested, struggled to keep up with me, and I found myself becoming a sort of unofficial lifestyle coach as they struggled to counterbalance the excesses of student life with a fitness programme.

Work was also bringing new challenges to my life, all of which were helping me to get back the self-belief and confidence I had taken for granted in previous years. True to his word, Norman had negotiated me a permanent position as a lecturer at the university, so no longer would I agonise over the insecurity of short-term contracts. This meant a fundamental change in my work life.

Whereas before my time was purely devoted to research, I would now have to spend half of my time teaching and this did present some problems. The fact was that I had effectively stumbled into the subject of pharmacology through a series of life events, and had never had any formal training in it myself. Now I was being expected to teach it at university level.

Of course, you can't spend 20-plus years in a hospital laboratory without coming across drugs, and what they are used for. Nevertheless, for a couple of years at least, I was learning on the job and, occasionally, flying by the seat of my pants in front of a class of students. But knowledge isn't neatly compartmentalised into separate subject areas, divided by fixed fencing. There are overlaps everywhere and pretty soon I realised I could draw on my previous experiences at the hospital to provide examples to my students which perhaps the purely-trained pharmacologists couldn't.

In truth, then, my life was really turning round. At work, at leisure and at home, everything seemed to be falling back into place after some fairly dark years. There was however one final parental duty I had to fulfil. Angela was by now firmly ensconced on a Library and Information Studies degree programme at the University of Brighton. Chris had passed through all the selection interviews for his long-yearned-for military career and had chosen the Royal Air Force Regiment as his destination. In common with all new RAF recruits, he would go first to RAF Halton in Buckinghamshire to be processed, kitted out and given a good haircut, and then be moved on to RAF Honington in Norfolk for the arduous regiment-based basic training programme.

I drove down from Birmingham to Sussex to pick Chris up from Gill's house and then took him to RAF Halton. After helping him into the barrack-room with his luggage I shook him by the hand, gave him a hug and left, as he clearly didn't want me to be hanging around. My boy was about to become a man.

I got back to the car, sat down and cried. Not just a few tears but real, full-on sobbing. I hadn't felt upset beforehand; it was just a spontaneous outpouring of all the emotion associated with being a parent, and then finally letting your child go. It was, if you like, the closing of a particularly difficult chapter in my life, but now many new chapters were opening up. It was a teary drive back up the M40 motorway to Birmingham that afternoon.

* * * * *

With my work and social life now being in a better place than they had been for over a decade, I could now start to look to the future with my running as well. First I had to re-evaluate what I might be physically capable of. For my previous marathons, and for my only ultramarathon, I had been in my late 30s. Now, I was fast approaching my 50th birthday. Could I reasonably expect to be able to replicate those performances?

The only way to answer that question was to enter some races and find out. A few ten-kilometre races as I built up my fitness suggested I might have lost a bit of speed, but I was still capable of running under 45 minutes. The same applied to half-marathons. I might never beat my one hour, 33 minute personal best again, but I broke the one hour, 45 minute barrier on several occasions.

The acid test was going to be a full marathon so, once again, I turned to London, and was fortunate enough to get a place in the 1997 race, just 11 months after moving to the Midlands.

I was unable to persuade any of my new youthful running partners to join me in the race but several of them did agree to travel down to London to show their support (I hoped!) from the sidelines. This had an unexpected consequence for I did not know who would be coming, or indeed, where they would be on the course. My deepest fear was that they would be standing just at the point where I might have to walk for a while, and I might just be subjected to some, albeit good-natured, banter from the sidelines.

As a result of this fear of being caught walking, for the very first time in my life I ran every single step of that marathon. Although I didn't beat my best ever marathon time, I did break the magic four-hour barrier and was three minutes quicker than I had been on my London Marathon debut 13 years earlier. Now I knew that, despite the advancing years, I was still capable of running these sorts of distances and could plan my future races accordingly.

While long-distance racing would always be my preference, there was one relatively short race in my back catalogue that my mind often drifted back to, and that was the five-mile run around Bryce Canyon on our last family holiday together. We would have visited the canyon in any case but probably from a public viewing platform to the sound of dozens of clicking camera shutters. However, the experience of running through the woods and emerging on to that narrow path on the canyon's rim had given me a perspective of that magnificent panorama which I might never have seen otherwise. Now I knew that I wanted to travel to other parts of the world, and see beautiful places such as this, and I wanted my running shoes to take me there.

Who knew what life had in store for me? Maybe I would soon meet a new partner and once more settle down to life as a couple but for now, I was on my own, and pledged to make the most of the extra freedom that that gave me.

* * * * *

Early August 1997 was when I sent off my deposit to enter the 1999 Marathon des Sables. I'd been apparently chewing the idea over in my head for about a month, ever since I'd come across the race within the pages of a running magazine.

The event, a six-day, 150-mile race across the Sahara Desert in southern Morocco, was the brainchild of a former concert-promoter, Frenchman Patrick Bauer. Competitors were required to carry everything they needed, including food, clothing and a sleeping bag in a rucksack on their back, although an overnight tent was provided and rations of water handed out at checkpoints.

Since the first running of the event in 1986, two competitors had lost their lives during the race, although the dangers were never better illustrated than in 1994 when an Italian Olympian disappeared during a sandstorm only to turn up nine days later in western Algeria, 44 pounds lighter.

Being a methodical sort of person, and rarely impulsive, I went through the motions of weighing up the pros and cons. I spoke to close family and friends – most thought I was mad. I sent off for an information pack. This began with the words 'Welcome to the world of lunatics and masochists', before going on to list 101 reasons why you wouldn't want to do the race, topping them all by informing you that, in addition to tormenting your mind and body for a week, it would cost you nigh-on £2,000 for the pleasure.

After apparently mulling over my dilemma for an eternity, I announced to those who mattered to me that I was going for it. In truth, the decision had been made at the moment I reached the final full stop of that magazine article.

In May of the following year, I would be celebrating my first 50 years on the planet and the usual alcohol-based festivities were already planned for the day itself, but I was also looking to mark this milestone in a more unconventional way. Despite many alternative and far more rational suggestions, the prospect of running 150 miles across the Sahara had caught my imagination and, after all, whose birthday was it anyway?

* * * * *

Twice during the remainder of 1997 I was able to develop my dream of taking my running shoes around the world. In the autumn, Angela and I took a long weekend break to Paris where I finished a 20-kilometre race in the shadow of the Eiffel Tower.

Then opportunity knocked again the following month when I was presenting some of my research findings at a conference in New Orleans.

Rather than flying directly home, I diverted to New York to run the city's world-famous marathon. Shelley, my ex-partner and now friend, was visiting her sister who lived in Manhattan so we were able to spend a few days exploring the city before race day itself. This included a visit to the Windows on the World restaurant at the very top of the North Tower of the World Trade Center, and I still gaze with disbelief at the photographs that I took on that day in the light of what happened there less than four years later.

The race itself was an unforgettable experience. The initial climb over the Verrazano-Narrows bridge, the passage through the diverse New York boroughs, each with its own cultural identity, the crescendo of crowd noise as you re-entered Manhattan at 16 miles after crossing the relatively silent Queensboro Bridge, and then a massive cloudburst that left us ankle-deep in water as we struggled through the final few miles in Central Park. My first overseas marathon could now be crossed off my to-do list, but now my greatest ever challenge loomed ahead.

* * * * *

Once committed to the Marathon des Sables, there were many decisions to be made, and these were not just confined to equipment and training regimes. If I was going to pit myself against a challenge of this magnitude I also wanted to help others less fortunate than myself.

My decision to run the race for charity was not made purely on compassionate grounds; I'd discovered in the past that the added pressure of having other people's money riding on you is a powerful motivational force in itself. On the other hand, fund-raising can be a time-consuming business and finding the right balance between this and training could be difficult. I opted to run for two charities.

Cancer, in its various guises, had had a major impact on my life, not least with the loss of my dear mum and dad. I would run this race for them. My father-in-law David, my cousin Carol and her husband each succumbed to bowel cancer before they had reached the age of 50, and Hillary, a very dear friend of mine and Shelley's twin sister, had lost her battle with breast cancer in her early 40s. Hillary had worked throughout her illness for the Cancer Research Campaign and this was my first choice.

My second choice reflected the fact that the most satisfying achievement of my life to date had been watching my two children grow up to become healthy young adults of whom I am deeply proud. Not all parents are as blessed, and when an illness beyond the reaches of modern medicine strikes a child, it can devastate whole families. I chose the Dreams Come True charity that helps families who find themselves in this appalling situation. I have always felt it to be unacceptable to use any of the money I raise to cover my own considerable expenses. Every penny would go to the charities, and every expense would come from my own pocket.

For much of the following year I maintained a steadily increasing mileage, ran the occasional half-marathon or 20-mile race, but mostly trained on my own or with work colleagues. However, health scares were never far away.

In March of 1998, I was woken early one morning with severe abdominal pain that I quickly realised was more than a trivial tummy ache. In agony, I called out an emergency doctor and was soon on my way to my local casualty department where an X-ray confirmed the presence of a stone lodged in my right kidney.

Once the excruciating pain had been relieved by the very drugs that I lectured about in my day job, I was discharged with the instruction of hugely increasing my water intake to try to wash the stone out of my system.

During this period, training runs were occasionally curtailed as further bouts of pain struck, although the stone did seem to be on the move. However, after a month of consuming volumes of water that would have bloated a camel, the consultant decided that it would need surgery to remove the stone, and I was admitted to a ward as a day patient to be assessed. This did the trick. Just one day before the planned surgery, the elusive stone made a natural, if somewhat painfully eye-watering, exit from my system.

Undeterred by this temporary setback, I continued to scour equipment catalogues for what would work best in the desert, and I threw myself into the fund-raising, posting out hundreds of letters in search of sponsorship; most falling on stony ground, but enough bearing fruit to make the effort worthwhile.

Of course, the higher the media profile I had, the greater was the interest from potential sponsors, so I made a point of keeping the local and regional media up to date with my progress. Soon I had built a collection of local radio interviews and newspaper cuttings with headlines such as 'Sands Wait for Doug' and 'Desert Dash for Charity'. In the mid-summer silly season of 1998 I even made the front-page story of my local newspaper under the banner headline 'Mad Doug Aims to Beat Sahara'.

As the autumn of 1998 approached it was time to get really serious and to lay a few demons to rest. Marathons I had done before, but never more than two in a year. The experts speaking from the pages of running magazines had drummed into me that marathons take a lot of recovering from. Run too many and you'll burn out.

Bowing to their knowledge, I had dutifully obeyed: one in the spring and one in the autumn was my limit. But now, in six months' time, I was going to ask my body to run virtually a marathon a day for six days. That nagging little voice in my head, that every long-distance runner is familiar with, would be screaming, 'What are you doing!! Anything more than two marathons a year is madness.' That voice had to be silenced.

I signed up to run four marathons in the space of ten weeks. The first, in Wolverhampton, was a real struggle for the last five miles but I scrambled across the line in a respectable three hours and 55 minutes – only five minutes outside my all-time best.

Three weeks later I lined up again, this time in Nottingham. Just as I had done in London the year previously, I managed to run every single step of the way, not once stopping to walk. There were tears of pride in my eyes as I passed under the finish banner with the digital clock showing three hours and 44 minutes. Fifty years old and I had just run the fastest marathon of my life. Confidence was on the up, and thoughts of a sub-three-and-a-half-hour marathon were now forming in my mind but, as so often happens, growing optimism tempted misfortune.

There were four weeks before my next 26-miler in Dublin, and for two of those my running fitness continued to blossom. Then, driving home from a speedy session along a local canal towpath, a car slammed into the back of mine as I sat stationary at a roundabout. Within an hour I was sitting in the waiting room of my local casualty department, my neck rigid and barely able to turn my head. No bone damage on the X-ray: rest, painkillers and try and keep the neck mobile was the verdict.

'Will I be able to run a marathon in two weeks?' I asked tentatively. Most doctors would have scoffed, but the young casualty officer was thankfully a sportsman. 'Not impossible,' he replied. 'Don't run for a week, then try a couple of short runs. If they go okay, try a longish run a couple of days before the race. If you get through that, go for it but take it easy and stop at once if you get any neck pain.'

I did make it to the start line when the Dublin pistol fired. I didn't stop when the neck pain arrived after about 19 miles, but it certainly slowed me down a lot. Five minutes after the four-hour mark I jogged uncomfortably across the finish line and immediately resolved that marathon number four in my mini-series was a non-starter. I had to give my neck a chance to recover properly but at least that irritating little voice in my head had been taught that I could now cope with three marathons in seven weeks. But six in six days? There was still a lot of work to do.

*   *   *   *   *

One Sunday, shortly before Christmas, I received a telephone call at home from a Steve Partridge, who was also running in the race in Morocco. Steve explained that there were a number of entrants from the London area who had already got to know each other. Not wanting to form a clique, he had decided to set up an email newsgroup for all those who were interested so that we could exchange ideas, information and even arrange to train together. I was very happy to join and immediately felt less alone in my preparations. At last I could communicate with like-minded individuals.

Steve was a project director, one of life's great organisers. Before long my email folder was bulging; dozens of printouts to read vying with fund-raising and training runs for what was becoming increasingly precious time. Although he subsequently took some good-natured teasing for his voracious appetite for organising others, it was very much due to Steve's efforts that a lot of bonding took place between the British runners long before we ever set foot on the sand in Morocco.

The new year arrived, three months to go, and I returned to work after a few days at a conference in Brighton to find the usual pile of telephone messages on my office desk. I fingered through them rapidly but one stopped me in my tracks. A Mr Miles Hilton-Barber had phoned. He had also entered the

Marathon des Sables and wanted to meet me to discuss a few things. He worked in Birmingham, so that was no problem, but it was the final few words on that note that I had to read several times. Mr Hilton-Barber was blind.

Now, in the 18 or so months since I had announced my intention of running the race, there had been a pretty broad consensus of opinion among my friends, family and workmates that I was stark, staring mad. I knew that I was setting myself probably the stiffest physical challenge I would ever have to face in my life, at an age when many were turning their minds to armchairs, slippers and a good book. I was determined to confound the doubters, and laid plans like a military operation, but if I was a lunatic to take this on, what did that make a blind man?

I picked up the phone. Miles was a softly-spoken gentleman in the true sense of the word; with just the hint of a southern African accent, a product of his early years in Zimbabwe. He was the same age as me and worked as a consultant for the Royal National Institute for the Blind. We exchanged a few brief details of our preparation and then arranged to meet for lunch a few days later. On putting the phone down my immediate thoughts were that what a shame such a pleasant man was going to have to face almost inevitable disappointment. I wouldn't hold that view for long.

We spent an hour or so over that lunch; Miles, his guide dog Ivor, and Julia, a bubbly, colourful work colleague of Miles whose enthusiasm for what we were planning only increased the schoolboyish excitement in our voices. Between mouthfuls of food we talked of shoes, food rations, energy drinks, backpacks and training. In terms of running experience, Miles was a relative novice, having only ever completed one marathon, but as we bade farewell before returning to our jobs, I knew that I had just met a man of such ferocious determination that nothing was going to stop him.

With only weeks to go the news came that Carlton Television would be making a documentary of the race, and the producer, Shaun Gilmartin, visited me at work to outline his plans. He would be focusing on Miles and his running guide, Jon, as this was clearly a powerful storyline, but he also wanted to highlight the mental demands of the race and, with my knowledge of the underlying brain chemistry, he hoped I might be able to provide some insight into this.

For the duration of the race I would be wired for sound and would put down, on a minidisc recorder, the thoughts that popped into my head as the race unfolded. It added yet another dimension of interest as we built up towards departure day. Nick Avery, Shaun's assistant, was assigned to filming some background material with me, and was soon arriving at my house at 5am to film me getting ready for the 16-mile run to work. Shaun meanwhile was flying off to Majorca to film Miles and Jon as they rehearsed in sun and sand.

The training mileage was now approaching its peak, and more and more of these miles were being covered with a backpack laden with barbell disc-weights wrapped in towels to stop them rattling around. It was a real eye-opener to discover just how much the weight slowed your normal running pace and rhythm, and this was without the heat.

Steve Partridge's newsgroup continued to recount the experiences and problems all the British runners were going through as they prepared. My morale would dip as I read of people training far harder than me, only to soar again as I realised that others were doing far less. But comparison was counter-productive. We covered a wide range of athletic abilities, and we all had commitments to our jobs and families to fit in around our training. Only as individuals did we know the limits of our bodies, and the best we could all hope for was to arrive in the desert uninjured having given ourselves the best possible chance of making it across the finishing line.

The first real get-together of the burgeoning British team had been a 50-mile run along the Thames towpath that I reluctantly had to pull out of because of work commitments. Nevertheless Steve ensured that even those who couldn't attend gained from the many painful lessons learnt by those who did.

The sand-dune running get-together in Norfolk was scheduled for two weeks later and this time I was determined to make it. Apart from the obvious benefit of running in sand, albeit sticky, wet British sand, it was a chance to put faces to the names that had now become familiar through the newsgroup. We were due to meet in the bar of the hotel in Hunstanton on the Friday evening, having made our way there from various corners of the land, and I pictured in my mind this group of finely-tuned athletes sipping mineral water as we talked of the following day's run.

I'd arranged to meet Miles and his running partner, Jon, at a service station on the M1 so we could travel together in my car, and at least leave their wives with transport to compensate them for the loss of their husbands for the weekend. We chatted about the race as I drove, and the more I heard from this remarkable duo the lower my jaw dropped.

Miles, I knew, had been running for 18 months and had just one marathon under his belt, although running round the streets of London is hardly preparation for the Sahara Desert. Jon, who lived in the same village as Miles, had been running for only seven months and had never taken part in a race of any description. Now what kind of person began their racing career with the toughest footrace on earth?

Jon was one of those remarkable people who would go out and do a 25-mile run off the back of no training at all. He was certainly the outdoor type, a youth leader and an experienced climber, including Himalayan trips and mountain rescue work. But a runner he was not, as evidenced by his dismissing a troublesome knee injury by saying he had a good one on the other leg. However, despite these reservations, there was something about the chemistry between these two that only increased my conviction that nothing was going to stop them giving this race everything they had.

A couple of hours later, two dozen of us were seated in the hotel bar and I was relieved to see the beer flowing freely; so much for a bunch of mineral water sippers. We were an unlikely mix from all walks of life; bankers, doctors, solicitors, editors, firemen, farmers, lorry drivers to name but a few, but there was already a discernible bond forming. We all knew how hard each of us had worked to come to this point and with that came mutual respect for one another. Team spirit was building.

After breakfast the next morning, and a quick briefing about the route, we piled into a coach and set off for Wells-Next-The-Sea from where we would run the 25 or so miles back to Hunstanton. For early March, the weather was kind, with the bitter wind and rain that had battered the north Norfolk coast for days beforehand finally relenting.

Within moments of us starting, Miles, who grasped a seven-foot long tape attached to the back of Jon's backpack, was being struck around the face by various items of Jon's clothing that were spewing through a broken zip. They stopped to repack. The rest of us had seen a line of dunes nearer the water's edge and doubled back to the beginning of them. We were going to make use of every yard of sand dune available.

Before long Miles and Jon cut across to rejoin us and I ran with them for a while. I was struggling to stay upright, the sand sloped this way and that, and the weight of the rucksack constantly threw me off balance – how on earth could Miles cope? Jon poured out a constant stream of instructions – downhill, now slopes to the right, steep up, moving left of a bush... To keep running, Miles had to have absolute confidence in the instructions he was being given. This was true teamwork.

We each settled into our own pace and gradually spread out as the miles went by. We passed round a headland at low tide, and turned inland to cross a muddy estuary. Head down, concentrating on where to put my feet, I was suddenly aware of a three-feet-wide ditch across my path. I leapt across it without changing stride but just yards later there was another, probably twice as wide and filled with water. I stopped, retraced my footsteps to the smaller ditch, and then running as fast as I could in the cloying mud, took off and, with some relief, landed upright on the far side. It was quite an obstacle but if I'd struggled to get across, how on earth would Miles manage?

Needless to say, Miles and Jon did manage. By early evening we again sat together in the warmth of the hotel lounge, some still wearing their mud-spattered clothing, while the faster runners had had time to shower and change. One by one we spoke of the lessons we had learnt during the day. What equipment, clothing and drinking systems had worked, and what had been a disaster? Did women's nylon pop socks pulled over your running shoes and ankles keep the sand out?

Three of the guys who had all rowed for Cambridge University had carried out a controlled experiment. Dick had worn pop socks on both feet, Tony had worn none and Andy had worn the nylon shield on his right foot only. The conclusion? Probably worth a try. I added pop socks to my mental kit list.

Soon we moved on to the restaurant and continued to get wiser as we chatted and worked our way through the courses. The wine flowed freely, very freely – probably a little bit too freely! As we made our way back home the next morning, many of our concerns and worries had been dispelled. New friendships had been forged and now we just wanted to get out to Morocco and do it. Just over three weeks to go.

* * * * *

Like me, Jon and Miles had missed out on the 50-miler along the Thames towpath and were keen to see just how their bodies would react to such a long distance with a pack on their back. I declined the invitation to join them on Derbyshire's High Peak Trail the weekend after Norfolk, as I had already planned to run 100 miles that week, surviving on nothing but the freeze-dried rations I would be eating in the desert – my own little dress rehearsal.

Steve North, a London fireman we had met in Norfolk, took up the challenge and, at 7am that Saturday, Jon, Miles and Steve set off to try and complete 50 miles in one session. It was a run that would have a big impact on their performance in the desert a few weeks later.

As the mile count built up, all could feel their feet blistering and Miles, in particular, was in considerable pain. When they stopped to examine the extent of the damage, nothing could have prepared them for what happened when Miles took his shoes and socks off. For some weeks, he had been hardening the soles of his feet with surgical spirit, a trick widely used by the military. When he had run out just the day before this outing, a friend had given him another bottle of what was claimed to be the same liquid. It wasn't – it was acetone and, of course, Miles hadn't been able to read the label.

As he gingerly peeled the sweat-stiffened socks from his feet, and as the accompanying Carlton TV camera rolled, so the skin on the soles came off in one piece, revealing raw flesh beneath. It was time for him and Jon to call it a day. Steve battled on for several more miles before driving back to his family home in Yorkshire, but he too had developed blisters that would return to haunt him in the heat of Morocco.

My own dress rehearsal week had gone pretty well according to plan. One hundred miles clocked up and my stomach had tolerated, but hardly enjoyed, the freeze-dried food offered to it. Okay, I was soon going to have to run half as far again in the same time, and in temperatures that I could only imagine but, on the other hand, I wouldn't be fitting the runs around a full week's work. But now was the time to cut the mileage, give my legs and feet a rest, get the obligatory pre-race medical out of the way and then launch into a final heat acclimatisation programme.

The medical would just be a formality as I had never felt fitter. It was a requirement that it should take place in the month preceding the race: yet another irritating little job that had to be fitted into an increasingly frantic schedule of work, training, equipment-checking and fund-raising. A simple one-page form for my GP to sign: height, weight, blood pressure, blood group, no major illnesses – the usual. We also were required to take an ECG trace to the desert with us, to show that we were at least going to start with healthy hearts.

The alarm bells started ringing with the nurse's first attempt at recording my ECG. 'How very strange – perhaps the electrodes aren't quite in the right place,' she smiled as she removed and then replaced them in seemingly identical positions. Again she watched my heartbeat being traced, this time giving just a knowing nod. We chatted amiably about the race as she took my blood pressure. Again, no comforting reassurance. Just a tight-lipped, 'I'd better check that again.'

There was a definite change in her affable manner as I put my shirt back on. The doctor couldn't see me for another hour, so she suggested I went back home for a cup of tea before returning to see him. 'Maybe I'll see you some time after the race and tell you how it went,' I remarked as I left the clinic room. 'We'll have to wait and see,' was the unexpectedly downbeat reply.

Wait and see. Wait and see. A creeping unease was replacing my earlier nonchalance towards the medical as I left the surgery. How could anything be wrong? I'd had a thorough check-up, including an ECG, at our local hospital less than a year before, during my kidney stone scare, and passed that with flying colours. Now I was fitter than I'd ever been. I'd just finished the most demanding week of my life – over 100 miles of running fitted around a full week's work, and I'd never felt better. Did I get chest pain? No. Did I get breathless? No. Did I get dizzy? No. Perhaps the nurse had just had a busy day and my imagination was playing tricks with me.

An hour and a half later I sat dumbstruck as my doctor spoke, 'You are not going to like me for this, but I cannot sign your form as things stand at the moment.' No form meant no race in the desert. He had known about my plans to run in this race for some time – we had discussed it in the follow-up to my kidney stone episode, and also when he had treated a minor hand injury caused when a delinquent treadmill had launched me into the air a few months earlier.

He knew how much it meant to me but he explained that my heart was considerably enlarged – left ventricular hypertrophy. My blood pressure was also a little high, not dangerously so, but the combination of this and the heart enlargement required further investigation and he would be failing in his duty to me, and indeed to my family, if he let me go to the desert as things stood.

There were barely two weeks before we departed. He would contact the local cardiologist as a matter of urgency, but I was obviously not a priority case as I was not clinically ill. Maybe I could see someone privately, but again there was no guarantee that investigations would be completed in time.

As I walked slowly from the surgery to my car, my mind was a whirlwind of scrambled thoughts. There was only one way to sort them out. I went home, got changed and went for a run.

The attitudes of others to my problems varied widely. There were plenty advising me to cut my losses; there was no point in going to the desert to die of a heart attack. It was a blessing: an easy get-out from a stupid idea. Others were angry with the medics. How dare they jeopardise my dream when I had trained so hard. 'But the medics can't ignore what they've found,' I tried to argue in their defence, although I desperately wanted to prove them wrong.

Days passed by and the prospects of my being properly investigated by a cardiologist in time for the race were diminishing. But I had come too far, and trained too hard just to let matters lie. I sought advice from anyone and everyone with a knowledge of sports medicine, even contacting the medical team of the now-defunct Birmingham Bullets basketball team, but the solution was closer to home.

There were many experts in sports and exercise science working at the University of Birmingham and, when I described my problems to them, the possibility of 'athlete's heart' being the cause was suggested. In simple terms, the heart is a muscle and, like any muscle that is exercised regularly and intensely, it can grow in size.

I was referred to a local physician who specialised in sports medicine. He asked questions about family history, my training and any symptoms I had experienced. There had been none. After a further ECG and a brief examination, I left his office with my race medical form signed. As a mediocre, middle-aged jogger, I felt quite flattered to be carrying an athlete's heart within my chest.

Joking aside, there were several people near and dear to me who already had concerns that I was biting off more than I could chew. The question mark over my heart only fuelled their concerns. With as much tact as they could muster, I was repeatedly advised that there was no shame in pulling out on medical grounds. I would be lying if I said that this had no effect on me. How would my son and daughter feel if I was to expire in the desert sun, knowing that the alarm bells could not have been rung more loudly beforehand? My riposte was: how would I feel if, after all my preparation, I was to withdraw from the race only to find out that on further investigation there had been nothing wrong with my heart in the first place?

One fact pushed me through this period of uncertainty. I had gone to my doctor only because it was a compulsory requirement of race entry to get an ECG and a medical form signed. Not once, in all my hundreds of miles of training, had I experienced any symptoms that would have prompted me to visit him.

The relief at finally getting my medical form signed was somewhat dampened by the time it had taken to sort it out, and this was time I had earmarked for more preparation. I did, however, have one secret weapon in my locker. Having recently returned from a tour of duty with the RAF in Kuwait, my son Chris was a mine of information about life in the desert.

'How long did it take you to get used to the heat?' I had asked. 'Two or three weeks,' came the reply. Two or three weeks! I would be back home by then. Having read reports of others who had completed this mad race, the importance of at least attempting to acclimatise beforehand had been repeatedly stressed. After all, we would only have about 36 hours in the desert before the running started. But how do you prepare for the Saharan sun under the grey skies of a typical English March?

Again, it was the sports scientists at the university who came to my rescue. Sweating was the key. Sweat cools the surface of the skin, and helps to dissipate the heat being generated, both from the inside by exercise, and from the outside by the sun. An acclimatised body can sweat 30 per cent more efficiently than a non-acclimatised one; so as long as you are rigorous in replacing the fluid lost by increased sweating, you will be kept much cooler out in the sun.

I had just about enough time to undergo a ten-day programme of riding an exercise bike inside a sauna – starting with 20 minutes and then gradually increasing the time and the intensity. It was torture, but it was also a good news story for the local press and TV. As I pedalled away furiously inside the pine furnace, the sweat dripping from me forming puddles on the floor, a succession of semi-naked cameramen and photographers crawled around the tight confines of the chamber, seeking the best angle and cursing as their lenses misted up. 'Next time I get a job like this, I'm going bloody sick,' muttered one.

The final days before departure were a blur of frantic activity. The bonus of TV coverage had provided a late surge in attracting new commercial sponsors and I spent my last weekend trekking around a number of hastily arranged meetings. For their money, the sponsors wanted visible logos that might catch the TV cameras and my kit was dispatched to various parts of the country for printing. Deadlines for return were missed. With a week to go, my shirt and Foreign Legion-style cap were in London and my rucksack in Wolverhampton. I did not get my shorts back until the day before I left. It was all added stress – no wonder my blood pressure had been high.

My kit was now laid out in the spare bedroom. Time and time again I went through the checklist to make sure nothing had been forgotten. When I finally got my rucksack back from the printers it was time to pack everything in.

Disaster. No matter how many times I tried, it just wouldn't fit. I rummaged in the loft for an old bum-bag that I could use for the excess. After a couple of days I would have eaten enough of the food to squeeze everything in the rucksack and then I could ditch the bum-bag. Another crisis passed.

Back in Derbyshire, Miles had other concerns. Losing the skin from the soles of his feet and vicious blisters had put paid to any more running since that ill-fated run on the High Peak Trail, but his ankle had also been causing him considerable pain since that day and, with time running out, he sought reassurance from his physiotherapist – reassurance he did not get. It was the beginnings of a stress fracture; the advice was to rest for a month and then perhaps some gentle walking on a nice friendly surface. The odds were stacking against him, but then Miles was used to that.

* * * * *

On the day of departure, I left home before 5am for the drive down to Gatwick. My son Chris was on leave from the RAF for a few days, and it had been after midnight the night before when I had picked him up from the rail station. We'd had a beer or two, a rare chance to catch up on news from each other, and then just a few hours of sleep. Chris would be looking after my car while I was away, but I chose to drive it down to the airport, if only to keep my mind from wandering forward to the challenges I would be facing in the coming days.

5

Tent 40

WE crouched beneath the black hessian cloth of the open-sided Berber tent, the cloudless blue sky clearly visible through the porous material. A dubious criss-cross of wooden poles and rope tentatively held the low roof in place over our heads as we squatted on blankets that provided only minimal protection against the jagged little stones that lay beneath.

Outside, the small wooden placard on the roof that identified us as 'Tent 40' flapped in the desert wind. The late afternoon sun had lost much of the heat of a few hours earlier but, even under the shade of our roof, its strength could still be felt. The air was dry and dusty. The sound of the drums and pipes of Berber musicians drifted across the plain; irksome camels groaned.

This would be our home for the next week and a bit and the nine of us sitting here were about to embark on one of the great adventures of our lives. 'Tent 40' was one of around a dozen British tents and these were joined by over 50 others of all nationalities in the giant semicircular village laid out in this desert wilderness.

Some in our tent had been friends for years. Others had met on a couple of occasions during preparations for the race and, for the remainder, introductions were in order. Of course, I already knew Miles and Jon and was delighted to be occupying the same tent as them as it made life easier for the Carlton TV crew to have all three of us under one roof.

We were joined by three London firemen, who formed the 'Blazing Soles' team. The youngest, Jerry Barker, had an infectious laugh and sense of humour that would help to sustain morale in the coming days. Steve Broomfield was a giant of a man, a tree surgeon in his spare time, and affectionately known as 'Lardy' by his two colleagues and the team was headed up by Steve North, the man blamed by the other two for 'getting them into this mess'.

The two Steves had both been on the Norfolk dune-running weekend with us and, of course, Steve North had also joined Miles and Jon on their ill-fated run on the High Peak Trail.

The other three occupants of our tent were new acquaintances at the outset, although they soon became part of a tightly-bonded team that would go to great lengths to look out for each other over the coming days.

Neil Chippendale was a garage owner from Leeds and was making a return visit to the Sahara having run the race the year before, finishing in a creditable 74th place. Derek Blackall was an aeronautical engineer working for the Civil Aviation Authority at Gatwick Airport and, finally, Henry Keighley-Elstub, the youngest member of our group at 27, was an Old Etonian who now taught at a prep school near Oxford.

But we were just nine of over 100 British competitors who were about to embark on what is touted as the toughest footrace on earth. In this, the 14th year of the event, a record 595 people from 28 different countries were about to pit themselves against the perils of the Sahara, and among the South African contingent was none other than Miles's own brother, Geoff.

Like Miles, Geoff had also lost his sight in his early 20s and, again like Miles, Geoff was an awesome adventurer. Just the year before he had sailed a yacht single-handedly across the perilous Indian Ocean from Durban, in South Africa, to Fremantle, in Australia. The Hilton-Barber dynasty was clearly an exceptional breed and, on this particular journey, Geoff would be guided by his wife, Carol.

The journey of the British contingent had begun at Gatwick Airport where a specially chartered flight took us all out to Ouarzazate. However, the air of excitement and tension as we boarded the aircraft was soon dampened as we then sat on the tarmac for a full four hours, as officialdom argued about how the solid fuel tablets we would be using to cook in the desert, could be safely transported in the hold. Finally a solution was found and within a few hours we were passing over the Atlas Mountains and getting our very first view of the sandy landscape below.

But before we would have to endure the discomforts of the desert, we were treated to one last day of luxury at a hotel in Ouarzazate.

We enjoyed plentiful food, a beer by the pool, and a pre-race briefing during which we were given the single most important document of the week – the Road Book. Although the total distance covered by the Marathon des Sables is the same each year, the route itself changes and is a closely-guarded secret until the eve of the race, to prevent anybody gaining an advantage by scouting it beforehand. Now we knew not only the lengths of the individual stages, but detailed step-by-step instructions, using landmarks and compass bearings that would hopefully guide us to the finish line.

The following day a convoy of rickety coaches ferried us out to the desert, edging uncomfortably around hairpin mountain bends, with precipitous drops falling away at the roadside.

For hour after hour, in unremitting, headache-inducing heat, we sweated, drank water and sweated some more. After a pause for a packed lunch, giving us our first opportunity to feel the heat of the desert terrain beneath our feet, the convoy eventually ground to a halt, seemingly in the middle of nowhere. From the horizon, a plume of desert dust heralded the arrival of the military trucks that would carry us onwards to our final destination at base camp and, for me and my new team, to 'Tent 40'.

As darkness fell that evening I lay in my sleeping bag, the thin foam roll beneath providing very little protection against the jagged stones that our tent had been pitched on. After all the months of planning and preparation, I was finally about to spend my first night in the desert. We had just enjoyed a wonderful meal and even a glass of wine courtesy of the race organisers, but very soon we would be entirely on our own.

The following day was to be one of final checks; our very last chance to decide what we would carry with us, the formal checking of our rucksacks to make sure we had all the compulsory equipment, and then a final medical check – something I had a certain amount of trepidation about, given my problems in the final weeks leading up to leaving the UK. It was cold that night, much colder than I had expected, and I immediately resolved that I would have to carry some thermal underwear with me during the race.

The following morning, a hearty breakfast was followed by a wander into the desert for a call of nature. There were no toilets out there, which meant that toilets were everywhere! On return, I had a few promotional photographs taken for my various sponsors, but then it was down to the serious business of the final pack. At lunchtime, our suitcases would be collected and returned to the hotel in Ouarzazate, leaving us with only what we intended to carry on our backs during the race. For the very first time, we could now see how much, or more often how little, our fellow competitors were intending to run with. Anything that fell into the category of 'might come in handy' was discarded – every single ounce of weight could be critical.

Once we had finally settled on our chosen burden, and carefully packed it to make sure it all fitted in, it was time to unpack it again for the final, extremely thorough, official kit inspection. There were a number of compulsory safety items we had to carry including a compass, reflecting mirror, whistle, distress flare and the rather ominous anti-venom pump. Failure to comply meant instant disqualification; the rules had to be applied rigorously as lives were at stake. We were also required to meet a minimum daily intake of calories during the race, so the calorific content of all the food in our backpacks was carefully added up for each competitor to make sure they complied.

My kit passed and then it was on to the medical tent. I gingerly handed over my signed form, the paper trace of my ECG, and then held my breath. The French medic stared long and hard at my ECG trace and then beckoned over his female colleague. They conversed for a while in French, pointing at the spikes and curves on the trace.

'You 'av a large art,' he exclaimed in broken English.

'It is an athlete's heart,' I countered, trying to sound as confident as I possibly could.

'It is very, very large,' he replied, puffing out his cheeks, as he passed the trace to his colleague so that she could store it in my medical folder. Then, with a wink, he spoke the magic words, 'You are OK.'

I was in.

That evening we ate a light supper, briefly checked our cooking stoves would light in the desert wind, and then settled down for a very early night.

* * * * *

I was awake at first light, the butterflies twitching in my stomach. From across the camp, the silence was broken by a hoarse cockerel crow emanating from the throat of a mischievous Italian runner. Some buried themselves deeper into their sleeping bags, trying to snatch just a few more moments of sleep. Others cursed, threatening to wring the Latin fowl's neck. Slowly, a steady murmur rose among the tents around us. The day of reckoning had arrived.

Even as we were coming to our senses, raucous cheers from the far side of camp signalled the demolition of the first competitor tent. In a steady wave, teams of Berber Arabs worked their way rapidly round the three sides of the encampment, cheerily lifting off our roofs as we still lay in our sleeping bags. They were enjoying it.

Within minutes, our belongings were being pulled off the rugs beneath us and dumped on to the stony ground. Tents and rugs folded, wooden props bundled together, our homes were hurled on to open trucks ready to move on to the next evening's campsite.

Then the morning routine began. Start drinking water from the word go. Get some water on the boil for breakfast. No more queuing for ham, eggs and cheese provided by the organisers now – from this morning we were on our own. I emptied three sachets of my isotonic drink powder into the plastic Camelbak bag and filled it up with water, massaging it into solution. With a few mouthfuls of water, I washed down painkillers, salt tablets and vitamin capsules.

The solid fuel tablet on my hexi-stove had burned out and the water in the mess tin was barely warm. I cursed my stupidity for sending the mess tin lid back to Ouarzazate in my suitcase the previous day. Yes, I'd tested the stove, and how long it took to boil a mug of water, before I left home. But that was in my kitchen. Now the desert wind was blowing the heat all over the place. I carried no extra fuel tablets – they were too heavy. It was luke-warm porridge and coffee for breakfast. First lesson learnt.

At the far end of our tent, Miles hauled himself to his feet. 'Am I standing in somebody's breakfast?' he enquired playfully, and a collective nervous chuckle passed between us. The routine continued. Brush teeth. I'd sawed the handle off my toothbrush to reduce weight. I produced one of my tiny airline tubes of toothpaste and squeezed a blob on to the bristles. The firemen fell about laughing.

'Doug, that has to be the smallest tube of toothpaste in the world.' They were right. Pack weight had become an obsession and you go for the smallest of everything that you can find, even if it is clearly inadequate.

Sun block. I rubbed it on to my arms, face and legs. Steve Broomfield rubbed some on to my back and shoulders and I returned the favour. There was laughter as we prepared. There was tension as well. Race vest. Race shorts. Pin on my number. I would be wearing this same vest and these same shorts for the next 150 miles. It didn't bear thinking about.

Prepare feet. Toes are my problem. Maybe it was those fashionable winkle-pickers that I crushed my feet into as a 1960s teenager, but my toes have always appeared deformed. Left to their own devices they climb on top of and cruelly abrade their nearest neighbours as I run, so I had taken to taping each of them up individually as added protection. It worked on the country lanes and towpaths of England, but how would they fare in the heat and sand of the Sahara?

A degree of caution was also necessary when putting on your running shoes each morning. Scorpions scuttling around among our belongings in the tent were not an uncommon sight and it was vital to check that they hadn't sought refuge inside a shoe overnight, before placing your foot inside.

The clock ticked on – time for our morning desert patrol. Armed with pads of biodegradable toilet paper, and wooden twigs to dig holes, I joined Steve Broomfield, Jerry and Miles as we wandered away from the camp in search of an unvisited bush. As we walked together, Miles asked each of us to convey our feelings into his personal tape recorder.

Anxious, nervous, apprehensive about the heat and the weight of the backpack – we shared the same concerns. For all of us, barely a day had gone by in the past year without somebody mentioning the race, and now that day had finally dawned. I also felt strangely aggressive – not a natural trait for me.

Not aggression towards my fellow competitors, but towards the desert itself. It enveloped us, and taunted us. It would do everything in its power to stop me, but I wasn't going to let it.

Miles took back his tape recorder and spoke firmly into it, 'I'm feeling the best I've felt since arriving. My ankle is feeling stronger and I'm feeling stronger. So we're going to go out and do it now, guys.'

We were into the final half-hour. I packed and repacked my rucksack. There was no room for my sleeping bag, bedroll, distress flare or flip-flops so I strapped them to the outside. I lifted it on to my back. God, it was heavy. I dropped it back down to the ground.

The British runners clustered together – handshakes, bear-hugs – this was it. The call went out for a team photo and we formed up obediently. Spontaneously, we began to sing the hymn, *Jerusalem*. 'And did those feet, in ancient times…' Three cheers for the Brits, and then we donned our packs and marched as one to the start and the first 30 kilometres that lay ahead of us.

From the top of his Land Rover, Patrick Bauer gave his final briefing in French, and then a colleague gave an English translation, both barely audible over the whirring of the helicopter hovering above. Cameras were everywhere.

We lined up under the banner. Dix, neuf, huit, sept, six, cinq, quatre, trois, deux, un, allez!

The helicopter dipped low over our heads. Land Rovers roared off over the parched ground, throwing clouds of dust into the air. The adventure had begun.

All the planning, all the training, and now this was for real. From the very beginning, the field spread out rapidly.

Some hared away at the front at a speed that seemed barely credible. Others had already taken the decision to walk the whole race. They were in no hurry and were going to soak up their surroundings as they slowly progressed.

As I broke into a steady jog, I settled somewhere into the middle of the pack.

It was hard to believe that this was really happening, but here I was, running a race in the Sahara Desert. Small stones, a crusty baked surface that looked solid but which gave a few centimetres under each stride – after only a few minutes I was already astonished by the variety of surfaces we were running on.

My backpack was heavy, around 25 pounds, but surprisingly stable and held in place by chest and waist straps. On one side was secured my Camelbak, possibly the most important piece of equipment I was carrying. 'Hydrate or die!' said the label when I bought it.

Out here, that was no idle threat. It consisted of a two-litre plastic reservoir holding my drink, a spongy felt covering to insulate it from the heat of the sun, and a long plastic tube curled over my shoulder ending in a valve that I could bite on and suck whenever I needed to drink. On my stomach rested my bum-bag, and this held all the bits and pieces that I might need during each stage: my anti-venom pump, compass, whistle, energy bars, carbohydrate gels and a disposable camera.

I also managed to squeeze the transmitter for the radio mike into this bag. I was going to be wired for sound for the duration of the race – black tape binding the leads to my rucksack straps, a furry little microphone sitting beneath my chin. A canvas and aluminium case was clipped to my waist strap, and this held the minidisc recorder – more leads, more jackplugs. As if running this race wasn't hard enough, I seemed to be carrying a small studio around with me.

We headed off through a series of passes, skirting around the rocky peaks that surrounded us. We were blessed with a breeze. I squinted at the tiny thermometer I had fitted to my shoulder strap but it was too high up to read without stopping – I'd have to shift it later. Occasionally we would swing round a peak that would block out the wind and my face would feel the temperature rising as if facing an open oven.

Less than an hour into the race and already I could feel the heat of the ground burning through the rubber soles of my shoes, but still I kept running. Despite the heat, despite the weight, I was enjoying every minute of it, devouring this unreal experience. I was on my first runner's high of the race – I wasn't to know there wouldn't be too many more.

Before I knew it, I was running across the soft sandy surface towards the first checkpoint. A dozen Land Rovers, a couple of tents and three lanes marked with our race numbers. Twelve kilometres under my belt and I'd run every step.

'How's it going, Doug?' called Nick, camera perched on his shoulder, as I jogged into my lane.

'Piece of cake!' I exclaimed with a grin. I searched under my vest to find the water ration card hanging round my neck. I collected a new bottle, and a hole was punched in my card.

Top up the Camelbak, change the minidisc, swallow a few mouthfuls of water and soon I was on my way again.

Almost immediately, we were into sand dunes. Compared to what we would encounter in the days to come, these were small, but they were my first Saharan dunes and they took my breath away. I paused for a photograph. It didn't take long for the penny to drop that if I continued to try to run in this soft powdery sand, my legs would soon turn to jelly.

But walking for a while had its rewards. For a start it gave me more time to take in the beauty of the dunes. The curves, the ridges – it was natural sculpture. Where footprints criss-crossed the glassy smooth surfaces, it seemed like a desecration. The temperature was now really climbing, and for the first time I was truly aware of the awesome power of the desert.

And then the dunes were gone, replaced by our first taste of what was to prove the desert's tour de force – the endless flat plain. Lulling you with the lack of hills, offering you a view of journey's end on the horizon, these plains would entice you in and then bake you alive as you realised that judging distance in the desert is like nowhere else on earth.

Now alternating jogging with brisk walking, I eventually dragged myself in to checkpoint two at the base of a substantial rocky climb over Jebel Hissima. There were no TV crews at this checkpoint. My feet were now feeling sore and, with only seven kilometres to go, there seemed no point in hanging around. I grabbed my water allocation, gulped down a few mouthfuls and was on my way again.

Soon I was scrambling up and down over huge slabs of granite-like rock. I feared for Miles on this section. This was what he hated most. For a while, I was joined by Robin, a fellow British runner. Like me, he felt he'd done his hard work for the day and now he was just going to coast to the finish. Together we reached the crest of the peak and there, less than four miles away across a sandy plateau, we could see the black and white tents of our new camp, a smoky haze shimmering above them. The end of day one was in sight.

As we picked our way down through the boulders to the plain below, Robin began to pull away from me. I reached flatter ground. Sandy mounds were everywhere, each only a few feet high and every one crowned with a thorny bush: some green, some brown. I zig-zagged between them. Where the ground underfoot was firm, I ran; when my shoes sank into the sand, I walked. There was little breeze now; the sun was still high overhead.

A patch of skin on my left arm was burning. I poured some water on it. I must have missed it with the sun block – I needed to be more careful. Every now and then I would catch another glimpse of camp, the camp that had seemed so near from the top of the rocky peak. It was no nearer. The first day had gone better than I could ever have hoped for, but I desperately wanted it to finish now. I really, really needed to get out of this sun.

The tiny, spiky dunes ended. More baked and crusty land. I was amazed at how much greenery was springing up from it. I sucked greedily at my drinking tube and ran again but five men blocked the way ahead. The two at the rear were hauling a rucksack slung between them as well as those on their backs. I passed them. Ahead were three, side by side, the Italian flag printed on their vests. The one in the middle, now minus his backpack, had his arms draped around the shoulders of his two compatriots. He was being dragged, his eyes glazed and pointing aimlessly upwards, bubbles of saliva running down his chin. I offered help but they shook their heads. I ran on. My sore feet now seemed so insignificant. For at least one man, the race was over already.

Four hours and 50 minutes after we had started, I eventually passed under the finish banner, punching the air with clenched fists. For me, the first stage was done: just five to go.

*   *   *   *   *

Back out in the desert, things were not going so smoothly for Jon and Miles. Barely into the race, and with the temperature already up into the nineties, Miles was suffering with his swollen ankle. Resigned to walking for much of the first day, Jon had kept a watchful eye on the Moroccan youngsters who gathered on the early mountain passes to shout encouragement. Given half a chance, they were also after anything they could snatch from your backpack.

They walked with some other members of the British contingent, including Denis and Sebastian Dovey, a father and son team with a combined age of 100! They also walked alongside the French team of hospital workers who were carrying 15-year-old, wheelchair-bound Sylvain Mahler around the whole course. There were some remarkable stories emerging from this crazy race.

By the second checkpoint, Miles was in serious trouble. His feet were in tatters. Already lacking the skin that had been burnt off just a fortnight earlier with acetone, the flesh now felt as if it was on fire. He visited the medical tent where the nurses tore more skin from his heel. Excruciating pain. Savages.

They patched and taped up the raw flesh and then, concerned about an infected toe blister, another relic of the ill-fated Peak District run, one of the medical team advised Miles it might be best to quit the race. As the medic wandered off to seek a second opinion, Jon urged Miles to get his shoes back on post-haste, and when the doctors returned, Jon and Miles were already hobbling towards the summit of Jebel Hissima.

Surely things couldn't get worse, but they did. Clambering down a rocky ravine below the peak, Miles went over on his weak ankle and cut his knee open. It was just what I had feared earlier when I had passed through this section. Jon patched it up as best he could and they pressed on. Miles tugged remorselessly at the tape hanging from Jon's rucksack; his ankle was agony. The knee felt badly damaged and might well need an X-ray. Flies buzzed around it, feeding at the bloody bandage. Beneath his right foot he could feel a huge blister squelching around inside his shoe, and he hadn't finished the first day yet.

* * * * *

Back at camp, it had been a real boost to get back to 'Tent 40' and find I was the third one home. As expected, Neil had led the way, finishing in around three and a quarter hours, but not without paying a price. A huge fluid swelling had appeared on his shoulder and he was just off to the medical tent when I arrived. Henry had been less than an hour behind him and appeared to have come through unscathed, although he had found the heat punishing and, amazingly, in all that open space, reported that he had felt claustrophobic.

I got some water on the boil, adding a few dry twigs to extend the life of the fuel tablet, and built a windbreak of small rocks around my stove. When the fire had gone out, I poured the hot water into a double-sized portion of dessicated Lancashire Hot Pot. Derek was next in – hot, happy and yelping with pride. Steve North followed a few minutes later and he was in a bad way. He'd also brought blisters out with him from the Peak District. How Steve, Miles and Jon must have regretted that Saturday jaunt.

Steve gingerly peeled off his socks and it wasn't a pretty sight – unless you were among the thousands of flies that swarmed around the camp. Another one destined for the much-feared 'Doc Trotter' medical tent. Half an hour later, Steve Broomfield and Jerry arrived, accompanied by two volleys of expletives. Steve, in particular, had really struggled in the midday sun and the soles of Jerry's feet were red raw. Day one and 'Tent 40' already resembled a battlefield hospital. Neil was now back, with his shoulders strapped up, and I joined him and Henry as we wandered over to the finish to wait for Miles and Jon – with the now cold stodge that claimed to be Lancashire Hot Pot still being spooned into my mouth.

Just over seven and a quarter hours after they had set out, Jon and Miles finally limped across the finish line to a tumultuous welcome. As we walked back with them to our tent, with TV crews and cameras milling around, applause and cheering broke out from every tent around us, regardless of nationality. 'What an amazing welcome,' gasped Miles, almost choking on the emotion, but the pain written across his face told the true story. He was completely spent.

Back under our hessian roof, 'Tent 40' was together again. 'That was the hardest thing I have ever done – and it's only the first day,' joked Steve Broomfield, and we began to recount our individual stories to each other. Jon told of how he and Miles had been forced to beat a hasty retreat from the medics threatening to pull them out of the race. He spoke of the fall that had cracked open Miles's knee, and he felt guilt that he had let it happen. We rallied behind him. He couldn't be expected to describe every step of Miles's dark journey. We could only imagine how hard it must have been for Jon.

Miles was quiet, uncharacteristically so. He had not imagined such pain, and there was mental anguish as well. Uncertainty. Self-doubt. Could he go on? He would sleep on it, but first it was back to those bloodthirsty medics.

It was dark by 8pm and most of us were tucked up in our sleeping bags, scribbling out our thoughts into diaries under torchlight, although Miles was still on the receiving end of a scalpel blade.

'Has anyone got a pen handy?' called Jerry.

'Here you are,' replied Steve North. 'And stop keep calling me Andy!'

It was a joke that would be repeated many times over the next week, but it always raised a smile.

My own euphoria had been dampened twice during the course of the evening. An explosive bout of diarrhoea had sent me scurrying off into the desert on a couple of occasions. Was it that Lancashire Hot Pot, or was it the salt tablets? I'd swallowed some loperamide and prayed that it would get to work during the night.

And then, on one of my hasty exits from the tent in fading light, I'd walked straight into low thorny scrub in my flip flops, the barbs slicing bloodily into two of my toes. Typical! I run 18 miles in the desert without a blister and then I cut my feet open going to the loo!

The camp rumour mill had been working overtime. The latest gossip was that 30 people had dropped out – the hardest ever first day – but none of us really knew. We did know that all the Brits were still in but, as we fell asleep, we were all silently praying for Miles.

6

Fluid in, fluid out

SOMETHING wasn't right from the very first moment I stirred. The exuberance I had felt at the end of the first day's run had now been replaced by a vague feeling of unease.

I'd been warm enough in my thermals overnight. The loperamide seemed to have done the trick with my diarrhoea – I hadn't had to get up at all during the night. The toe that I had torn on the bush the previous evening was throbbing but nothing more.

I managed to ease myself up on to my elbows before our tent was once again dragged from above us. Sitting up, still in my sleeping bag, I rummaged among the chaotic pile to my right for my hexi-stove, fuel tablets and lighter to get some water boiling up for breakfast. Eating was the last thing I felt like, but there was no place for stupidity in this race. Calories in your stomach now would mean the difference between success and failure later in the day.

Around me, the two Steves and Neil were stirring. Steve Broomfield complained of having been too hot overnight in his sleeping bag. You pay your money and you take your choice. We had all researched our equipment carefully but until you get it out into the desert you just don't know. At the far end of the tent, Jon was still fast asleep; Miles was awake but, again, uncharacteristically subdued.

I went through my usual morning routine: eat breakfast, swallow some multivitamins, painkillers and salt tablets, mix energy drink and fill my drinking reservoir, slap on the sunscreen, brush teeth, wash feet with wet-wipes, tape up toes. I wandered slowly across camp to pick up my morning's water ration. My legs and feet were certainly heavy with the effect of yesterday's stage, but when I looked around at others hobbling and limping, I knew I had got off lightly. I paused at the board displaying the first day's official results – 369th – yes, I was well pleased with that, but even as I ambled back to our tent, the unease I had felt on waking would not go away.

By 9am we were again gathering around the start banner – my pack felt much heavier than the day before, although I knew that was impossible. The sun was stronger, and I sought shade behind one of the hot-air balloons surrounding the start area as I waited for the daily briefing.

Although I'd only been a few minutes before, a sudden urge for a pee sent me scurrying off across the plain, to conceal myself behind a jeep. The nerves were really jangling – I felt so much more apprehensive than I had done the previous day. I stood with Jon, Miles and the Carlton TV crew as we listened to the briefing, and then we waited for the countdown. Nothing happened. People were just milling around – nobody seemed to know what was going on.

God, I can't need another pee already! Again I hurried away to find a secluded spot. I guzzled at the water bottle in my hand – if so much liquid was wanting to come out, I needed to make sure enough was going back in. And then an announcement. The start would be delayed by an hour – no reason given. Shaun pushed the TV camera towards my face. 'What do you think about this delay then, Doug?'

'Bloody ridiculous,' I snapped irritably. 'The sun's getting hotter and hotter, we've all got our packs on and they're getting heavier by the minute, and for no reason they're keeping us waiting here.'

Of course, there was a reason. A few minutes later it was announced that one of the lorries carrying our tents to the site of the next camp had crashed on a mountain road. It seemed that some of the Berber Arabs had been injured, although thankfully, none seriously.

My anger subsided and I felt guilty about my earlier outburst. These were people of the desert, and this race could not happen without them, but even they were not immune from the dangers surrounding us.

The race eventually got away only 40 minutes late, and the moment I broke into a run I knew something was definitely amiss. The previous day I had been in awe of my surroundings, scarcely able to believe that here I was, running in the Sahara Desert. Today, I was so internalised, that I might as well have been running on a treadmill surrounded by four blank walls. I berated myself – 24 hours just couldn't make that much difference to my psyche. Every time the surface became at all sandy underfoot I would slow to a walk, whereas the day before I would have run through it. Surely I wasn't losing the mental battle already.

Very, very gradually I began to build a rhythm. The ground became stony, covered in tiny loose pebbles, and this I found a bit easier than the crusty sand that gave way under my weight. Another quick toilet stop, and then we were heading south towards a small mountain, Jebel Ammessoui. Now I was about to confront the one thing I really feared in this race.

The heat, dunes, sandstorms, snakes and scorpions I believed I could cope with, but I have an irrational fear of heights and, when I knew this race included crossing small mountains, I broke out into a cold sweat of apprehension. It doesn't need to be an enormous height, but a steep unprotected drop of any sort can turn my knees to jelly. Face your fears, Richards!

I wasn't going to let this phobia stop me running the race, and knew that at some stage I would have to confront it. Now, as I approached Jebel Ammessoui, that time had come. As I scrambled over the rocks leading to the first peak, my intense focus was blocking out the discomfort I had felt earlier in the day. I reached the top and gasped at the scene that lay ahead of me. A steep rocky descent, a wide flat valley and then an awesome rocky climb on the far side. I could just pick out the tiny figures of the faster runners scrambling over the boulders ahead. It was time to face my nemesis. I switched on the minidisc recorder attached to my bumbag. I was going to talk myself through this and I'd have a record of the conversation for future reference.

Determined not to look back down behind me, I picked a route through the scattered rocks, muttering into the furry microphone beneath my chin as I went. Photographers and cameramen seemed to pop up everywhere as I scrambled towards the top. Shaun called out to me but I ignored him; my concentration was solely focused on planting my foot in the right place for the next step. And then I was at the top. A huge wave of achievement swept over me as I surveyed what I had just climbed and I exalted into the microphone.

I knew that to most people in the race this was just a pimple on the landscape, but it had been my Everest. I had taken on and beaten my one big fear and, as I began the descent, such was the mental boost I had given myself, I was already thinking ahead and picturing myself crossing the finishing line in five days' time. Foolish. Once down off the mountain we entered a valley that curved away south-eastwards, with a clear path emerging among the scattered pebbles, and now I seemed to have recovered the enthusiasm that I had had the day before as I approached the first checkpoint.

There were no TV cameras to talk to at the checkpoint. They were obviously waiting at Jebel Ammessoui to see Miles and Jon come through what must surely be one of the toughest sections of the race for them. My fear-of-height problems were as nothing compared with what Miles was facing. My mind went back to just how dispirited he had been that morning and I muttered a little prayer for him as I topped up my Camelbak with water and isotonic drink powder. I ripped open the velcro fastener to see how much recording time I had left on the minidisc. It was still full.

The recorder hadn't even started and all the words I had muttered as I cajoled myself up to that summit were lost forever. Damn, damn, damn! But what was done was done. I wasn't going back. I hauled my pack on to my shoulders and set off again. I'd had a slow start to the day and now I wanted to make up some time.

The boost in spirits I had enjoyed from my climb was short-lived. The course now headed out across the centre of a wide valley: a massive plain full of nothing but hot, dry air, with not even the slightest prospect of any shade from the relentless sun. I was now stopping every ten minutes or so for a pee, and each time my bladder was full to bursting. Where was it all coming from? What the hell was going on? I had to drink to replace the fluid, but at the same time I knew that my drinking was only fuelling the problem.

As midday passed, the temperature continued to soar and the bursts of jogging became fewer and shorter. I tried to swallow an energy bar but it was devilishly unpalatable out there – like eating hot, sticky, corrugated cardboard, and it just induced a bout of retching. And still the valley stretched ahead. I could see a line of mountains in front of me, but they seemed no closer than they had been an hour ago. As I pressed on, my head was spinning; my mind seemed to want to detach itself from my legs – to disown them. Panic began to rise from within me; drink more water, drink more water – God, I need to stop again.

I fought to drag some of the motivational phrases I had memorised beforehand from my scrambled memory, and then recited them out loud, over and over again. I berated my own athletic ability like a grumpy sergeant-major and, when I couldn't take any more self-criticism, I would sing myself a song out loud. Yes, this race was one big mind-game.

Very gradually the path started to climb and, as I came round the base of a large rocky hill, the joyous sight of the next checkpoint was directly ahead. Nick was there to greet me, his camera perched upon his shoulder. 'How's it going, Doug? How are you feeling today?' I snarled a few choice words in reply and then beat a hasty retreat to the shelter of a tent. The sun was crushing me. Nick followed but filming from a healthy distance. 'Look, sorry mate, I just feel like shit. Just give me some time.'

I filled my drink reservoirs and then just lay back, pulling my hat over my face. How easy it would be to call it a day here, but deep down I knew that wasn't an option. A few minutes passed and I sat back up again. Nick was still there and now I felt a bit more sociable. He told me that Miles had been through the first checkpoint and seemed to be going better than the first day. I told Nick of my burst water main problem, and he suggested I visit the first aid tent. Now why hadn't I thought of that? Leaving my pack on the ground, I scrambled across to the tent and tried to explain my problem to the young, French nurse.

'Ah, diarrhoea!' she exclaimed.

'No, no, no!' I retorted, before going on to depict a gushing fountain using only hand signals.

'Ah, I understand,' she replied before rummaging around in a large bag and producing two different kinds of pills. 'Take two of these, and one of these, now. Take one more blue one the next time you have to stop, and then one of each at the next checkpoint.'

I didn't ask what they were, I didn't even want to know. I just did as I was told and prayed they would do the trick.

I'd taken a long time out at this particular watering hole when I eventually set off again, far longer than at any checkpoint in the race so far, but time was no longer a factor – I just wanted to get the stage over with. People were passing me who had finished way behind me on the first stage, but that was to prove the way of the race. We'd all have good days, we'd all have bad days, and I hoped that I wouldn't have any worse than this.

We now continued along a dry riverbed, and then up and down over an endless stretch of small sandy mounds, sapping what little strength I had left in my legs. The sun had lost a little of its power but still there was no hiding from it. I still had to make several stops but they didn't seem to be quite as frequent – perhaps the pills were doing something.

I was in better spirits when I reached the final checkpoint – Shaun and Nick were there to greet me. Shaun suggested I went to see the chief medical officer who happened to be in the medical tent at that time.

Again, in a fractured mixture of French and English, I described my troubles to him.

'Ah, diarrhoea!' he exclaimed, and once again I had to resort to hand signals to point him in the right direction.

I took the glass of Dioralyte he offered, toasting his good health before downing it. I would have got the same treatment even if it had been diarrhoea.

Only six kilometres remained to the overnight camp but they seemed to be unending. Much of the route was slightly downhill, meaning the camp was in sight for much of the time, although it just seemed to be drifting further away on what little breeze there was. I was now feeling really nauseous and the mix of walking and jogging was now more and more heavily biased towards the former.

My relief at eventually reaching the finish was tempered as I took on the added burden of three one-and-a-half-litre bottles of water, and an unexpected can of Coke. Clutching them to my chest, I staggered across the site towards 'Tent 40' which always seemed to be pitched further away than anyone else's tent.

There were the customary warm greetings as I eventually reached the welcome shade of our desert home, hurling my water bottles towards my patch at one end. A much larger reception party than the day before. Aside from the two speed merchants, Neil and Henry, both Steve North and Derek had beaten me across the line today. From my terse responses to their questions, the penny soon dropped that I just needed a little time on my own to reflect on my day. Without words, the 'Tent 40' welfare machine swung into operation and helping hands were there to unroll my sleeping mat and bag and tidy up my water bottles. I lay down, too exhausted even to take off my shoes.

Twenty minutes later I was feeling half-human again. The Doc Trotter tent was the next stop; I had to find out what was going on with my kidneys today. I just couldn't tolerate that for the rest of the race. I was soon in front of another French doctor but again the language barriers hindered any useful dialogue – just keep drinking and keep taking the salt tablets was his only advice. As I hobbled back to our end of the encampment, cheerful American voices called my name. It was Dave and Debbie from Arizona, who I'd met at the hotel in Ouarzazate.

'How's it going, Doug?' enquired Debbie. 'You're not looking so good.'

As I started to recount my day, I suddenly remembered that Dave was a medic. At last, a medic who could speak the same language. He listened attentively and felt I hadn't taken enough carbohydrate on board. I just had to keep swallowing the energy bars and gels, even if I did think I might throw them straight back up again. More carbohydrate, and perhaps a little less salt, was his verdict. At least now there was something I could change in my routine that might just make the difference.

I wandered back to our tent. Steve Broomfield and Jerry were back now, and they told us that Miles and Jon weren't too far behind. It looked as if we were all still in the race, something that had looked far less than certain earlier that morning when Miles had been in so much distress.

I was just about ready for food but first it was time to lever my shoes and socks off and clean my feet up a bit. The sight of the four huge blisters on my toes took me quite by surprise. So immersed had I been with my peeing problems, and immersed is not an inappropriate word, I hadn't been picking up the pain signals my feet must have been sending out. There was no alternative; it was another trip to the dreaded medical tent. Dinner had to wait.

Before long I was lying on my back on the rug, my feet up on a stool at the mercy of the delightfully pretty French nurse. One by one she pierced the blisters with a scalpel blade, drained them and then, with abandon, she pulled away the loose skin with forceps. Just when I thought the pain couldn't get any worse, she swabbed the raw exposed flesh underneath with iodine solution and I almost bit through the peak of the cap that was clenched between my teeth. The wounds were then dressed, taped up and I was sent packing so that the next victim could take my place.

I dallied a little in the medical tent afterwards, delighted to see my friend Miles lying just a few yards from me. Not delighted to see him back in the hands of the nurses, for again his feet were a terrible mess, but delighted to hear him laughing and joking with those around him. Such a contrast to that morning. Miles was bouncing back, and for that reason alone, we all slept better that night.

* * * * *

Day three was Dune Day. Marathon des Sables legend has it that the first two days are just a gentle warm-up. Dune Day was when it really began to get serious: 37 kilometres, and a glance at the Road Book showed that the serious dunes were all around the midpoint of the stage when the sun would be at its fiercest.

I'd had a far better night, with the added bonus of not even having to get up for a pee. It had been dark when I'd got back from Doc Trotter's the previous evening, but feeling better had given me an appetite and, under torchlight, I set about preparing a meal of sweet and sour chicken and rice, followed by bananas and custard.

Now, after a breakfast of sweetened porridge, I was standing once again on the start line, only this time feeling raring to go just as I had been on the first morning. As we meandered around waiting for the briefing I came across Andy Elder, a doctor at a London hospital, and I sought yet another measured opinion of my problems of the previous day. As Andy racked his brain to recall how kidney function is regulated by a complex interaction of three different hormones, we were called forward to the start.

'Leave it with me,' he called. 'I'll work it out as I run and see you later. It will give me something to think about and take my mind off the pain,' he grinned.

A couple of hours later, at the first checkpoint, I caught up with Andy again. 'I reckon you're taking too much salt,' was his advice. 'Because you're so slim, the four salt tablets a day they recommend is probably too much for you. Try cutting it to two.' Similar advice to Dave, my American medic friend, and it turned out to be sound advice, because that particular problem never recurred for the rest of the race.

The first half of the stage had been uneventful for me. I had still been peeing more than usual, but it was nothing like the floodgates of the day before. Small dunes, scree ridges, stony plateaus – nothing too demanding, and I'd been able to run large sections of it.

At checkpoint one I'd loosened the straps holding my Camelbak to the side of my rucksack to allow me to refill it and mix the drink powder in. I'd wasted as little time as possible but, within two minutes of leaving, I felt the Camelbak slip through the straps and flop to the ground. Stupid mistake – I'd forgotten to re-tighten the straps. Idiot. Stopping was a major operation. Disconnect my sound wires first. Take off the minidisc recorder. Then the rucksack could come off. Feed my Camelbak back through the straps, tightening them this time. And then everything back on in reverse order. Minutes had been wasted just because I'd forgotten to do a simple job that took seconds. I was angry with myself, but it served a useful purpose as I quelled it with a sustained spell of harder running.

Now the dunes were bigger, but soon a respite – checkpoint two.

From there it was straight back into powder sand and, for the first time, the dunes towered above me. The Sahara Desert of the cinema screen. It was awesome. To my left a hill of sand soared 200 feet into the air with a solitary set of footprints running up its face to the very summit. A wicked waste of effort by one runner, but then I was envious of the view they must have had from the top.

I stayed low and wound between the dunes. A camel and her calf nibbled at some greenery. I paused to take a photo. High above me, a herd of six goats wandered from bush to bush rummaging among the dry, brown thorns for the occasional succulent green shoot beneath. Another photograph. Such a desolate place, but still so much life.

Climbing, climbing upwards; feet sinking into the sand that sucked at the shoes on my feet. Scorching heat, abrasive sand, glittering views. Across a dry riverbed, another steep climb through a mountain pass packed with deep, golden, drifting sand, and then, from the top, a view that took my breath away.

Below lay the dried lake of Iferd. It could so easily have been another planet – it was stunning. It shimmered like a mirage, violet and then cream below the wide blue sky and blazing yellow sun. Again I reached into my pouch for the tiny disposable camera. A tap on my shoulder; it was a Japanese runner. We didn't share a language but we did share a sense of wonderment at what lay below us. We took each other's photo in front of this stunning background before plunging down the sandy hill to the checkpoint at the edge of the lake.

Replenished with water, and feeling far better than I could ever have hoped for on the previous day, I left the checkpoint and set off across the parched lake. It was as if it had been placed there to aid our recovery after the exertion of the dunes. Flat as a pancake; firm but slightly springy, just like a tartan track. I raced across the lake, the thought of walking not even entering my head. From there, the ground became sandy again, but no big dunes. Gentle undulations, scattered bushes, the heat now receding.

As I covered the final six kilometres to our new camp, my morale was sky high once more. I had overcome Dune Day. Certainly, my legs were really heavy but I could feel no new blisters, and mentally I was strong. Just 24 hours earlier all sorts of black thoughts had been crossing through my mind. Could I really have continued if every stage had been as psychologically tough as yesterday's was? But now that was history. I ran under the finish banner, and had a spring in my step as I lugged my new water allocation towards our tent.

Something was different. The tents were laid out on the ground but most hadn't been erected yet. I found 'Tent 40'. Neil and Henry were in, crouched under a small canopy of shelter propped up on a solitary branch. I was the third one back, just as I had been on the first day: another morale boost. It seemed that some of the lorries transporting the camp had got lost in the desert and, until all the equipment and men had arrived, they couldn't finish erecting the camp. If this had happened the day before, it would have been the last straw, but today it just didn't seem to matter. Such are the ups and downs of the Marathon des Sables.

Neil and Henry set off towards the finish to welcome the rest home. I got some water on the boil. I was hungry.

7

The longest day

A BRIEF stage summary of my race so far might have been good, bad and then good again. I could not allow that sequence to continue into stage four. Although we had been given the Road Book two days before the race started, one of the secrets of the race was not to let your mind stray forward to the days ahead. Each and every leg was a massive enough challenge without wasting valuable energy worrying about what lay over the page.

As the, by now familiar, Italian cockerels across the camp stirred my senses, a sinking feeling in my stomach told me that it was now time to confront the big one: the 74-kilometre stage.

My mind was turning over the options as I prepared. My body was sore and aching from the efforts of the previous stage, but the same distance on this day would only get me to the halfway point. I had two choices. Run and walk as far as I could until nightfall, snatch a few hours' sleep wherever I happened to be at that time, and then finish the rest of the stage in tomorrow's daylight; or much more appealing was the prospect of finishing the stage in one go, even if that meant travelling some of it by night.

That would have the huge advantage of giving my body the best part of a day off the following day, but was I physically capable of it? It was going to be a question of pace. Even if I felt good, I had to conserve energy for the later miles, so, by the time I lined up behind the start banner, I had made a conscious decision that for this stage only, I would only run the easier flat sections, and power-walk the rest.

Speed-wise, there was probably little to choose between my power-walking pace and the slow jog that my still weighty backpack imposed, but from a mental point of view, choosing to walk most of it was a great relief. For this day at least, the two conflicting voices in my brain, that screamed 'walk' and 'run' alternately, would be temporarily silenced.

I felt good from the beginning, despite the exhausting dunes in the early miles. We had left the leading 90 or so runners back in the camp – they would start some three hours behind us with the idea that this would help to keep the field relatively compressed so that the helicopter that swept up and down the line of runners could spot anybody straying seriously off-track.

Neil was among this elite group and, as I held myself back from breaking into a jog too early, I tried to calculate in my head what time he might come past me; it all served to take my mind off the pain. Checkpoint one came surprisingly quickly but the heat was building rapidly and I was grateful for the new bottle of water. Just beyond the checkpoint we actually crossed a small stream, tiptoeing carefully over the stepping-stones, and then the course opened out on to a dried riverbed.

The heat intensified. Mile followed mile and now I was happy to be walking. The field was increasingly spread out and there were several occasions when no one else was in sight, either behind or in front. A tiny bush covered with delicate white flowers appeared in my path. Amazing. How could anything flower out here?

I again broke into song. Very little was living round here so there wasn't much to offend! What a magnificent venue this would make for a Pink Floyd concert, I fantasised. I imagined vast banks of speakers spraying drifting guitar solos over the endless plains. Is there anybody out there?

I started to climb towards a sandy pass alongside the small mountain of El Abhet. As it got steeper, so the sand got softer and deeper. My feet were sucked in and my thighs screamed with the effort of repeatedly pulling them back out again. A local family group of at least three generations stood at the top of the pass, urging me up, and then I was there and the view on to the vast lunar-like landscape immediately repaid the effort. Not for the first time I felt privileged to be in this race. I paused briefly to take a photograph of this fantasy world and was then on my way again.

On the horizon I could now see the first real signs of habitation we had encountered in four days: the village of Jdaid. As I approached across a stony field, a young mother stood by the wayside and watched in silence and, seemingly, bewilderment. On her back was strapped a tiny baby, only weeks old, and swathed from head to toe in clothing to protect against the intense heat. A young boy danced excitedly at her feet and held out a hand as I approached. All I had that was easily accessible was about a third of a sticky energy bar, so I placed this into the youngster's fingers and he held it high above his head, screaming and dancing with delight. The mother nodded her approval and, as I strode on, I wondered whether he would find it as unpalatable as I did.

Compared with what we had passed through before, Jdaid was a thriving metropolis. The locals were out in force, the helicopter swept up and down and film crews seemed to be everywhere. Palm trees abounded and the area was clearly irrigated, with cultivated patches of crops lining both sides of the track that wound through the village. Both Nick and Shaun homed their cameras in on me and we exchanged pleasantries, as well as a few barbed comments about who was working the hardest.

Soon the village was behind me and it was back to the hot, dusty open spaces. The next checkpoint stood on a vast dried lakebed as flat as a snooker table and this gave me the opportunity for a little gentle jogging as I approached it. I paused for a few minutes in the shadow of a Land Rover to top up liquid containers. I had been on the move now for more than four hours, and was still only just over a quarter of the way to the end of the stage.

There were now almost 14 kilometres to the next checkpoint and the heat from the sun was powering down relentlessly. Mostly flat ground but endless, absolutely endless. I strode on, and occasionally broke into a gentle jog, which seemed to be a relief from the relentless power-walking. The distant chatter of voices and ripples of applause from behind snapped me out of the internalised world I was gradually drifting into. I turned to see Lahcen Ahansal, the race leader, coming up behind me. A tiny figure, he seemed to glide effortlessly across the desert surface at a pace I would have found impossible on the finest running track. A grin, a wave of acknowledgement from the great man, and he was gone.

Again I pushed on across the stony infinity. The land ahead shimmered with the heat. Far to my right, several sandstorms spiralled into the sky at the base of a range of dunes. In this heat, drinking was my lifeline.

The electrolyte drink that I sucked down the tube from my rucksack was becoming increasingly sickly and I alternated it with mouthfuls of water from the plastic bottle I carried in my hand, but this was exposed to the full force of the sun, and was becoming increasingly tepid. Each mouthful of warm liquid induced retching so I poured the water over my forearms in an effort to cool them.

About 200 yards to my right a Land Rover passed by in the opposite direction and then suddenly and skilfully spun round. It was the Carlton crew. As I jogged on they filmed from a distance through the windows. The vehicle then accelerated ahead and Nick leapt out with his camera on his shoulder and ran across towards me. As I plodded forwards, so Nick ran backwards, just feet away from me, his camera pointing into my grimacing face. Imperceptibly, I picked up the pace.

There weren't too many opportunities to have a bit of fun out here but this was one. Nick's legs were moving faster and faster but he stuck to his task with the utmost professionalism – film crew didn't have it easy out here either. And then I spotted a large boulder beside the track and Nick was heading straight at it. I caught him just as his feet hit the boulder, and together we managed to keep both him and the camera upright and intact.

'I think I've got enough footage of that,' he grinned, and set off back to the shelter and comfort of his Land Rover. I pressed on.

Perched on top of a rocky embankment, checkpoint three didn't arrive a moment too soon. Still not halfway through the stage and I felt burnt out in more ways than one. I just had to get out of the unrelenting sun and take a break. I crawled into one of the low Berber tents and threw my head back on to my rucksack. Sleep would have come easily, but even as I stared aimlessly at the hessian cloth above my head, I could sense Nick's lens discreetly recording my every move.

Neil arrived, having set out with the elites three hours behind me, spoke briefly, and then moved on. How did those guys do it? Twenty minutes drifted by and I knew I had to get going again; if I stayed any longer, I might never move from there. Steve North arrived just as I was scrambling to my knees. He had started out with Steve Broomfield and Jerry but they were both really suffering in the heat and he had decided to press on at his own pace.

I pulled on my rucksack, said my goodbyes to Nick, and set off down a steep, rocky slope. The sun seemed hotter than ever and its reflection bounced back off the smooth rocks and drilled into my eyes.

Despite my long rest, I was feeling worse than ever. I squinted to pick out my route through the glare of the dazzling rocks and then the penny dropped. Damn and blast! I had left my sunglasses back in the tent.

Of course, it was uphill back to the tent and, for a moment, I wondered whether Nick might have picked up my profanities on the radio mic, and might just bring my glasses down to me. But the TV crew weren't allowed to assist us in any way, so I set off back up the rocky hill. Over 38 kilometres to go and here I was, going in the wrong bloody direction.

My sunglasses were still on the rug where I had laid them and I left the tent again, this time with Steve North. We travelled together for a couple of kilometres but Steve was on a roll and I was struggling to keep up. I let him go and plodded on through yet more debilitating sand dunes. At least I was now past the halfway point of the stage.

I stayed at checkpoint four just long enough to top up my liquid supplies and bolt down yet another sickly energy bar. We were also given a green lumistick to make us visible once darkness had fallen, and I snapped this to activate the contents before putting it into the mesh pocket on the rear of my backpack.

There was still maybe an hour and a half of daylight left, but the stick would give off its greenish glow for a good 12 hours. I rummaged in my front pouch for my penlight torch and the headband it fitted into: when night came, I would be ready.

Steve and another British runner, George, had been setting off just as I arrived at this checkpoint so they were probably only five to ten minutes in front by the time I was ready to leave. I really didn't want to be travelling alone in the desert at night.

If there was a group of us, at least we'd all get lost together. I set out after them.

I'd covered more than a marathon on that day already, but the decision I'd made earlier in the day to power-walk, rather than run, most of the stage seemed to have paid off. I still had some energy left, but was it enough to complete another 30 kilometres, most of it in pitch darkness, or would I have to get my head down until dawn?

Soon I caught sight of two figures ahead of me and gradually increased my pace to close the gap. As I neared, I realised it was not Steve and George – these two were far too good-looking. As I sped past the two French girls, yelling out a greeting, they gesticulated urgently, pointing at my head, 'Torche, torche!' In squeezing my torch into the headband, I'd inadvertently turned it on even though there was still an hour of sunlight left. Another stupid mistake, and one that might cost me later; an hour of battery power could make a lot of difference in the dark hours ahead. I thanked the girls and sped on. There was no one else in sight.

The sandy path bent round to the left and there, maybe a quarter of a mile ahead, I could make out three figures. They'd picked up more company. My legs moved with renewed vigour, rapidly closing the gap. Again I was disappointed – it was not them. Two Italians and a Japanese runner. We exchanged greetings and reassurances in a universal sign language, and I ploughed on again. The sun was now low on the horizon – glowing orange, then red, then purple. It threw my shadow yards across the sandy plain. For so much of this race my shadow had been a tiny patch of black between my feet. Now it stretched away as the last few minutes of daylight passed. I took another photograph.

Then I saw them. Up and over a succession of stony mounds they strode, their trekking poles driving into the surface. I'd been in two minds about trekking poles; were they a help, or a hindrance? They would certainly have taken some of the workload off of my legs and on to my arms. Great for fast walking, but another encumbrance when running. In the end, like the majority of competitors, I'd decided to do without poles.

I caught Steve and George just as the sun slipped below the horizon. The transition from daylight to darkness was incredibly rapid. We walked together the last couple of kilometres to checkpoint five and, by the time we reached it, it was pitch dark. Now, it was decision time. To slip into our sleeping bags, and join several other runners already stretched out under the tents that had been erected, or to plough on into the darkness?

I felt weak from lack of food. I pulled an energy bar from my front pouch and peeled back the foil wrapper. The bar had snapped in two and I cursed as half of it fell to the ground. I picked it up; sand and fine grit was glued to its sticky surface. I was hungry, but I wasn't that hungry. I ate the remaining half.

'What's it to be then?'

Twenty-two kilometres remained, with one further checkpoint at the halfway point.

'Let's take it one stage at a time. We'll push on to the next stop and decide again there.'

We hauled our backpacks on to our shoulders and set off in single file up the darkened, rocky path.

'Entrance to the dunes of the Erg Znaigui,' the Road Book decreed next. Following a bearing of 32 degrees would see us to the next checkpoint. Easier said than done.

As I fumbled for my compass and turned to face in the correct direction, I was confronted with a wall of black. Within yards, we were in powdery soft sand. I started to climb, my thighs screaming as I drove my legs upwards. Each footfall would plunge deep into the sand and then, as my weight shifted on to the other leg, would slide back downwards again. If we could just get to the top, then surely we would see the way ahead.

The gradient worsened. Now my hands were plunging into the sand as well. Drive with the legs, pull with the arms. My shoes were in danger of being sucked off my feet, and I had to curl my toes inside them to hold them in place.

And then, suddenly, we were there: on a pinnacle of sand. Unbelievably narrow – the dune was topped with a razor-sharp edge. I straddled the peak sideways – each foot sliding down the steep, slippery slope, threatening to split me in half. Overhead the sky was awash with a zillion stars but no friendly moon to light our way. I looked ahead on the bearing we were following. The sand plunged away below our feet but ahead was just more blackness. Another dune? Possibly even higher than the one on which we were standing.

As Steve and George came up alongside, we scanned the darkness ahead looking for the tell-tale glow of a white lumistix that we had been told would mark the route: white for the route, green for the runners. Nothing. In daylight, we could have moved to the right or the left to skirt round the bowl of the dune, but there was no light here to illuminate our passage.

Steve pushed on and I followed. Giant strides down the slope, I started running, tried to put the brakes on, but couldn't stop. Legs thrashing through the loose sand out of control and then, bang – face to face with another wall of sand. Again we started to climb.

'This is bloody stupid,' called George. 'This can't be the way – there's no markers, there's no footprints. Let's go back to the checkpoint and start again.'

We paused to take stock. Check the compass – we were heading in the right direction. There were many runners in front of us but most would probably have passed this way in daylight and would no doubt have opted for a less direct route through the dunes. We were probably one of the first groups to come through here in pitch darkness.

'Let's climb this next bastard,' urged Steve. 'We might see more from the top.'

'We'll end up killing ourselves,' grumbled George, but he pushed on regardless, although less than convinced we were on the right track.

The higher we climbed, the more powdery the sand became, and the deeper we sank into it. Higher and higher we clawed our way up, and then again another razor-sharp ridge. We gasped in the rapidly cooling air as the exertion of the climb caught up with us, but now we could see tiny dots of light in the dunes below us, but moving in all directions. There were other runners lost in the dunes.

Then we heard voices from behind. It was Andy, the London doctor, and his colleagues, Dick and Tony, who together formed the Cystic Fibrosis team.

'We're lost aren't we?' pleaded George, 'Let's turn back.' But the fact that we had arrived together at this point, despite travelling as two separate groups, encouraged us to push on. The six of us stood together surveying the pinpricks of light in the blackness below our feet. The runners were pale green, the route markers white, but at this distance they were both just a speck of light in the darkness. We would focus on any pinprick of light that appeared stationary and then, just as we had convinced ourselves it must be a marker, it would move.

Tony took the lead. 'Come on, all we've got to do is to keep following the 32 degree bearing,' and he plunged over the brink into the sliding sand. The rest of us stayed put, still uncertain. I again gazed overhead in awe of the myriad of stars. Here we were, lost at night in one of the most inhospitable places on the planet, but the overwhelming emotion was not of fear, but of wonderment. For want of a better idea, we followed Tony's lead.

Another valley, another dune. We began to fan out, looking in vain for that elusive speck of light that would signal we were back on track. Voices called out across the dark landscape in all languages, and shouts came back in response, but no one was really certain who was doing the calling, or who was replying. Minutes flowed by, but time was of no consequence and then, gradually, the dunes seemed to be easing in their ferocity. We were coming out the other side and we were still holding our compass bearing. Soon the six of us were together again and we paused to empty our shoes of the abundance of sand that had worked its way in, grinding away at our already raw blistered feet.

We were now on a relatively flat, dried lakebed and, according to the Road Book, the next checkpoint was just eight kilometres away, on the same bearing. Sure enough, through the gloom ahead, lights could be seen shimmering in the distance. We were back en route and, as a group, our spirits were lifted as we strode out towards our target. Dick, in particular, seemed to be limping badly, but the proximity of our goal was sucking us all towards it.

With less chance now of straying off track, we could each move at a pace that was comfortable to our individual conditions. Andy, Dick and Tony upped their pace and gradually pulled away. Steve, his trekking poles tap-tap-tapping into the stony surface, fought to keep up with them. I let them go. For a while I walked with George, surveying the ground in front of me with torchlight, aware that this was a time we might well encounter a snake among the still-warm rocks. Little was said as we employed every ounce of energy we had to keep moving.

The lights ahead still beckoned and we fought on – and on and on and on. Judging distance in the desert was hard enough; at night it was impossible. Surely the lights were receding. I forced my gaze downwards in the hope that this might make the checkpoint arrive sooner. My feet were screaming to be let out of the confines of my shoes. The sound of George's trekking poles grew fainter as he fell behind, but I knew he could still follow the light on my rucksack.

And then suddenly we were there. Tents, water, friendly faces lit by flickering flames. I fell to the ground, absolutely exhausted. The Cystic Fibrosis team had already set off on the final leg, but Steve was still there, once again emptying the sand from his shoes and socks. I rummaged in my front pack for my last energy bar. George came in and just wanted to keep moving.

Just 11 kilometres now stood between us and the finish line but the temptation for me to call it a day and to sleep here was overwhelming. Steve reminded me of the home comforts of 'Tent 40', my warm sleeping bag, and the prospect of a whole day off in the morning, and this tipped the balance. I agreed to press on. Steve and George set off as I munched my bar, swallowed some more water and tried to massage some life back into my toes through my shoes.

As I set off again, I could see the faint glow of their two green lumistix just a few hundred yards ahead and then, suddenly, the whole landscape was momentarily awash with light. The photographers were still awake. I coaxed my legs through those agonising first few yards that followed every rest break in this mad race, before the body's own medicines gradually washed the worst of the pain away.

'Ca va?' an invisible female voice called from the shadows.

'Tres bien,' I replied in my strongest voice, just in case it was one of the wandering race medics looking out for people they considered to be unfit to continue.

'Doug?'

'Ah, Cathy. I thought you might be a medic. I'm absolutely done in.'

'You're doing great. Last leg – you're nearly there. Good luck.'

Cathy was reporting on the race for the *Sunday Times*, and that brief exchange of words gave my spirits an immediate lift. I struck out after George and Steve and soon caught them again.

We walked together as the ground was now more hilly and strewn with large rocks. Route markers were again less frequent and hard to locate.

'We'll have to stop,' called George, 'I need to change batteries in my headlamp.' Steve and I walked on the spot to keep our legs from seizing up as George rummaged in his bag. He put new batteries in, switched on the lamp – nothing happened. 'Can you bring your light over here?' he called. I began to get irritated by the delay, and could see that Steve was champing at the bit as well. At last George's lamp burst back into life and we set off again.

Ten minutes later my own beam of light faded away and now it was my own turn to call a halt. Steve and George waited patiently and I felt guilty for showing impatience earlier.

As we strode on, George was beginning to suffer and again started to fall behind. 'Are you OK, George?' Steve called back. 'Just tired. I'm OK – I'll make it. You two go on.'

Steve upped the pace, his sticks setting a rhythm that I struggled to maintain. Few words were spoken, but from time to time we would feed each other brief bouts of encouragement. Heads down, our petrol tanks were on empty, our feet were on fire, but now we both knew that we were going to make it.

A strange glow appeared ahead. At first sight it appeared to be the dipped headlights of a Land Rover, and then it dropped below a rocky mound before reappearing like a mini-sunrise. It was much further away than we'd first thought, so we cajoled each other onwards. Again the glow dropped below the skyline as we forced our legs up a sloping incline, but this time a phosphorescence lit the sky. As we reached the brow, we saw the camp spread out in front of us, a cluster of lights surrounding the finish banner, the rest enveloped in darkness. As if choreographed, we simultaneously punched the cold desert air with clenched fists, and struck out briskly for the line.

Just before 1am, after a struggle of nearly 16 hours, Steve and I jogged side-by-side over the finish line, and immediately embraced. I will remember that moment for the rest of my life.

'You might not look it, but you're a fucking tough cookie,' muttered Steve. I knew that, without Steve's urging, I might well be asleep by now at the final checkpoint, but together we had pulled each other through.

We located 'Tent 40' in the darkness and threw down our rucksacks. Just Neil and Henry had got in before us. They stirred from their sleeping bags to offer congratulations, but now it really was time for sleep. Eating and foot surgery could wait for the morning – we'd earned a lie-in.

Our race was run, but, as we rapidly slipped into a deep slumber, we were blissfully unaware of the dramas that had already happened behind us.

*　*　*　*　*

Despite the crushing fatigue, I still had a very broken night's sleep. My feet throbbed and burned constantly. I'd had the energy to prise off my shoes, but examining the damage that had been inflicted by 74 kilometres of hot desert was a job that would wait until morning. My feet remained hidden from view beneath socks stained with sand, sweat and blood; every movement during the night was accompanied by jolts of pain.

As first light crept into the tent there was the consolation that, for this morning at least, our shelter was not going to be pulled from above us. As I peeped through the open sides of our tent from the relative comfort of my warm sleeping bag, I took in my first real view of the location of this new camp. I was stunned to see that we were nestling at the foot of an awesome range of dunes: Erg Chebbi. These would provide the first eight or nine miles of our next marathon stage, but I had a day off to enjoy first, so I put that thought to the back of my mind.

No one else from the tent had come in during the hours of darkness – somewhere out there Derek, Steve, Jerry, Jon and Miles were still battling and I did not envy them. I tried to get more sleep but the hubbub grew in intensity as the camp returned to life.

Just before 7.30am there was a whelp of delight as Derek celebrated his return, throwing his rucksack to the ground and punching the air. Within minutes, he was silently enveloped within his sleeping bag. Neil and Henry were soon up and about and I managed to empty the contents of my backpack and get some water on the boil, without leaving the confines of my warm bag in the chilly morning air. Hunger was now striking hard and I frantically rushed to mix up some porridge.

Having eaten that, I could delay no longer – it was time to inspect my feet. Gingerly, I peeled back the crusty layers that yesterday were a new pair of socks. Every time the stiffened material stuck, I gritted my teeth and tugged tentatively. What a mess! Even the blisters seemed to have blisters and these were going to have to run a marathon the very next day.

Between my toes, clods of sand were bound together by dried blood. Fortunately we had picked up more water rations on arrival during the night and, with having a day without running, I could afford to spare a little more of the precious liquid on cleaning up my feet. Coward I may have been, but I was determined to avoid the scalpel blades and iodine swabs of Doc Trotter if at all possible.

It was during this delicate operation that I glanced up to see Steve Broomfield trudging towards us, rucksack hung over his shoulder.

'Stevie, mate,' I called out. 'Great to see you. Well done, mate.'

He paused in front of the tent, dropping his bag to the ground. He looked good, he looked cheerful; Steve always looked cheerful.

'It would be well done, boys, but…' He paused briefly to gather his thoughts. 'I'm afraid I've binned it. I've just been brought back in the Land Rover.'

The news stunned us into silence. In the space of just a few days, the shared hardships of our desert existence had bonded our little community together in a manner that might have taken years in 'the real world'. Not one of us could have felt worse had it been ourselves.

'Now let's get one thing straight,' bawled Steve, as we sat shaking our heads in disbelief. 'I'm not going to put up with you bastards walking round with long faces. Yes, I'm disappointed, but if I can deal with it, then you bloody lot can. I've got to go and hand all my food in, but they say I can still stay with you guys. I'll just get carried round in the jeep the last couple of days and have to eat good food with wine and beer! So cheer up. I'll be out there with you in spirit.' Lardy was a big man in more ways than one.

Between us we began to unravel the sequence of events that had evolved on the previous day. Steve North had started in agony with his horrendously blistered feet, although he felt strong otherwise. He set off at a very slow hobble and soon fell behind Lardy and Jerry. As so often happened, what seems like intolerable pain at the outset soon subsides once the adrenaline starts pumping through the bloodstream and, shortly before checkpoint two, Steve North caught and then passed his two colleagues.

They shared a few minutes together under the shelter of a tent at the checkpoint. It was approaching the hottest part of the day and Lardy wanted to take it steady until around 4pm, when the temperature would begin to diminish, and then he would put a spurt on. All seemed to be fine.

Lardy was not fine. The heat had been his big bugbear right from day one, and the long haul between checkpoints two and three was to be his downfall. The sun blazed remorselessly.

Unbeknown to him at the time, he was already developing a throat infection and his body temperature was climbing. He became vague and disorientated. When he and Jerry reached an isolated tree, they sat in its shade for as long as they dared, but once back in the unforgiving inferno, every forward step became a massive effort.

At one point he toppled over into the sand and it took a mighty combined effort to get his huge frame upright again. When they eventually staggered into checkpoint three, Steve knew in his own mind that his race was run. Miles, Jon and the Carlton crew came in shortly afterwards and suggested he lie down in the shade and reconsider his decision once the sun was lower, but by then, Steve was vomiting and shivering. He could not continue.

As we sat in the shelter of the tent listening to Steve's tale, it was impossible not to feel admiration for the man. After all the months of preparation, it must have been absolutely gut-wrenching to make the decision to pull out, but only he knew his limits and, deep inside, he knew he had surpassed them. Now he had the hardest job of all to do: to phone his girlfriend, Laura, on the camp satellite phone and tell her the bad news.

'I'm dreading this,' he sighed, as he pulled himself to his feet to make his way over to the communication tent, 'but I've got to do it. I'm not going to have her find out by reading it on the internet!'

We returned to the task of foot repair and our thoughts now passed to Jerry, Jon and Miles who were still out there. The mood was sombre, but was temporarily lifted when the email lady called on her daily 'post' round; our individual messages having been printed on little slips of paper. I had four that morning and it was such a lift to know that people at home were thinking of me. My sister-in-law telling me that my cats were OK and surmising on the colour of my underpants by the end of the week, a friend's young son urging

'Doug the Thug' to keep running, a workmate worrying about my blisters and another friend encouraging the 'Mad One' to go all the way.

And then the temporary mood of relaxation around the camp was suddenly interrupted as a cluster of dust-devils, mini-whirlwinds of fiercely abrasive sand, swept abruptly across one corner of the camp, picking up items of clothing, shoes and equipment and dumping them haphazardly out into the desert beyond. Without instruction, runners of all nationalities fanned out as a giant search party in order to retrieve as much as they could find and hopefully return them to their rightful owners so that they could continue their race. Most of the time we were competing against each other; on occasions like this we were in it together.

Time passed, a diminishing trickle of runners was still crossing the finishing line, all being given the hero's welcome that each and every one of them deserved. News filtered through that Jon and Miles were not far away, but Jerry was not with them. The whole British contingent gathered together under the shade of the balloons at the finish.

Shortly after 2.15pm, two tiny figures, tethered together with a strap, appeared over the crest of the rocky slope, and headed down to the line. A crescendo of sound built up from all corners of the camp, and somehow Jon and Miles found the energy to jog the final few yards. They were understandably elated, and amazingly, they seemed to be getting stronger as each day passed. They had cracked the big one and, as we helped them carry their water and bags back to 'Tent 40', tears were running down my cheeks. Never before in my life, and perhaps never again, would I be in the company of such a large group of people with such a shared common purpose.

'But what about Jerry?' we asked. We already knew he had left checkpoint three with Jon and Miles after Steve's collapse, but with the soles of his feet little more than raw meat, Jerry just hadn't been able to maintain the pace of the dynamic duo, who were gaining in strength as the race progressed.

We were later to learn that Jerry had teamed up with Allister McWilliams, a sergeant from the Royal Logistic Corps who, in his own way, was developing into one of the heroes of the race.

After a steady first day, Allister, or Mac to his army mates, had been struck down by a vicious bout of diarrhoea and vomiting. He had battled through day two but nothing, not even water, would stay down and he was growing weaker by the hour. Ignoring advice from the medical team and from his own colleagues, Mac was determined to make it to the finish. Like many of us, he stood to make a lot of money for charity, and it was this that was driving him on in the face of increasing dehydration and debilitation.

Jerry and Mac had decided to stick together in joint adversity. Just as I had found with Steve North, the combined efforts of two people struggling over this nightmare landscape was worth more than the two individual efforts added together. Slow they may have been, but their determination and grit matched that of anybody else in the race.

Thirty-one hours and 11 minutes after they had set off, Jerry and Mac finally hobbled the last few yards to the finish line. They were the last of the 565 runners to complete this murderous stage but they had made it comfortably inside the official cut-off time of 40 hours.

As ever, Jerry was ebullient as he covered those final steps. Mac was grey, drawn and silent. The reception they received at the line exceeded even that given to Jon and Miles – television cameras from across the globe were pressed into their haggard faces, and virtually everyone in the camp was there to greet them.

The effort Mac had put in was etched in deep lines on his ashen face. His legs were buckling, and he was hastily carried back to his tent by his concerned army colleagues.

Yes, Jerry may have been able to go a bit faster on his own, but there was no way was he going to leave Mac, and condemn him to almost certain failure. Jerry had stayed put, and never was the spirit of the Marathon des Sables more clearly demonstrated.

* * * * *

That evening, after darkness fell, the Berber Arabs who had so cheerfully transported our camp around the desert lit a huge bonfire and danced and chanted fervently around it to the frantic rhythm of their drums and pipes. For them it was an evening of celebration. For we competitors, premature celebration would surely tempt fate, but, as the flames of the bonfire danced on our faces, our ultimate goal now at least seemed to be within touching distance.

Miles asked me to describe the scene to him. He could feel the heat, smell the smoke and listen to the crackle of the bonfire and was bouncing to the flow of the music, but he just needed a few words to complete the picture in his mind.

'It's a beautiful scene, Miles,' I began. 'A huge fire, maybe ten feet high, in the middle of a hollowed-out area and surrounded by sand. There are clouds of glowing embers billowing off into the desert wind and up into the sky – it looks like a huge firework. Patterned rugs all around it, people sitting, standing and dancing on them, and a group of musicians playing on the far side. Hundreds of people are watching – competitors, organisers, medics, media, everybody. There are TV cameras filming it, and people in traditional Moroccan dress kneeling down on one of the mats.'

'How far away is the fire?' asked Miles.

'Thirty feet, no more,' I replied, and Miles exhaled deeply. 'Wow! In the middle of the Sahara Desert.' Jon sidled up to us, and together we listened to the pipes and gyrated our battered bodies to the rhythmic pounding of the drums.

'Where in the world would you rather be at this moment?' murmured Jon. It was a question that didn't require an answer.

We spent about an hour by the bonfire, only drifting back to our tents when the fire had died down, and the music had faded away. Overhead, a panoply of diamonds studded the night sky. It had been one of the first occasions where competitors and media were free to mingle with each other and we had shared anecdotes of what had been an unforgettable experience for us all, whichever side of the camp we came from.

With their late finish, and further suffering at the hands of the foot nurses, Jon and Miles had still not eaten and set about preparing a meal. By half past eight, I was tucked up into my sleeping bag, pencilling brief memories into my notebook. Just outside the tent, Jon cursed as he battled to keep his stove alight, as gusts of wind sent more mini sandstorms scuttling across the camp. Their long-overdue meal would be delayed a little longer. From some parts of the tent, snoring could be heard already. Others fidgeted restlessly, trying desperately to find a comfortable position for their battered feet.

As hush gradually descended, I wondered whether my day off had been a good or a bad thing. Despite the day of comparative rest, every part of me still hurt like never before and in some ways I envied those who'd been running that day, for they would still have that unrelenting momentum that somehow defied all logic, and carried you through from one impossibly hard day to the next. Tomorrow would provide me with my answer.

8

The sands of time

S TAGE five of this unforgiving race covered the classic
marathon distance, 26 miles and 385 yards, but there
were no tarmac roads, no mile-markers and certainly no
cheering crowds. It was a duel under the sun with the desert
throwing down the gauntlet.

Normal practice for a marathon would be to taper down
training in the build-up to the race. Well, we had been tapering
up. The previous four stages had seen us run around 19, 20,
23 and then 46 miles on consecutive, blisteringly hot days.
Indeed, as the camp stirred in the early morning haze, and I
wearily poked my head from the cosy confines of my sleeping
bag, there was almost a sense of, 'Well, at least I only have to
run a marathon today!' But this was to be a marathon like no
other.

Having breakfasted and somehow forced our swollen and
disfigured feet into shoes that now seemed ridiculously small,
the remaining members of the 'Tent 40' team once again hauled
their rucksacks on to their backs. At least these were now a little
lighter, as we had now eaten most of our food rations. As we
trudged painfully towards the start, we bade a fond farewell to
Lardy. He had been allowed to spend the night with us in the

tent, but would be completing this day's stage in the back of a four-wheel drive. Despite his intense personal disappointment, and his fragile state of health, Steve had spent the previous evening urging us all on, and demanding that we didn't let him down by feeling sorry for his plight.

Standing waiting beneath the start banner, another of my marathon mantras drifted into my mind, 'Don't set off too fast.' There was no chance of that today! Towering above us, within yards of the start, was the Erg Chebbi, the largest range of sand dunes in the Western Sahara, and the second-largest on the whole African continent. The first nine miles of our run that day would be through these dunes; that should put a brake on an overenthusiastic start.

Trois, deux, un, allez! We were on our way again and immediately, every painful footstep was being sucked into the soft sand. Twenty minutes later I was in another world; menacing, but oh so beautiful. Bulwarks of soft, powdery sand soared hundreds of feet into the air as far as the eye could see, sculpted into perfect curves and basins by the busy desert wind. Yes, we had spent a lot of time in sand dunes over the previous four days, but these giants were of an order of magnitude more imperious.

Following the line of the razor sharp ridges was the only way to progress. Miles of sand stretched to the right, miles to the left, but we advanced in single file along the narrow ridge, for to step on to the downslope on either side meant an inevitable slide to the depths of a sandbowl, and another Herculean climb back out again.

My mind wandered back to the struggle we had had trying to follow a compass bearing across dunes in pitch darkness just two nights previously. How much easier that journey would have been if we could have seen where the contours of the dunes lay and they were just a fraction of the height of what extended in front of us now.

The heat of the sand burned through the soles of my shoes, the sun bore down from above; a glance at the thermometer on my backpack showed the red liquid nestling into the overflow bulb above 50°C. We were later to learn that the temperature in the dunes had reached 58°C on that day.

The sand that had penetrated any tiny openings in the gaiters around my shoes and socks ground remorselessly at the grisly wounds on my feet. It was a cauldron, it was Hades, but, as we sucked in the hot air and pushed onwards and upwards, it was also a privilege to be there. Panoramas that few people ever get to see; pitting yourself against the full repertoire of desert perils – the experience was so uplifting that it hauled me above and beyond normal reactions to pain and exhaustion.

Three hours had elapsed when I finally emerged from those breathtaking dunes, pausing yet again to empty my shoes and socks of the incessantly infiltrating sand. Three hours – and I had only completed a third of my marathon. From here to the end, the Road Book suggested that the route was more encouraging – sandy, stony plateaus, dried river and lakebeds – surely an opportunity to make up for lost time.

I stumbled up and over a sandy bank and saw stretched in front of me a rock-strewn plateau. Flat ground at last, a chance to get back into a running rhythm, but some of the boulders were quite large and the chances of turning an ankle over were high. I paused at the foot of the bank to assess the situation – were the rocks spaced far enough apart for me to jog my way through without slowing to a walk?

As I looked ahead for the answer, I felt something moving across my feet. I froze. I was running a marathon in the Sahara Desert, and the organisers' insistence that we all carry an anti-venom pump had not been an encouraging omen. Glancing down, I was relieved to see that the two-foot-long lizard didn't appear to have noticed that it had just crossed a pair of size 11 trainers, rather than yet another rock. As it sought shelter from the blazing sun under a pile of desert rubble, I breathed a sigh of relief and sent instructions to my legs: it was time to start running. Either the message didn't get through, or my legs were becoming mutinous, for there was no response to the command. This was a marathon like no other.

The desert seduces you with immeasurable beauty and then, in the space of minutes, it rips away the vista and presents an expanse so vast and empty that there is nothing, absolutely nothing, that will distract your mind from the relentless task of putting one foot in front of another. No longer could the beauty of my surroundings lift me above the heat of the day. I again urged my legs onwards but there was nothing there. I had hit the wall not ten miles into my marathon.

Auto-pilot took over. Repeated gulps of electrolyte drink, a bite of a stodgy energy bar, but my stomach was sick of sweetness, and it was a battle to keep anything down. Even the bottle of water that I carried in my hand was baked by the sun and each warmed mouthful induced further bouts of retching which were inconveniently captured by my minidisc recorder and transmitted onwards for Nick's amusement.

The landscape ahead was now so flat that the 16-mile checkpoint shimmered and beckoned in the distance, but as fast as I urged my legs onwards, it grew no closer. The desert was blunting my ability to judge distance – tempting me with an unattainable vision. I was a donkey following a carrot on a stick.

There really was no point in trying to run. I could barely walk, and certainly not in a straight line. As on the second stage, there were now serious doubts in my mind as to whether I could continue, or even if it was wise to do so. Every step forward took a massive effort, yet took me no closer to that shimmering mirage on the horizon. I recalled another quotation I had read from a previous competitor in the race, 'When you get to the point where you just can't take another step and want to lie down and sleep, you have probably used about 80 per cent of your available resources.' Where was my remaining 20 per cent?

And then I heard footsteps behind me. It was Dick from the Cystic Fibrosis team. He had also come close to quitting in the furnace that was the Erg Chebbi dunes but he was now moving more freely again.

He could have sailed past me, but he didn't. He walked with me for a while, cajoled me, praised my persistence, reminded me of just how close we were to the end of the race, and then, when he was finally satisfied that I wasn't about to quit, he moved away at his own pace. Another demonstration of the spirit of the Marathon des Sables; no matter how difficult your own personal journey was, you could always find time to help a fellow runner in distress.

When I eventually struggled into that elusive checkpoint, I sought the shade of a Berber tent to provide a brief respite from the sun, but was soon back to being scorched again – still ten more miles to go. But now there was a transformation. Whether it was Dick's pep talk, the sight of a primitive dwelling to the left, a battered water-well, or a tiny cluster of palm trees, it was just enough to persuade some inner mental harbinger that the desert was not going to be allowed to beat me.

My remaining 20 per cent had finally surfaced; the mind and the body became one again. I broke into a gentle jog. Could I keep it going for two minutes? Yes, I could. Okay, what about five minutes? No problem. In that case, let's see how long I can jog before I have to stop. On and on I went; my surroundings were every bit as barren as they had been earlier when I had seemed so bereft of any energy, but where before everything seemed uniform, grey and lifeless, now there was shape, texture and colour all around.

I wasted no time at the final checkpoint, pausing only briefly to collect more water. On I ran. As the end approached, the ground rose and fell as we passed between mountains, the terrain underfoot becoming rockier and more hazardous, but now I was flying.

As I reached the brow of each hill, I imagined the finishing line just beyond, only to be confronted by yet another rocky outcrop to clamber up.

And then it was there. Half a mile away, surrounded by those four, so familiar, coloured hot air balloons. I raced for the line, ripples of applause coming from the runners who'd finished ahead of me, but who now stood and welcomed the rest of us home.

Seven hours and 50 minutes it took me. Never before had I run a slower marathon, and indeed never since, but never have I felt such extremes of wonder, pain, elation and despair, all in the space of those few hours. Every single marathon is an experience in its own right, and the stopwatch is just one part of that story.

As I joyously staggered my way back to 'Tent 40', the realisation suddenly dawned on me that I was now just one ten-kilometre stage away from completing this race. So, so close. As per usual, Neil and Henry had been back for some time, and greeted me as I approached. Derek had also beaten me in again, just as he had on the second day, but he had paid a heavy price as the abrasive sand and heat in the dunes had shredded the skin on his feet. In flip-flops, he hobbled solemnly towards the Doc Trotter tent.

Outside the cover of our hessian home, Steve North was already busily preparing his evening meal. Steve had paid dearly for his final training run on the High Peak Trail with Jon and Miles, starting this race with badly blistered feet that rapidly deteriorated further once the heat and sand got at them. On one visit to the medical tent his feet had been described as 'just about the worst they had ever seen', which was some reference coming from a place that sometimes resembled a medieval hospital.

However, the turning point of Steve's race had been the long night stage that we had finished together in the early hours of the morning. Just as I had felt that I could not have completed that stage without the encouragement and support of Steve, he felt exactly the same about me: the synergistic effect of joint effort. And now on this day, Steve had beaten me home by over an hour and, for the first time, had now overtaken me in the overall standings.

Eating seemed like a great idea and I soon had my little hexi-stove alight and boiling a mess tin full of water to prepare yet another freeze-dried delicacy. Little did I know, or indeed expect, that I was about to enjoy a culinary experience that would live long in my memory. Rummaging around in my rucksack, I found a packet of sweet and sour chicken and rice which I knew would provide the necessary nutrition, although little satisfaction.

Whatever the meals, whether it was porridge for breakfast, or shepherd's pie and bananas and custard for dinner, the result would always have the same stodgy consistency, with just slight variations in colour and flavour.

On this day I also pulled out a small packet of dried mushroom soup, but this was not just soup; it was soup with croutons. Deciding on a soup course before my main dish, I emptied the soup powder into my plastic mug and poured on the hot water. I watched as the croutons began to swell in the steaming liquid, and waited impatiently for it to cool enough to drink.

Even years later, I find it difficult to put into words just how good that soup, or rather the croutons, tasted. After days of ingesting nothing but liquids, or the mushy consistency of my dehydrated meals, the experience of crunching a crouton between my molars was pleasurable beyond belief: so pleasurable that I munched the croutons just one at a time, in order to prolong that little period of indulgence.

I still devoured my sweet and sour chicken meal, if only for its calorific value, and it was while eating this that the peace and quiet of our tent was shattered by the 'whoop, whoop' of Miles and Jon returning. What a difference a few days had made. On the brink of a compulsory medical withdrawal from the race on the first day, Miles had struggled on the many rocky mountain sections of the early stages, but, as sand and dunes took over, so Miles became stronger and stronger.

Only the evening before, around that desert bonfire, Miles had spoken into his personal tape recorder, 'As I cross rocky ground, I am just waiting for my toes to jar against the next big rock. When I am in the dunes, they cushion my footfall. The silence and the solitude of them absorbs all the sound; they are like great big empty amphitheatres waiting for something to happen. Even though it's such a pain getting up and down their loose sandy slopes, it just takes your breath away. Awe-inspiring!'

We were now waiting only for Jerry to come in, but even as we spoke of him we saw him limping towards us, accompanied by Lardy Steve. It was to be another tale of heartbreak. Following their epic completion of the long stage together the previous evening, Jerry had continued the journey in the company of Mac. Jerry could barely stand on his feet, let alone walk on them, and Mac was still dangerously dehydrated. He had received one intravenous drip from the medical team; a second meant instant disqualification.

Progress was slow, dangerously slow. Each checkpoint on a Marathon des Sables stage has a time cut-off point. At the rear of the field, two camels plodded and grunted slowly across the desert landscape, timed to arrive at each checkpoint at the cut-off time. If the camels caught up with you, you were out of the race. Between checkpoints two and three, on the long section that had come so close to ending my own personal ambitions, the camels passed Jerry and Mac. A helicopter was summoned to fly Mac to the medical tent where he could at last receive the intravenous fluids his body was craving.

Jerry climbed aboard a jeep that would carry him the remaining miles to our new camp, but his race was run. If he wanted to, the organisers would allow him to take part in the final stage the following morning, and cross the ultimate finish line, but his time wouldn't be officially recorded, and he would not be taking a coveted Marathon des Sables medal home with him. There was no room for sentiment in the Marathon des Sables.

There was a genuine mixture of emotions in 'Tent 40' as we chatted on that final evening. For seven of us, we were just ten kilometres away from the glory of finishing the toughest footrace on earth, and nothing could be allowed to stop us now. Even had I fallen and broken my leg on that final stage, I would still have tried to drag myself to the finish. For Jerry and Lardy, there must have been intense disappointment, but not for one moment did they show it.

They were taking a lot of positives from their respective performances and had both achieved feats way beyond their wildest dreams before setting out on this adventure. They had not failed; they had just succeeded a little less than the rest of us and would still be taking home memories that few could even dream of.

* * * * *

Dawn broke and the rituals of preparation were followed for the last time. On cue, the tent came down on top of us, our Berber friends having one last joke at our expense. Today, they would not be moving on to a new campsite, but would be returning to their families and friends, hard-earned cash in their pockets, and with respect from the international group of runners for whom they had provided so cheerily.

We gathered under the start banner for the final time and there was a mood of celebration in the air. Everybody hugged everybody. It didn't matter if you didn't share a language, a hug is a hug and an international signal of mutual respect. Where tension and pained grimaces had ruled the start lines of previous stages, laughter and smiles were the order of the day on this morning.

Bang on time, we were away and en route to the oasis town of Erfoud; a deliberately shorter stage to allow time to ferry the huge caravan of competitors, organisers and media the near-200 miles back to Ouarzazate before nightfall.

My thighs burned with the pain of movement, my calves were tight and on the very brink of cramping with every step, and my poor bruised, bloodied, blistered and battered feet just could not believe that they were once again being expected to perform. Above my waist, the contrast could not have been greater. Even the backpack, and the trailing wires and pouches of my travelling studio, seemed much lighter that morning and my head was singing with happiness for I knew I was almost there. There would be no walking breaks today – this was the day I would run every step of the sixth and final stage of the Marathon des Sables.

After a few kilometres of sandy plateaus littered with sand mounds and loose rocks, we turned on to a road. Not a desert track compacted by the tyres of four-wheel-drive jeeps, this was a true tarmac-covered road. Soon we came across a few isolated houses by the roadside, the occasional green tree or bush, and even a few poles carrying communication wires. Don't stop running now.

Another couple of kilometres passed and the density of housing grew greater. At the roadside, there were people going about their daily business and looking quizzically at us as we ran past. Shirt-sleeved men labouring in the hot sunshine; young women, many wearing full black face veils, guiding small children along the edges of the road. We were returning to civilisation. Don't stop running now.

And then there were traffic signs and signposts pointing to the town centre, flags and bunting. There was a buzz around the town; it was coming to life. The crowds at the roadside were now more packed, young children eagerly holding out their hands to slap palms with the runners as we passed. No longer were our spectators interested in their daily chores; they were now engrossed in this stream of colourfully-clothed men and women running into their town, each wearing a wide grin from ear to ear.

I came to a crossroads and a blue-uniformed policeman pointed me to the right. We were now in the main street of the town and the crowds at the roadside were packed several deep. Shouts of 'Bravo, bravo!' echoed from all around. I rounded a slight bend in the road, running now as fast as my messed-up legs would carry me, beneath a large blue inflatable arch that was stretched across the street, and there, 400 yards away, was the finish line: not just any finish line but the finish line of the Marathon des Sables.

With tears running down my cheeks, I took off my desert cap and waved it wildly around my head to acknowledge the deafening wall of noise that the crowd was generating. I was now sprinting without a hint of pain in any part of my body, my mind ecstatic with what I had achieved, and then I was there. I crossed the finish line, and fell into the arms of Patrick Bauer, the father of this unique race. He gave me an enormous bear-hug, congratulated me in a mixture of French and English, and then placed the very large and heavy medal around my neck. I tried to look at it but the tears that were filling my eyes made it very difficult to see anything clearly.

Denise, the representative of the travel company that had organised the arrangements for the British contingent, gave me a hug followed by Cathy from the *Sunday Times*. They were very brave ladies as I must have smelt awful.

Nick, from Carlton, with whom I had developed a really close relationship both in my preparations beforehand in the

UK and then out in the desert in Morocco, offered me his mobile phone to call home as he now had a signal. Angela and Chris were out, but I was able to speak to Gill to pass on my news. I had done it!

One by one, or two by two in the case of Miles and Jon, the remaining runners in our 'Tent 40' team arrived at the finish line, Derek bringing up the rear on this day, finding just enough energy to drag his exhausted and injured body to the line. Together with our intrepid TV colleagues from Carlton, and Lardy and Jerry who had been such integral elements of our cooperative effort, but who would sadly be returning home without medals around their necks, we gathered together for a group embrace and team photo, before finally boarding the coach for the long, hot and sleepy journey back to Ouarzazate.

Back at the hotel, a week's worth of ingrained sand and grime was painfully scrubbed from sunburnt skin, matted hair, and from behind torn finger and toenails. A week's worth of stubbly facial hair was gently shaved from the tender skin beneath. As I slowly teased off a variety of medical dressings from the still raw wounds, I could scarcely believe the amount of filth my bathroom's plumbing system was having to deal with and this was being repeated across so many rooms in that hotel at that moment. It cannot be fun to be a hotel chambermaid or plumber the morning after the Marathon des Sables arrives back in town.

Then it was time to be reunited with clean clothing. My sweat-stiffened running vest, shorts and socks were at last consigned to the depths of my suitcase, and the feeling of freshly laundered fabric on clean skin was a stark, but pleasing contrast to what we had endured during the previous week.

That night we partied. In the ornate grounds of the hotel, dozens of tables were laid out for a giant open-air banquet for organisers, media and competitors alike. Even grumpy camels came along. As we feasted on a variety of delicious, freshly-cooked Moroccan dishes, the wine and beer flowed freely. Colourfully-robed musicians energetically pounded out their rhythms, although there was little appetite for dancing among the exhausted competitors.

The final results were displayed on a large board for us all to view. Of the 595 competitors who had set out on that incredible journey, I had finished in 408th position, in a total time of 42 hours, 26 minutes and 30 seconds. Yes, it was a long way behind the absurd 17 and a quarter hours taken by the race winner, Lahcen Ahansal, but I was actually closer to him than I was to the defiant Japanese lady who battled those malevolent conditions for over 71 and a half hours, before becoming the final competitor to cross the line in triumph.

Patrick Bauer himself brought proceedings to a close with a moving speech, and then handed out trophies to the leading runners, and also to those who had brought something special to the race, including my amazing unsighted friends and their guides, Miles and Jon, and Geoff and Carol. Sleep came easily that night.

A final breakfast together the following morning and then it was time to bid our farewells to the many friends we had made from other nations before heading to the airport. In contrast to the outward journey, where the aircraft cabin buzzed with excitement, the prevailing mood on the flight home was one of calm and tranquillity, and this gave us our first real opportunity for some personal reflection on what we had achieved.

So what life lessons could be learned from running this race? From a personal point of view, I could do no better than quote the words of T.S. Eliot, 'Only those who will risk going too far can possibly find out how far one can go.'

I would certainly never be the same person again. We all live most of our lives within a personal comfort zone, and some people's zones are broader than others. Now I knew beyond doubt that I could achieve feats way beyond what I previously believed I was capable of and that I could use that knowledge in all aspects of my life. So where did this undiscovered fortitude come from?

There were various pillars of support out there, not least the camaraderie between all of the competitors in the race. Nothing breaks language barriers quicker than shared adversity and one of the great strengths of this extraordinary event was the way it brought together people of all races, cultures and creeds. At the same time as we were running across the desert, a fierce air-war was raging not 1,000 miles away in the Balkans and the international community was deeply divided.

Out there in the hot sand, we ran as one. Yes, there was also a good-natured nationalistic element to the race, in part created by the organisers who had divided up the competitors' village country by country, with the tents soon becoming adorned with national flags and jingoistic banners, but when the chips were down, nobody in trouble would be left marooned.

Then, of course, was the tier of support that we came to heavily rely on, and this was the group within our own tent, 'Tent 40'. These unofficial 'teams' had been thrown together almost by chance on arrival at base camp, but living under the same roof in the most rudimentary of conditions would mean that, by the end of the race, we would have no secrets from one another. If you snored, farted, overslept or got up several times during the night for a pee, there was no hiding place.

Each of us had initially staked a claim for a few square feet of matting under our roof, positions that would be strictly honoured for the remainder of the race, and the bonding process had invisibly begun. We had each prepared in different ways. We had different goals; some to finish in the top 50 or top 200, but for most, just finishing was the Holy Grail. We were all athletes; we just covered a wide spectrum of athletic prowess. But whatever our differences and personal ambitions, a team spirit had been evident from the very beginning and grew perceptibly as the race progressed. We were always there for each other if needed.

Partnerships had also been an important source of support at critical times, whether by design, as in the formidable teamwork of Jon and Miles, or by serendipity, when two people happened to be in the same place together in a moment of crisis. The courageous, but ultimately fruitless, efforts of Jerry and Mac epitomised this and, from my own experience, the alliance with Steve North that dragged us both to the end of the long stage without an overnight sleep stop stood out, as well as Dick's inspirational support after the Erg Chebbi dunes had seemingly sucked every ounce of energy from me on the marathon stage.

However, the very last line of defence would always remain your inner resolve. If this failed, your race was over. As forbidding a physical challenge as this race presented, it was even more a battle of the mind. A bruised and blistered limb could be coaxed onwards with the power of positive thought, but even the fittest of bodies would be useless with a broken mind at the wheel.

In the not-too-distant past before setting out for Morocco, I had been crippled by the lack of self-esteem and confidence that accompanies depression. Now I could look myself in the mirror and see a person who had battled through all kinds of adversity, in the most inhospitable environment, and yet come out on top. I was proud of myself.

*   *   *   *   *

My brother, Dave, was there to meet me at Gatwick Airport and to witness the emotional scenes as tired and battered competitors were reunited with their nearest and dearest before it was time for these same competitors to say goodbye to each other and go our separate ways. It was inconceivable that this would be a final farewell. We had shared too much, bonded too tightly, for this week to have been a fleeting coming together on our respective life journeys. We would surely meet again, but for now it was time for us all to return to what, in many respects, suddenly seemed a pretty humdrum way of life.

It was as we drove from the airport on the road back to the Midlands that a conversation between Dave and me, and my reaction to it, seemed to perfectly illustrate just how much this experience had changed my outlook and priorities in life.

'I hate to dampen your celebratory homecoming,' said Dave, with caution in his voice, 'but I'm afraid there is one piece of bad news that you need to know about.'

'Go on,' I replied, with trepidation.

'Your new car that you left with Chris,' Dave continued. 'He crashed it on Brighton seafront. He asked me to tell you as he's too scared to tell you himself.'

'Was Chris hurt?'

'No, he's fine, but the car was pretty smashed up. It's being repaired at the moment.'

'Then, there's no problem,' I replied instantly, and turned the conversation back to tales of my desert adventures.

9

To buried warriors

THE return to the UK was every bit as busy as the final days before departure had been. The regional newspapers were eager to run stories of my exploits while radio stations, both local and national, were keen for me to come into their studios for live on-air interviews. All of this boosted the fund-raising, even after the event, and also attracted a host of invitations to speak to various clubs, societies and schools, with any proceeds further beefing up the charity coffers. Of course, this brief period of near-celebrity status had to be fitted in around a return to work and very soon life was back to normal, or as normal as it could ever be after such a cathartic experience.

I had known all along that I would inevitably meet up with some of my fellow desert competitors before too long, but even I was surprised at just how soon that would be. Only a few days after returning to the UK, I was contacted by Rory Coleman, who had cheerfully lugged a large Union Jack across the Sahara, to entice me to run an invitation-only marathon along the canal towpath between Birmingham and Stratford-upon-Avon.

Still euphoric from my desert achievement, I immediately agreed, and less than one month after the final stage of the

Marathon des Sables, I was running another marathon, this time along the muddy towpaths of central England in the company of several of my desert colleagues.

A couple of weeks later, the vast majority of the British contingent were together once more, this time in more salubrious conditions as we met at a Northampton hotel to see a preview of the documentary that Shaun and his Carlton TV crew had made and that would shortly be broadcast on ITV. It was a moving story, focusing on the courageous journey of Miles and Jon, but capturing many of the key moments that punctuated our various individual journeys. With most of us staying overnight, it was a perfect opportunity to rekindle the memories we had all shared and I'm pretty certain the hotel bar had record takings that evening.

And there was more. A little later in the year there was a reunion of many of the 'Tent 40' team at the London Fireman's Ball, as guests of the two Steves and Jerry. With Miles and Jon, and a couple of the other British runners in attendance, it was another great evening of celebration and reflection.

However, although this was largely a period of recognition of past achievement, my running shoes were already getting restless and wondering what was to come next. If Bryce Canyon had been the spark that had ignited my interest in running in wilderness settings, then the Marathon des Sables had fanned the flames into a full-on forest fire. How on earth could I follow that?

I still had every intention of seeking out the big-city races in foreign climes as a route to seeing the world; if you want to discover all the best bits of a new city that you have never visited before, then enter its marathon.

It's a bit more tiring than the open-top tour bus, but a lot more rewarding! However, what I wanted to do more than anything was to run tracks and trails far beyond where a tourist might normally venture.

For a period of time, I very seriously considered going back to the Marathon des Sables and running it again. I felt strangely drawn to the desert but this was an option that wouldn't expand my horizons, so I looked elsewhere. Patrick Bauer and his team had a second desert race in their repertoire: the Jordan Desert Cup. This was of a similar length to the Sahara race, but, instead of being run in six stages, it was a non-stop event with the clock ticking from the very start and continuing to tick even while you slept. The earliest available place would have been in the 2001 race, but even a year beforehand, the deteriorating situation in neighbouring Iraq had placed the race under threat and it was eventually removed from the adventure-racing calendar.

Another possibility was a race in the Kalahari Desert, based on the same format as the Marathon des Sables, and about to be launched by one of the South African competitors I had met in the Sahara. However, the date he had chosen was in October and I was unable to take leave from work during term-time because of my teaching commitments. Thwarted again!

Eventually, the internet threw up another intriguing possibility: a multi-stage race in various locations throughout China, including some running in the Gobi Desert! Once again, the race organisers, Sport Développment & Performance Organisation (SDPO), were a French company, and this time were led by a husband and wife team, Jean-Claude and Dominique Le Cornec. The race itself, Les Foulées de la Soie, loosely translated as the Silken Footsteps, was based around locations on the ancient Silk Road trade route.

It was a very different beast to the Marathon des Sables; still 100 miles of running in little over a week, but hotel beds and regular cooked meals were part of a gentler package. However, the itinerary was very demanding, with sightseeing visits and extensive travel, by coach, train or plane, linking the individual stages over a huge geographical area. It certainly ticked all the boxes regarding my desire to run and see the world.

SDPO was a much smaller operation than the organisation behind the Marathon des Sables, and a brief trawl of their website revealed that most of the past competitors had been French, and indeed there was no English translation on the website. Like many people of my generation, I had studied French at school but had done nothing to advance, or even maintain, that knowledge in the 35 years since. Would that be a problem if I entered the race?

I tentatively put together an enquiry email in the best French I could muster, apologising profusely for my deficiencies in this respect, and was hugely relieved to receive a reply in perfect English from Sabine, one of the organisation's administration staff. Within a few weeks all of my questions had been answered and I had signed on the dotted line to run the race in August 2000. This gave me a year to prepare for the event, both physically and also by brushing up my French language skills, as Sabine had informed me that I was the only British runner to have entered the race at that stage.

In the meantime, another unexpected, but nevertheless exciting, running opportunity had arisen. The wide media coverage of my efforts in the Sahara, and most notably the TV programme that had resulted from it, meant that my fund-raising efforts for my chosen two charities far exceeded my expectations. One of the charities, Dreams Come True, was so pleased with the several thousand pounds that I had raised for it that it offered to send me to the Honolulu Marathon, provided I could cover its costs with further sponsorship.

This I was pleased to agree to, even though it meant going back, cap-in-hand, to many of the same people who had supported me just a few months earlier. Happily, many of my supporters felt that I had somehow earned an 'easy' run in Hawaii and were happy to put their hands in their pockets again.

After a warm-up September marathon in Edinburgh, which that year began in Dunfermline and involved a spectacular but blustery crossing of the Forth Road bridge, I was en route to Honolulu just a couple of weeks before Christmas. Fortunately, given the 16 hours of flying time to get there, with a short stopover in San Francisco on the way, I had a few days before the marathon to adjust to the humidity and to the very different time zone.

There were a number of unusual features to this big city race that set it apart from any marathon I had run before, or indeed since. The first became apparent when I joined hundreds of other runners for a short jog the day before race day, to acclimatise to the warm and sticky conditions; the vast majority of my fellow competitors in the race were not American, but Japanese.

Although Hawaii is an American state, geographically it is closer to Japan than it is to many of the most populous cities on the US mainland. Also, at that time, mass participation marathons had not really taken off in Japan, with their key races being confined to elite athletes, so Honolulu was, and continues to be to this day, the premier event for Japan's enthusiastic running community.

Another curious feature of the Honolulu Marathon was that it started in the middle of the night! As I alluded to earlier, there is no better way of discovering a new city than to run its marathon, although Honolulu may be an exception to that maxim, as much of the race was run during the hours of darkness. Whether it was to avoid the steamy humidity of the midday sun, or the inevitable and massive traffic jams that characterise every new day in the city, the race started at five o'clock in the morning. This of course meant getting up several hours earlier than that, in order to get to the start line in time, so this was a marathon that challenged not only my cardiovascular system, but also my body clock!

Race day dawned, and the weather was as un-Hawaiian as it was possible to be with heavy, driving rain and strong blustery winds. Nevertheless, I trudged forlornly in the darkness to the Ala Moana Beach Park, not far from the Waikiki hotels where most of the runners, including a tiny British contingent, were housed. In the glow of a massive fireworks display, we set off on time, initially heading west through Downtown Honolulu to the harbour, with the historic Aloha clock tower peering out of the gloom. The route then swung back eastwards, cutting through the vast shopping precincts of Downtown that were vividly illuminated with extravagant Christmas decorations, before then heading towards Waikiki and its spectacular beaches, although these were of course invisible in the darkness to the drenched runners.

At this point I felt comfortable with my pace and coped well with the steep climbs around the eight-to-nine-mile mark, as the route made its way round the extinct volcanic crater of Diamond Head. However, as the route continued onwards through the eastern Honolulu suburbs, most of the running was on an endless highway where we were exposed to the full force of the storm that was battering the coastline. This was unequivocally not how I had envisaged my Honolulu Marathon experience to be, and there wasn't even the consolation of taking in the magnificent scenery as it was still dark. My pace slowed, my motivation dipped.

At around 16 miles the route took a loop through Hawaii Kai before returning us westwards along the same endless highway that we had just run along. However, now dawn was beginning to break, so at least there were sandy beaches and palm trees bending in the fearsome wind to view. Not a day for the Waikiki beachcombers, but it was very apparent why the island of Oahu is a surfer's paradise.

As Diamond Head came back into view, with just three or four miles to run, the rain at last relented and the sun pushed through the clouds. Within minutes, the heat and humidity were oppressive and the hills in the final two miles around that extinct volcano seemed so much steeper than on the outward journey.

Suddenly I was missing that rain and wind that I had spent so many miles berating. As the sun now blazed down on to a roadway swimming in puddles, I relished a long downhill section, and a final flat, straight stretch to the finish banner, with boisterous but drenched spectators lining the tree-covered avenue. A pause for breath and that wonderful warm feeling of achievement as another marathon medal, hanging from a string of seashells, was placed around my neck.

Looking back now, I wouldn't place Honolulu in my top three of big-city marathons, largely because of the rather uninspiring route on such a beautiful island, although the grim weather and darkness didn't help. However, my trip to Hawaii did leave me with one abiding memory which will forever linger and that was a visit to Pearl Harbor.

Although never having achieved anything more than being a reluctant corporal in the army cadets at school, the armed forces have been a feature of my life throughout the years. My own son, Chris, has served in many of the world's recent trouble-spots, and I have felt that inner apprehension that every parent with a son or daughter on tour in a war zone feels.

Looking further back, I lost an uncle who I never got to know during the Second World War and, if my own father had not been plucked from the Mediterranean by Italian fishermen after his minesweeper had been torpedoed, then I would not be here now to tell this tale. Indeed, as a child, I vividly remember family visits to historical military sites on the Channel Islands and European mainland, and listening in awe to my father's tales of life in those troubled times.

The opportunity to take in a visit to Pearl Harbor, a location of such military significance, just couldn't be turned down and was indeed a humbling and emotional experience. Still a thriving and busy naval base, a massive modern aircraft carrier towered above our small boat as it took us out to the floating memorial above the submerged USS *Arizona*.

As we gazed down at the superstructure of the stricken vessel lying just below the surface, tiny droplets of oil spiralled their way upwards every few seconds, spreading out into rainbow-coloured ripples. Over 58 years after reaching its final grave, entombing over a thousand souls, the shattered battleship was still not entirely at rest.

*   *   *   *   *

But in the year 2000, a new millennium, attention was firmly switched to China. Without the involvement of a television crew, training was much more low-key, although local radio and print media took a keen interest and the UK edition of *Runner's World* magazine commissioned a post-race article, as this was the first it had heard of the event. In comparison to preparations for the Sahara, the build-up was relatively uneventful with heavy mileage, several half-marathons and just the one hot and hilly full marathon in the Potteries of Staffordshire. I even managed to get my medical consent form signed off without any dramas, my GP reasoning that if I had survived the perils of the Sahara then, in his eyes at least, I was indestructible!

Before I knew it I was en route to Charles de Gaulle Airport in Paris to meet up with the SDPO team for the first time, armed with a French phrase book, a pocket electronic translator and an abundant supply of cough remedies to tackle the malaise that, as so often happens, had struck just a few days before departure. It was a relief to be greeted in Paris by Sabine, with her impeccable English language skills, and to then be introduced to Jean-Claude and Dominique Le Cornec, who could both speak English far better than I could speak French. I felt a good deal happier as I settled into the long flight to Shanghai.

A word about SDPO and its ethos. The rallying call for SDPO on its website is '*Si courir était notre seul but, nous passerions à côté de moments inoubliables*' which translates to, 'If running was our only goal, then unforgettable moments would pass us by.' Yes, competitive running was still very much part of the package, but it shared equal billing with the cultural aspects of the journey, and that didn't just mean viewing the local sights as a tourist would, but embracing and interacting with the local population as well. On every stage of an SDPO race, local people were invited to run alongside the touring athletes.

It was in this spirit of sporting harmony that the running began in an early morning Prologue around the streets of Shanghai. We had arrived in the hot and humid city just the day before and spent several hours exploring the contrasts between the typically eastern architecture of 'Old Shanghai' and its westernised modern counterpart.

By day: the exquisite Yuyuan gardens; weeping willows, oriental pavilions, rockeries, lakes and twisted tree branch furniture being committed to canvas by talented pavement artists at their easels. By night: the flashing lights and billboards of the city centre rivalling the displays of New York's Times Square.

After a leisurely hotel dinner, I joined the other 92 competitors at a race briefing. I already knew I was the only British competitor in the race; what I learned now was that I was the first British competitor in the event's five-year history. With a Union Jack already embroidered on to the front of my running baseball cap, I appointed myself national team captain, with the sure knowledge that, however well or badly I did, I would be setting a new British record for the event!

As part of the competition, the 93 runners were split into teams of four or five, and I was allocated to the International team along with two Swiss ladies, Sandra and Hala, and two Stefans, one Italian, the other German. Indeed, it was the

German Stefan, Stefan Schlett, who I would room with for the duration of the China trip, and this was an opportunity for me to get inside the mind of an athlete whose long-distance running achievements would dwarf those of almost any other on the planet.

For me, running was a regular hobby that occasionally transported me from the stresses and strains of my daily life to far-off places and to meet amazing people. For Stefan, running *was* his life, spending most of his year racing around all corners of the planet, and the rest of the time writing, broadcasting and lecturing about his feats, in order to raise the sponsorship that funded his unique lifestyle. Among his many extreme exploits were trans-continental runs across the USA and Australia, as well as a 5,000-kilometre run across Europe, from Lisbon to Moscow, in the space of 64 days.

Fortunately for me, Stefan could speak perfect English and I would spend many an hour during the trip listening in awe to tales of his running travels. Indeed, Stefan had won Les Foulées de la Soie the year previously and was now out to retain his crown.

It was Stefan who, in the early glow of dawn, was given the honour of carrying the large, pale blue flag of SDPO for the Prologue, alongside the bright red flag of the Shanghai Marathon, hoisted aloft by a Chinese athlete. A large cavalcade of SDPO and Chinese runners, all dressed in the white and red race T-shirt, jogged alongside one another in a non-competitive, but nevertheless sweat-inducing, procession from People's Square to the Huangpu river waterfront of the Bund and then back again.

Even so early in the morning, and despite the gentle pace, the sticky, humid heat made breathing difficult and was in such stark contrast to the dry heat of the Sahara.

The rasping cough I had carried with me to Shanghai was silent during the run but burst back into life as soon as I had finished. However, the relentless schedule left no time for dwelling on this. Back to the hotel for a post-Prologue breakfast, a visit to the Temple of the Jade Buddha, the air rich with the aroma of burning incense, and then a Mongolian buffet lunch, where our chosen ingredients were cooked in seconds on a sizzling, circular hotplate before being launched into the air by the chef and landing perfectly in a bowl held several feet away. No sooner had the food been devoured than we were back on a coach to the airport for a flight onwards to the ancient capital of Xi'an. Such was the pace of a typical SDPO day, everything planned and executed with military precision – it was impressive!

It was on arrival in Xi'an that evening that it first began to dawn on me just how much interest our race series was generating among the Chinese people. Our coach was escorted for the entire one-hour journey from the airport to the hotel by four police outriders on motorcycles, their lights flashing and their sirens wailing. Even though it was now dark, the contrast to the bright lights of Shanghai was immediately apparent.

Tiny shops with their wares lying on the pavement outside, scruffily clad children sitting at the edge of the gutter waving cheerily to us as we passed; bicycles were everywhere, many of them bearing a pillion passenger sitting side-saddle – this was more how I expected China to be. At the hotel we were greeted with applause by the staff, a massive welcome banner stretching across the entire reception area – we really were being treated like celebrities.

The true running competition was now only hours away but there were nagging doubts creeping into my psyche. I am not one of those people born with an abundance of self-belief and confidence; I need to work on it. Of course, my success in the Sahara was proof of what I was capable of achieving, but there were still periods of self-doubt when I had to give myself a good talking-to. This was one of them.

Despite the creature comforts of hotel beds and regular meals, there were different challenges ahead of me here. The tent banter that had seen me through the dark times in the Sahara just wouldn't be there this time. The language barrier between me and the vast majority of my fellow competitors left me feeling somewhat isolated. While I could speak in my own tongue to Stefan, we were on different planets in terms of running pedigree and I could not relate to him in the same way as I had done to my more modestly talented 'Tent 40' chums.

I was also feeling less than 100 per cent fit with my cough continuing to trouble me, particularly at night. At least I could do something about that, so I made a late-night, last-minute visit to the race medics, emerging with antibiotics and cough suppressant tablets, and the comforting reassurance that there was no evidence of an infection on my chest.

The following morning, I stood on the start line for race one, the 18-kilometre Grand Emperor stage. If such a thing was possible in China, it was a typical English morning – driving rain, humid but still chilly, a low mist drifting across the fields beside the roadway. With a few dozen Chinese runners among us, we set off into the gloom and the twisting road immediately began to climb.

As we rounded each bend, a new climb came into view. One mile, two miles, three miles and still we were running uphill, and the swirling mist and drizzle became an impenetrable fog the higher we climbed. It could hardly have been a more difficult introduction to this new running adventure but, despite the laboured breathing and my legs crying out for some flat sections to run on, my pre-race self-doubts were already being washed away by running's happy hormones. This wasn't just another wet and hilly training run in the Midlands; my running shoes had taken me to China, on the other side of the world!

After almost five miles of ascending, there were no more hills above us; whatever we had climbed, we had reached the top.

An SDPO official cheerfully directed us off the tarmac surface on to a muddy, rural footpath, winding between fields of crops. The further we ran along it, the muddier the path became – a winter cross-country race in August.

From the swirling mist ahead, the lead runners emerged, running back along the same footpath in the opposite direction; a moment to acknowledge Stefan who was well-placed in this group. With thick mud clinging to my trainers, I was grateful that I had had the foresight to bring two pairs with me – these were not going to get cleaned and dried before another race in the morning.

We passed through a tiny rural village, with clusters of people standing by the wayside yelling what I trust were words of encouragement. I paused for a moment, opened the pouch around my waist, and pulled out a tiny notebook and a pack of coloured pencils. We had been encouraged by SDPO beforehand to bring a few small gifts if we had room in our luggage. I handed them to the smallest child of a family group and will never forget the look of surprise and glee on her face. I ran on.

Before too long we were back on the same tarmac road that had brought us to the summit of this great hill, but now we were running down it. The pace picked up. I was now relishing every minute of this experience. With just over a mile to go, I was caught by a young Chinese runner, maybe 15 or so years old. He held out his hand. I took it, and together we ran at a pace that was a lot faster than I was really comfortable with.

There were tears of joy in my eyes as we crossed the finish line together, urged on by an exuberant crowd sheltering beneath a kaleidoscope of different-coloured umbrellas, and supervised by a surprisingly heavy, but friendly, police and military presence to keep everyone in check. Within moments, Sabine was interviewing me in front of a TV camera, reviving memories of my Sahara experience. SDPO were producing a film of the race series, and it was to be curiously amusing, at a later date, to see my breathlessly garbled and ecstatic words on the final DVD, subtitled in French!

There was no time to return to our hotel to freshen up, although I had brought a fresh T-shirt and shorts that I changed into on our coach. We were now about to embark on a visit to arguably the greatest archaeological discovery ever – the Terracotta Army of the Qin dynasty, that had lain buried and unknown for around 2,200 years before being unearthed, initially by a small group of farmers in 1974. It was a visit I had eagerly anticipated from the moment I booked my trip to China, and it did not disappoint. Once again, my strenuous hobby was transporting me to a wondrous place that I might never have visited otherwise.

Now, from what you have read so far and indeed, from what you will read in later pages of this book, you will appreciate that my 'Wow!' response is generally activated by the beauties of our natural world. Only very rarely is a man-made construction capable of dropping my lower jaw in amazement. The Terracotta Army provided one of those moments.

I am old enough to remember the earliest reports of the chance discovery of the site by farmers digging a well in 1974. I watched in amazement as news programmes and documentaries revealed the growing extent of the find and once I knew our travels through China would give me the chance to view the warriors with my own eyes, it just had to be one of the highlights of the whole trip. To say I was not disappointed would be a massive understatement.

Along with Stefan, I joined a small tour with an English-speaking guide as we slowly made our way around the halls and three large trenches, marvelling, at one extreme, at the sheer magnitude of the whole site, and at the other, the unique and intricate detail on each and every one of the thousands of excavated warriors, their weapons, their horses and their silver and gold-gilded bronze carriages. These were no mass-produced figures made from a mould; each warrior was individually crafted with unique facial features and uniform trimmings. How long had it taken to construct this army, with many still remaining to be excavated even to this day? How many people must have been involved, and what must the working conditions have been like? So many questions. From that moment on, for every step I would run on Chinese soil, I would wonder what might just be lying beneath my feet.

* * * * *

The rain had still not relented by the time we congregated on the ancient 700-year-old city wall that surrounds Xi'an for stage two of the race the following morning. After returning from our visit to the Terracotta Army the previous day, we had been treated to an evening of spectacular and colourful Chinese theatre, with exotic costumes, acrobatic dancing and an astonishing variety of musical instruments, the majority of which I couldn't begin to name. This musical theme continued when our coach was greeted at the city wall on that very morning by the rhythmic pounding of a 30-strong percussion band, clad in bright yellow tunics and vivid red headscarves. Once again the city of Xi'an was pulling out all the stops to make us feel welcome.

Now, this Les Foulées de la Soie race series had begun with a prologue, and that is a word more commonly associated with a rather more well-known French multi-stage race – road cycling's Tour de France. The similarities between these two events were not to end there. Before running commenced on the second day, the race leader from the first stage was presented with a yellow jersey, the 'king of the mountains' a red one, a green jersey was awarded to the fastest runner over a designated sprint section, and even a pink jersey for the leading lady.

Similar award ceremonies would now take place at the end of each day of running and, to make the cycling theme complete, this particular day's running along the city wall would be in the form of a time trial. Competitors were to be released on to the nine-kilometre course at 30-second intervals, in the reverse order in which they had finished the first stage. An interesting and energising format; knowing that those following immediately behind you were just that little bit quicker than you on the first stage.

Having finished 60th of the 93 competitors during the first stage, I didn't have too long a wait in the rain before I joined a short queue to be called forward to the starting gate. 'Six, cinq, quatre, trois, deux, un…allez! Now where had I heard that countdown before?

Although there were to be no hills today, the flint slabs underfoot were tricky; fragmented, uneven and slippery with the rain that was finally beginning to ease. Concentration was key to avoiding a slip or a trip. I adjusted to a pace that I thought would be competitive, but was dismayed to hear rapidly closing footsteps behind me within only a couple of minutes of my start. The rival sailed past, so I stepped it up a notch. It was a hard pace to maintain, my breathing was heavy, but the humid and damp atmosphere seemed to be keeping the coughing at bay. Soon I was beginning to catch and overtake some of the slower runners who had started ahead of me. From the ramparts of the wall, I could glance down on to the ancient city; some stunning oriental architecture but also no shortage of slum dwellings, with bare mattresses lying beneath dilapidated corrugated roofs, providing little protection from the elements.

Pushing on, I would spot another runner ahead and slowly, step by step, reel them in – the time trial format had certainly galvanised my competitive instincts. Then half a mile away, on a long straight section of the wall, I spotted the 'Arrivée' banner, stretched between two pagodas. I picked up the pace again, arms aloft as I passed triumphantly beneath it. It had been a good day; I had caught and passed at least eight other runners, and the only one to go past me had been that single nemesis in the early stages. Now, I even had a few moments for a little raucous spectating as we cheered the faster runners home to the drumbeats of our oriental percussionists. But time never stood still for long on this trip; we had another plane to catch.

10

A puddle
in the desert

DUNHUANG, an oasis town in China's Gansu province in the vast western desert region, was strategically placed on the ancient Silk Road trade route and was at one point in history the most westerly point of China. Indeed, its name translates as 'The flamboyant lookout tower'. No western-style glittering billboards here – there was a much more medieval feel about the town.

As our flight from Xi'an had drifted down towards the desolate airport, the view from my window seat was oh so reminiscent of the descent into Ouarzazate: sand, sand and yet more sand. The journey had at least provided a couple of hours of much-needed rest and relaxation, although the plane had clearly seen better days as my lap-tray was secured by pieces of string; I hoped that the mechanical maintenance was rather more rigorous.

The airport barely justified that status: no terminal building to speak of, just a few isolated portakabins, our plane lonely and isolated as the only aircraft out on the tarmac. We waited patiently in the hot sunshine as a tiny team of perspiring baggage handlers lifted our suitcases down from the aircraft hold, placed them on trolleys and then manually hauled them across the sandy airfield towards us. However, once again the evening welcome at our hotel was both spectacular and uplifting: firecrackers exploding all around as a guard of honour of immaculate young men in red-belted tan tunics, and exquisitely-costumed young ladies, their heads adorned with intricate ornamental tiaras, applauded us through the entrance.

Just time for dinner and then yet another visit to the medics. The cough was beginning to relent, but now diarrhoea was a new problem; already my bedside cabinet was beginning to resemble a small pharmacy and I still had almost 100 miles of running to do.

Fortunately, by the time we lined up for the third stage the following afternoon, the medication had already begun to work its magic. We were starting from outside the main entrance to the Mogao caves, yet another astonishing archaeological masterpiece that almost defied belief, and one we had visited that very morning. Suspended like honeycomb on the cliffs of the Mingsha hills, over 500 caves had been sculpted out by Buddhist monks, over a period of 1,000 years, and filled with thousands of paintings, statues and sculptures of spine-tingling size and complexity. In one cave alone, a Buddha statue, carved from the rock, towered into the gloomy chamber above me at 115 feet high. It was enough to take your breath away, but I was now going to need every ounce of that, as I faced two tough desert runs within the space of 15 hours.

For the first time on this trip, I carried my trusty bladder of electrolyte drink on my back; the distances might not have been as great as in the Sahara, or the location as remote, but this was still the desert and, as I stood on that start line, the sun was bearing down on us relentlessly.

And then we were off again. A gentle climb for the first couple of kilometres alongside a dried riverbed, but it was tricky underfoot. Loose shingle and scattered larger pieces of rock turned my ankles this way and that as I ran and threatened a more catastrophic twisting, but gradually the surface turned finer and we began to climb more steeply into a convoluted mountainous section.

Now, as I have mentioned previously, the Achilles heel of my adventure running pedigree is a disproportionate fear of heights. Had I known what I was to encounter over the next few kilometres, I might never have signed up for this race in the first place. This was a small mountain range, and we were running in the foothills, but the steep and twisting pathways were slippery and narrow, and the drops either side, while not Alpine, were plenty steep enough to cause serious damage should I lose my footing.

Once again, the running hormones took over – rather than tip-toeing nervously around the route as I almost certainly would have done at home, I found myself prancing around like a mountain goat, a grin across my face. I was running in China; fears and phobias were going to have to take a back seat.

In time we were running back downhill and out into the desert. The temperature increase over such a short space of time and distance was proving hard to cope with, and I drank thirstily from the fluid on my back. Towering dunes all around us now, but the path that we followed was relatively flat. Scattered tombstones in the desert, a primitive metal bridge being built across a deep ravine, the construction worker's aged bus almost disappearing from sight in a sudden swirling sandstorm. Then, from nowhere, a temple appeared, attached to the side of a mountain and we turned past it to run downhill back towards Mogao. But this was no time for celebration; we had to run the same circuit again.

I paused briefly to top up my drink bladder, aided by one of the French runners who had fallen on the Xi'an wall the day before, sustaining some knee damage that had already ended his race. Back alongside the dried riverbed towards the mountain stage, but now the sky had turned from blue to black. Lightning flickered between the peaks and thunder rumbled in the distance; just how many microclimates could we pass through in a couple of hours of running?

I knew what was coming next but, in a strange way, was now looking forward to it. The rollercoaster mountain section was again accomplished with a smile on my face and I even had the confidence to pass another runner on a particularly narrow section. Back to the desert, the merciless heat, and a long toil to the finish line as the nimble exuberance of my rock-hopping subsided, to be replaced by unadulterated fatigue.

Even two bottles of water failed to quench my thirst as I waited under sublime tree cover at the entrance to the Mogao caves for the slower runners to finish, but that wonderful post-run glow of satisfaction, that every runner will understand, was flowing through my veins. No time for triumphalism though; the next stage was just hours away.

Dunhuang is bordered by two deserts: the Taklamakan to the west, and the Gobi to the east. Despite the arid location, the town was well irrigated and was an important agricultural centre. Indeed it was harvest time in the farmlands surrounding our hotel and the fields were alive with dozens of workers labouring in the heat. No modern-day combine harvesters here; in this part of China the pitchfork and horse-drawn cart ruled.

With most of those of working age grinding away in the fields, it was largely children and their grandparents lining the roadside as we set off through the streets of Dunhuang on the Crescent Moon Lake stage early the following morning. For six kilometres we ran along fairly flat tarmac roads, just the surface I had done most of my training on, and I passed runner after runner as I made my way through the field. Then we hit sand – soft, deep, powdery sand. First a lap around the lake – yes, a lake, a true oasis in the desert. Shaped exactly as its name suggests, and overlooked by trees, vivid green shrubs and beautiful pagodas, the Crescent Moon Lake, fed by an underground spring, is a natural paradox, its blue waters reflecting the yellows and golds of the surrounding Mingsha dunes.

Being just a few miles from a seat of civilisation, the lake attracts a number of tourist visitors, and as we ploughed our way through the powdery surface around the lake, we passed trudging trains of camels sulkily carrying sightseers to the edges of the drifting sands.

For us the onward journey would not be so restful. Marco Polo had named these dunes the 'grumbling sands' in recognition of the noises that could be heard when the wind blows across them; the sounds of thunder or drum roll. As we climbed higher and higher from the lake, in single file, along the narrowest of razor-sharp ridges, our hands clamped to the fronts of our thighs to maintain momentum, I was once more totally captivated by the peaceful beauty of running in such wondrous surroundings. I have had the privilege of being able to run in all kinds of environments and climatic conditions, but nothing, absolutely nothing, comes close to the fearsome tranquillity of a giant sand dune.

Far ahead, I could pick out the tiny figures of the runners in front of me as they struggled up to the top of the ridge, but one figure seemed to be at a standstill. Surely not a spectator up here? As I approached I noticed the backpack on his back, and then the growing realisation that one of our medical team had climbed all the way up here, just in case one of us needed help. What some people will do in the line of duty!

On reaching the top, I paused for a few seconds to take in the wondrous view that my little disposable camera could not possibly do justice to: rolling waves of golden sands as far as the eye could see. But I had a race to run and the route-marking arrow appeared to be directing me over what I can best describe as a cliff face. Was someone having a joke by moving the direction sign around?

I peered over the near vertical drop and there, almost 200 feet below me, was a tiny figure. It was Sabine. I yelled down to ask which way we had to go and she beckoned me towards her. I stepped over the edge. It was a crazy, crazy descent. There was no way I could slow my momentum but the soft, powdery sand applied the brakes as, with each stride, my feet and lower calves disappeared beneath the surface. In no time at all, I was standing alongside Sabine, both of us grinning from ear to ear.

'That was fun, yeah?' she smiled, before directing me on into further dunes. I just felt so at home in that environment, but at the same time was acutely aware of just how draining it was to run in. I felt I was getting pretty close to my limits of exhaustion, yet these desert stages were nowhere near as long as those I had tackled and overcome in the Sahara just 16 months earlier. Was age beginning to catch up with me?

The ground was gently falling away from me, and I began to increase my pace. Steady, steady, not too fast, but my legs were now moving faster than I was comfortable with. I tried to dig my heels in, but this sand was much more compacted and my legs continued to move faster and faster as gravity took over. I was running out of control and, in a flash, my mind went back to a similar experience in my childhood when a gentle canter down a grassy slope turned into a mad gallop that was only halted by a painful and bloody collision with a hedge. There was no hedge here; this was the Gobi Desert, and I was racing towards another near vertical drop.

I desperately wanted to fall to the ground but that is so difficult to achieve when you are running so fast. Panic was rising within, and my heart pounded like a jackhammer in my chest. Just as I had resigned myself to a very painful and dire conclusion, the sand beneath my feet suddenly loosened as the precipice approached and I was able to anchor myself to a halt.

I sat down in the sand shaking like a leaf. I vomited. There were no other runners in sight and I waited a couple of minutes to let my heart rate settle. I gingerly got back to my feet and began to move forward again at a very gentle pace, and when I say gentle, believe me, I mean gentle.

After a few more miles of sweat and sand, albeit without the dramatic ascents and descents I had already encountered, it was some relief to see the 'Arrivée' banner up ahead on the edge of a small village. As I sat in the shade of a small building, emptying my shoes and socks of the sand that had penetrated every tiny opening, I again ruminated over my experiences that day, both awe-inspiring and scary, and couldn't help but think I was coping less well with the challenges facing me than I had the year before. Nevertheless, I had now completed four of the ten stages on this journey and a real treat lay ahead for me the following day: our one and only day off.

It was back at the hotel that I began to realise just how shaken I had been by my 'runaway train' experience, and that perhaps this had contributed to my unusually negative mindset at the finish line. There had also been another unfortunate consequence. In emptying the sand from my shoes, I had managed to leave one of my orthotic devices behind in the desert. I had worn these in my running shoes for a number of years and they had magically cured the knee problems I had endured previously. There was no way of going back to look for it, so I would have to run the remaining stages without them: a setback, but not an insurmountable one.

With a rest day beckoning it was a chance to relax at last for the evening. Our International team, together with some of our French colleagues, wandered around the bustling streets of night-time Dunhuang, the strip-light illuminated market still filled with dozens of stalls selling everything from fabrics, ornaments, intricate jewellery and even barbaric-looking knives and other assorted weapons. Around them, fruit vendors jostled us, desperate to sell the last of their produce from their tricycle-borne displays, and there was even time to sit and enjoy a couple of large glasses of a very palatable local beer at a price so ridiculously low that one wondered how there could be any profit in producing it.

As a driver used to British motorways, traffic dawdling through mile after mile of plastic cones is not an uncommon sight. In China, they adopt a different approach – they just close the road completely while they repair it. We had left Dunhuang for the 200-mile journey across the Gobi Desert to Jiayuguan in a convoy of three coaches and I sat alongside Jean-Claude and Dominique in the final one of these. Whether it was a problem with the vehicle, or a driver who was in no mood to rush, our coach soon lost sight of the other two, much to Jean-Claude's frustration as he sought to co-ordinate the transfer and, presumably, the welcome reception at the other end.

The long, straight road stretched away into the distance across the barren landscape, but if losing visual contact with our colleagues was bad enough, Jean-Claude's temper reached boiling point when two labourers waving giant red flags brought our journey to an abrupt halt. A quick interchange between them and our translator confirmed that the road was being closed for resurfacing and we would be going nowhere for the next two to three hours. Worse still, a phone call confirmed that the other two coaches had got through so, for the first time, the clockwork organisation of this trip had come unstuck. It was no great deal, but obviously a blow to Jean-Claude who took such pride in maintaining a meticulous itinerary.

While four-wheel-drive vehicles could circumvent the obstruction by driving off into the desert, our aged coach just sat where it was, the interior getting hotter by the minute. With little drinking water on board, we wandered around the arid landscape, where at least there was a little breeze, the air pungent with the smell of hot tarmac. There was no sense of urgency from the workmen, as they engaged in leisurely chatter, leaning on their shovels, with some actually taking a nap in their wheelbarrows. Just another example of an altogether different pace of life from the one we were accustomed to.

We did, of course, eventually reach Jiayuguan, although our civic welcoming committee had long since departed. First impressions were of a town devoted entirely to the locals. No souvenir shops here; just bustling street markets displaying meat, fruit and giant tanks with large fish swimming freely around in them and animated men crowding around pavement games of checkers, all with a different opinion of which move to make next.

* * * * *

As dawn broke the following morning, the view from the hotel bedroom window was one of contrast. To the west, the stark and brutal landscape of the Gobi Desert, but turn 90 degrees to the south, and there were the giant, snow-capped mountains of the Gilian Shan, towering to a height of over 5,500 metres. Soon, altitude was going to be a new factor that we runners had to adjust to, but first we had one final half- marathon encounter with the Gobi Desert.

We started at a Buddhist temple overlooked by the modern-day western extremity of the Great Wall, hanging at a seemingly impossible angle from the north-west face of the Heishan mountain. A fast, downhill start on very loose and stony ground and then a thoroughly enjoyable long, flat section in the shade of the Great Wall itself. Once again I had to pinch myself just as a reminder of where my running journey had taken me now. After several miles of increasingly hot sunshine, we reached the imperious 14th century Jiayuguan fort, built during the Ming dynasty to resist the advances of the Mongols and to defend the strategic Jiayuguan pass. On this occasion it served as a massively overstated water station. Then we headed off uphill through a sublime tree-lined oasis, providing temporary respite from the sun, before emerging into the dangers and demons of the Gobi Desert.

It was here that, two-thirds of the way through the stage, I suffered a mishap that I have dined out on on many occasions since – I fell into a puddle in the desert. This wasn't water from an underground spring, like the one feeding the Crescent Moon Lake. This was rain from the sky! My trusted dictionary defines a desert as a region that is almost devoid of vegetation because of limited rainfall. Note the word 'limited' – not 'no' rainfall, but 'limited' rainfall.

Now this particular section of the Gobi Desert must have had its full quota of 'limited' rainfall just a couple of days before we arrived and, with the Great Wall providing a bit of shade from the relentless sun, large pools of the precious liquid lurked in sandy hollows. They lay in wait to lower my runner's high.

As I skirted around the edge of one particularly deep accumulation, my foot slipped sideways on the muddy surface and, before I could say Marco Polo, I was on my back, immersed up to my neck in a thick sandy sludge. I emerged looking like a modern-day terracotta warrior. As the old proverb says, the sun loses nothing by shining into a puddle and, take it from me, if fate ever has you running in a desert, then to spend a few seconds immersed up to your neck in a cool, sandy broth is no bad thing.

My pride might have been dented but I was a lot more comfortable than most of the runners out there, and this was cruelly brought home to me in the final stages when I passed a stricken runner lying in the sand, the medics busily inserting an intravenous drip into his arm.

We faced a spectacular, although exhausting, conclusion to the race. The finish was back at the fort and the towering structure could be seen from far out in the desert sands. Just as in the Sahara, it stubbornly refused to get any closer, no matter how much running you did towards it. Eventually, I passed under the great arch of the Gate of Conciliation on the western wall of the fort to puzzled looks from spectators, organisers and camels alike, who couldn't quite comprehend why only one of the competitors had returned with a substantial coating of the desert sand caked upon his skin.

A final sting in the tail, as I pounded up a flight of 150 steps to the finish line on the ramparts, and then a thoughtful costumed archer managed to find a bucket of water from somewhere so that I could at least remove the worst of my encrustation before the journey back to the hotel. There were a few new blisters on my insteps, possibly from having to run without my orthotics, but I could deal with those.

I felt good, really good. I'd needed that rest day from running, and the doubts and insecurities I had struggled with at the end of the previous stage were now a distant memory. My sand-caked appearance had been the source of much hilarity among my fellow competitors, and that day went down in my running memory bank as one of the most enjoyable ever – the day I fell into a puddle in the desert!

* * * * *

As ever, time never stood still. A bath, a meal and then an overnight train journey on to Lanzhou; battered and bone-weary competitors crammed into tiny bunk beds, although spirits remained high. The camaraderie of communal adversity was breaking though the language barrier. Lanzhou, a frantic, smog-laden city, was just a breakfast stop at this point. We would return. The desert was behind us; now it was time for the mountains.

This time managing to remain in convoy, our coaches edged up steep boulder-strewn roads as we climbed towards our next stop: Linxia. On several occasions we ground to a halt completely, as the drivers disembarked and manfully levered large rocks to the roadside so that the vehicles could edge round them. Clearly landslides were a major feature on this route and perhaps we were fortunate that none were severe enough to stop us entirely.

Eventually we reached Linxia, a town that had played a central role in the propagation of Islam from central Asia to China, becoming known as the Small Mecca and as a place of pilgrimage for Muslims of other Chinese provinces. The centre of town was dominated by a large mosque and the streets filled with old men in long, white robes, white caps and long beards – yet another astonishing contrast to the towns and cities we had visited before.

After checking in to our hotel rooms, it was time to get stripped for action once again and this time the stage was nothing more, and nothing less, than a 10-kilometre road race taking in four laps of the town centre. Now, I have run many dozens of 10-kilometre road races, but this one stands head and shoulders above all the others in terms of memorable moments. That we were in for a treat was apparent from the moment I emerged into the hotel car park that was protected by both a low wall, topped with spiked steel railings, and a line of shoulder-to-shoulder police holding a vociferous crowd at bay. Inside the railings with us, a number of local athletes, wearing the Foulées de la Soie T-shirt, were busy limbering up, obviously intent on demonstrating their running prowess to their visitors. The crowd, which was several deep, pressed harder at the railings, amidst a cacophony of blaring horns. With small children being in danger of being crushed at the front, the police opened the hotel gates to allow the little ones into the car park, and they ran gleefully towards us, autograph books and pens in hand.

For the one and only time in my sporting career, I had a line of young fans queuing for my signature! Their parents screamed through the railings, cameras held aloft, and we posed with their young ones as shutters and flash guns fired all around. For five minutes, I lived the life of a celebrity, but then it was time to run. The line of police drew their batons, the exuberant crowd dutifully parted to allow us out on to the road and we were away.

It appeared that this 10-kilometre race was one of the highlights of the Linxia year and virtually all of the route was lined by enthusiastic crowds that any big city marathon would have been proud of. Although the spectators were keeping to the roadside, the town was still going about its normal business, and we shared the narrow and pot-holed roads with battered cycles, tractors, and carts laden with sheep fleece, and we had to swerve around the many dogs, cattle, donkeys and chickens that littered our path. Only on the final lap of this crazy circuit was I lapped by the two leading runners, and, by the time I finished, my palms were sore from high-fiveing every child in town – four times.

It was by far my highest finish on an individual stage, and I felt absolutely elated at the finish, despite a bit of discomfort from my fresh blisters, and some nagging twinges from my left knee. Yet again, running had given me an experience that is as fresh in my mind today as it was at the time, and now we were headed for Tibet.

*　*　*　*　*

Tibet. For as long as I can remember, Tibet has been right up there near the top of my bucket list. I have always been fascinated by the very highest mountains on this planet and would have loved life as a mountaineer were it not for my acrophobia – that's a fear of heights in plain English. My bookshelves at home sag under the weight of illustrated volumes describing expeditions, successful and tragic, to the Himalayas and the sheer mention of the name of Tibet, the Roof of the World, conjured up all sorts of magical images in my mind as a youngster. Indeed, the fact that this trip included two stages in Tibet, albeit not at the top of its highest mountains, was a major clinching factor in deciding to go. Tibet did not disappoint.

The coach transfer from Linxia to Xiahe was every bit as picturesque and tranquil as the images I had painted in my mind. Initially along the Diaxhe river valley, a fast-flowing torrent called the 'Bowl of Treasure' by the Tibetans, we edged gingerly over fragile river crossings, before attacking the mountainous regions where Tibetan shepherds, under their wide-brimmed hats, watched over their herds of yaks. It was a journey of cultural contrast, with Islam and Buddhism living side-by-side and yet very separate. One village would be centred around a mosque; two miles down the road the next village would be decorated with Tibetan prayer mats.

Xiahe itself, beautiful Xiahe, was dominated by the gargantuan Labrang monastery, grafted on to the face of Feng mountain, and home for 1,700 red-and-purple-clad monks of the Yellow Bonnet sect studying Tibetan medicine, esoteric teaching, astronomy, high and low theology, and the time wheel.

As we gathered in the courtyard, the monks, their yellow bonnets glistening in the bright sunshine, sat on the steps opposite clutching colourful prayer flags and chanting in harmony. High above them, on the ramparts of the monastery, an elder monk wailed out a call for prayer that echoed off the mountainside. The air was full of incense from giant burners. A massive bell chimed deeply and the monks threw off their footwear, leaving boots scattered everywhere on the monastery steps, before disappearing hurriedly inside for prayer.

In time, when they had completed their worship, we were quietly ushered inside the temple. Concise guidance was provided in many languages at the entrance; in English it read simply 'Need ticket, no smoking, no picturing, no spitting, don't make noise please.'

Even our hotel in Xiahe was a place of beauty, if that can ever be said about a hotel. On stepping down from the coach, we had each been presented with a white, silk scarf to hang round our necks: a traditional welcome for visitors to Tibet. The luxurious cabin-style accommodation rooms were each enveloped in a decorative woven fabric cover, the delicate colours and patterns complementing the kaleidoscopic wild flower beds in the hotel gardens.

And yet, from our hotel windows we could see what life was like for the people who lived in Xiahe. Bubbling mountain streams served as playgrounds for the children and laundrettes for their mothers. They waved cheerily at us. A lifestyle that was both medieval, and yet seemingly so peaceful. Who has it right?

The run that afternoon was the Yellow Bonnet stage: 12 kilometres, with a very testing mountain section, but that was not the main adversary. From Dunhuang to Jiayuguan to Linxia, we had been steadily climbing in altitude. Now, even in the foothills of Tibet, there had been a dramatic increase to over 3,000 metres and we had had only a few hours to adapt to this before having to run.

Even on the relatively flat road of the first two kilometres from our hotel into Xiahe, I was gasping for air at what should have been a very comfortable pace. Light-headed, heart pounding in my chest, this was a good deal higher than I had ever run before, and the effects were stark. We reached the Labrang monastery, passing purple-clad monks gently spinning the prayer-wheels that lined its walls. Once again the villagers and children were out in force to support us, but here the costumes of the indigenous Tibetans were so different from anywhere we had visited previously. Women in vividly bright coloured blouses, white-brimmed hats and long-trailing skirts – almost Latin American in style.

The road became a pathway, and we began to climb towards a distant mountain top. If running on the flat had been gruelling, then trying to climb became practically absurd. As the path gave way to loose shale, and with my hands clamped to the fronts of my thighs to provide extra strength and support, I could just about manage a fast walking pace as I drove on upwards, the sounds of my rasping breath causing some alarm to the occasional yak.

There were no flat sections to provide any respite; the ascent was relentless, and the summit seemed so impossibly far away. And then, just as I was beginning to doubt that I could continue, or at the very least that I needed to take a rest break, the loose rock gave way to a steep grassy pasture and a distant figure came into view above me, standing beside a large red flag. It was the turning point! Oh joy, we weren't going to be expected to go right to the top of this mountain. The organisers had managed to get a limited supply of water up there, but my measly ration was as pleasurable as any drink I can remember, and now my spirits were lifted by the thoughts of the descent ahead.

It was only when I began this descent that I fully realised just how steep the climb up had been. With my out-of-control plunge down the Mingsha dunes still very fresh in my mind, I adopted a very cautious attitude, digging my heels in hard to act as a brake; a similar escapade on this rocky landscape would be very unlikely to have such a positive ending. Indeed, my prudence was perfectly illustrated on the way down by passing three other runners being attended to by first-aiders for a variety of cuts, grazes and swollen joints after taking painful tumbles on the jagged and loose surface.

Finally the rubble gave way to a well-worn path and, as I rounded a green hillside, the roof of the monastery came into view below me. Now I could pick up the pace to the finish line of yet another stage – just three more stages to go. The 'Arrivée' banner was alongside a fast-flowing bubbling mountain stream, traversed by a primitive wood and rope bridge, decorated in coloured scarves blowing wildly in the wind. Mothers, children, even the monks showed wild excitement as they cheered in the runners, one by one.

This was the Tibet I had dreamt of visiting, and it was to these wonderful people that I wanted to give the remaining small gifts I had bought with me. As I delved into my waist pouch for the last few crayons, notebooks and tiny plastic toys, I was suddenly enveloped by a forest of tiny faces, eagerly holding out their hands. There was no way I had a gift for everyone. I handed out what I had as fairly as I could. Some of those faces left with broad grins on them, others with bitter disappointment.

*   *   *   *   *

After the exertions of running such a strenuous race at altitude, I would happily have returned to our hotel and crawled straight under the covers of my bed. But no, this was Les Foulées de la Soie and our Tibetan hosts had arranged a special treat for us; an outdoor meal on the high Himalayan plains.

Our coach driver struggled with the vehicle as it ground its way up the steep and twisting mountain passes, until we eventually reached a remote, tented encampment just as darkness began to fall. Now, there are two aspects of life at high altitude that cause difficulties to those not adapted to it. The first is with breathing the thin air, particularly if you are planning to do anything at all energetic, which of course we were, and indeed had been. The second was coping with the rapid changes in temperature between day and night.

Our mountain run had been bathed in warm sunshine, but, as we stepped out of the coach, it was suddenly unimaginably cold and we shivered collectively as we huddled around bare wooden tables inside a small, unheated tent. Our hosts were as pleasant and friendly a people as I have ever met on my travels and were quick to reassure us that we would all soon be feeling much better once we had downed a bowl of warm, sweetened yak's milk.

Wherever my running journey takes me, I like to eat and drink the local cuisine whenever the opportunity arises. I did finish my bowl of warm yak's milk, but will not be scouring the shelves of British supermarkets in order to repeat the experience. The following meal, however, of a meat and vegetable stew, and copious amounts of warm bread, was very welcome, and soon we were being toasted even further as we danced around a huge bonfire with the local people trying to teach us, rather unsuccessfully in my case, the secrets of Tibetan folk dance.

I was also afforded a rare opportunity on this trip for a prolonged conversation in my native tongue, when Jean-Claude introduced me to a local family of mum, dad, brother and sister, who had together been studying the English language, and were eager to practise their new-found skills. It was a heart-warming ending to a heart-warming day.

The following morning's stage was the longest of the whole series: 25 kilometres, finishing at our colourful hotel in Xiahe. The good news was that it was a net downhill route; the bad news, of course, was that our coach had to climb even higher up into the mountains to ferry us to the start. We were now at a debilitating and freezing cold 3,500 metres, the thin air rich with the aroma of wild mint. Even running gently downhill on a wide sandy track was draining and the cumulative effect of all the miles on such a variety of surfaces was increasing my blister count.

At least conditions underfoot were a lot more runner-friendly than the mountain rubble of the previous stage and, as we gradually descended on a succession of dusty trails, so the temperature gradually crept up to a more comfortable level. This was a hushed countryside: green and tranquil, but with very little evidence of habitation or agriculture. Solitary and serene running. After 15 kilometres we turned on to a narrow road. Despite the thin air, I had run every step of the way, albeit at a very leisurely pace, but pride was keeping me going. Now we started to see glimpses of civilisation – the occasional small farm, grunting black pigs pressing their snouts against the wire fencing that separated them from we runners on the roadway and an isolated apiary, row upon row of white beehives, with jars of honey stacked at the roadside, and a young girl holding out her hand, eyeing me with a plaintive look. I carried no money, so high-fived her outstretched palm and hoped that would suffice. There were no cars on the road, just the occasional donkey-drawn cart piled high with straw. And then the Tibetan equivalent of an out-of-town supermarket: an open-sided tent in the middle of a field, with vegetables, bottles of water and other farm produce stacked inside, away from the glare of the sun.

With five kilometres to go I could run no further. Whether it was the altitude, the extra distance, or the cumulative effect of so many hard runs, my legs were screaming at me to stop. Sandra, from our International team, caught up with me and for a short time I jogged along with her as she spurred me onwards, but I couldn't keep up and, in the end, urged her to run on. Several others caught and passed me but no amount of encouragement could elicit a further response from my frazzled legs. It was a spent and temporarily discouraged version of me that finally stumbled across the finish line on that sunny afternoon, but as was so often the case on this trip, 30 minutes of rest and some calm contemplation of what I had just experienced soon had the batteries recharging.

*   *   *   *   *

Lanzhou, the location of our penultimate stage, will not stay long in my memory. Don't get me wrong, the people were as warm and welcoming as ever, we were joined on the run with the customary group of enthusiastic and amiable local athletes, and the flags and bunting flew in a colourful display around the start and finish areas. It was the city itself. After the extraordinary history that lay beneath our feet in Xi'an, the hostile beauty of the Gobi Desert stages, the chaotic absurdity of our road race around Linxia, and the charm and arresting beauty of Tibet, my principal memory of Lanzhou is of an acrid brown smog that lay over the city, with traffic chaos and a proliferation of industrial chimneys collectively belching out their contribution.

The race itself was named 'The Ascent of Goa Lan', and this was something of a misnomer for they had left the letter 's' out. It should have read 'Ascents'. Goa Lan was the massive hillside that overlooked the city, and we did at least start above the brown blanket that encased everything other than the tips of a few of the tall, smouldering chimneys standing out like candles on a birthday cake.

For me, this was one stage too far. My calves burned with lactic acid after the long stage of the previous day, and my legs still felt like jelly. I'd also been up in the night with a tummy upset, not an uncommon occurrence on this trip, and had skipped breakfast for fear of aggravating the problem. It wasn't an easy run to do on an empty stomach. For five kilometres we climbed towards the summit; I ran with a couple of my French friends to begin with but eventually had to let them go, as I was reduced to a walk. No longer could the surrounding scenery take my mind off the pain; it was just a road, climbing up and up and up. Near the summit, we turned off the main road on to a well-trodden track and began to descend the far side of Goa Lan.

I ran again. I ran again at a good pace. It was downhill, and suddenly energy seemed to be seeping back into my weary legs. For four lovely kilometres, I ran down that hill. The green slopes were steep, but that hadn't stopped them being used for cultivating crops, with layer after layer of large flattened plateaus being chiselled out of the hillside. Running was now fun again, but at the back of mind was the name of this race, 'The Ascent of Goa Lan'.

That meant finishing at the top, and I was heading downwards. Sure enough, the track twisted round and soon we were climbing again, this time from the other side of the hill. As the gradient increased, so the fun factor decreased. Once again, my journey was becoming something of an ordeal. Dig deep, don't stop moving forward and you WILL eventually get there. After another hour of relentless hill-climbing, forcing myself to run for two minutes, walk for two minutes, the ornamental arches that topped the summit of Goa Lan finally came into view and I jogged over the finish line.

In 74th place out of the 93 runners, this was my lowest finishing position in any individual stage of the whole race, but I was a finisher, and that was all that mattered. Submitting myself to a painful, but much-needed leg massage, stretched out on a cold marble slab, I now realised that this particular journey was coming to an end. Just one more stage to go, and for that, a flight to Beijing was waiting for us.

* * * * *

Three kilometres, just three kilometres. Now for any distance runner, even one of my modest pedigree, that is barely a distance worth getting changed for, but that is what faced us on the final stage. But this was to be 3,000 metres like no other; this was a time trial on the ramparts of the Great Wall of China.

From our hotel base in Beijing we had travelled the 80 or so kilometres to Mutianyu, where the majestic Wall wound over a backdrop of wooded mountains as far as the eye could see. Even as I stood on the start line, waiting for my cue to start, the sweat was pouring from me. To get on to the Wall we had had to climb over 1,000 steps through humid, steamy woodland, our eardrums battered by a screeching insect cacophony.

Allez Doug! I was off. The Wall seemed to plummet almost vertically downwards at my feet as I struggled to find an appropriate pace, somewhere between tip-toeing and an appointment with a hospital bed. And then I was going up; some steps barely warranting the name, others for which a small ladder might have been useful. And so it continued, a bit of down, a lot of up, and up, and up.

I was running on the Great Wall of China. Reality check. Yes, I really was running on the Great Wall of China. A big wide grin spread across my face, and then, a mischievous thought occurred to me. What would the millions of soldiers and peasants who had hauled huge blocks of rock up steep mountain slopes over 2,000 years ago have made of us using the fruits of their labour as a running track?

Just occasionally, the endless rollercoaster of steps was briefly broken by a flat section as I passed through one of the fortified watchtowers that punctuated the snaking ramparts. Then, high above me, I could see the 'Arrivée' banner at the very top of what seemed to be an unhelpfully lengthy and near perpendicular stairway. This was not only the finish line for this day's stage, this was the finish line for Les Foulées de la Soie.

My hands once more clamped to the fronts of my thighs, I drove on up that stairway, with an inner sense of achievement growing with each pace forward. I had passed more runners than had passed me, so I knew that, despite the growing fatigue of the previous two days, I had done myself justice on that final, almost theatrical stage. Indeed, to add to the surrealism, costumed warriors bearing mighty swords were there to welcome us at the finish. It was a fitting climax to a ten-stage challenge that had been demanding, emotional and cathartic all rolled into one.

We spent a final day and a half in Beijing. We visited art galleries, the Temple of Heaven, conical roofs capped with blue, varnished tiles; the Forbidden City and Imperial Palace with acres of wonderfully ornate gardens and exquisitely furnished chambers. We walked the parks, alive with groups of people practising Tai Chi in the sunshine, and admired the beauty of the endless lines of weeping willows that hung over the canals. And we strolled around Tiananmen Square, under the watchful eye of the military police, and of the portrait of Chairman Mao at the Gate of Heavenly Peace.

There was a boisterous celebration meal in a Peking Duck restaurant, and a more formal and sedate prize-giving ceremony in the French Embassy where trophies were awarded to the leading runners and teams. Commemorative plaques tracing our 3,500-mile journey across the breadth of China, over 100 of those in running shoes, were presented to all competitors. I finally finished in 61st place of the 93 runners, and our International team were placed in a noteworthy fourth position out of the 18 teams, although this was largely due to the efforts of the two Stefans.

It was the end of yet another remarkable running venture. From a personal point of view, my French language skills had certainly been enhanced, but that would likely fade. The sporting memories would not. Les Foulées de la Soie had been a very different type of event from the Marathon des Sables, but just as rewarding. To run on such a variety of surfaces, in such different conditions, to meet so many amazing and different cultures, and to visit so many memorable places, and all in the space of ten days, was testament to the organisational abilities of Jean-Claude and Dominique, and the SDPO team.

It was with some sadness that I finally said farewell to them at Paris's Charles de Gaulle Airport and I pledged that I would spread the message of their unique adventure through the UK running community. I also promised them that I would run with SDPO again at an event in the future. It was a promise I was able to keep just five years later.

11

One extreme to another

THE prospect of running again with Miles and Jon was one just too inviting to turn down. I'd kept in regular touch with Miles since our Saharan adventure and we'd shared a few meals together. In fact, it was at one of these that the idea of running in Siberia was cemented.

Geoff, Miles's blind brother from South Africa who'd run with us in the desert, was on his way back home from running the New York Marathon and had returned via the UK to see Miles and his family for a couple of days. Miles had invited me to his home town of Duffield to join them and a group of friends for a pint and a bite to eat and, as we chatted of adventures past, present and future, the possibility of an icy Siberian half-marathon began to crystallise.

Many months previously, both Miles and I had read the same *Runner's World* magazine article about the previous year's race (these articles have a lot to answer for!). Runner after runner dropped out as their eyes froze shut in temperatures of 42 degrees below zero! That represented a 100-degree difference from the scorching 58 degrees we had endured in the Erg Chebbi dunes: the difference between frozen ice and boiling water. It sounded just our sort of event!

Since the Marathon des Sables, Miles had continued his amazing quest to show that blindness, or indeed any physical handicap, need not be a barrier to achieving anything that you really wanted to. Unlike myself, who kept my feet firmly on the ground, Miles was looking upwards as well. After Morocco, he and Jon took up ice climbing in Scotland, before scaling Europe's highest mountain, Mont Blanc.

A climb to 17,500 feet in the Himalayas was cut short by a high-altitude health scare, which thankfully turned out to be a false alarm and, while I was running in China, Jon and Miles were summiting on Kilimanjaro, Africa's highest peak.

Their greatest triumph was to follow just a few months later. Accompanied by an American, an Australian and Jon, Miles set out from the coast of Antarctica, hauling a sledge weighing over 400lb, with the goal of becoming the first blind man to reach the South Pole. Sadly, 400 kilometres and three weeks later, Miles's journey was brought to a premature end by frostbitten fingers.

Without his eyes, his fingers tapping on a keyboard were essential for his communication with the sighted world, and the risk of permanent damage to them was just too great. Miles was airlifted to safety. Jon faced the ultimate dilemma: to return to the UK with Miles, with whom he'd shared so many adventures, or to continue on the journey they'd started together. Before being evacuated, Miles was insistent that Jon should continue and, 62 days after setting out, Jon planted the flag of the Royal National Institute of the Blind at the South Pole.

Back in the UK, Miles was delighted and proud to hear of the success of his sidekick, but inside he hurt. Despite holding the world distance record for a blind man trekking across Antarctica, he still felt a sense of failure and was already planning a return visit to the White Continent. In the meantime he kept himself in shape by following my footsteps, and joining several other Brits in running Les Foulées de la Soie in China the year after my venture, this time accompanied by his son, David.

The appeal of Siberia to Miles was that it would give him a chance to assess how his frostbitten fingers would face up to the intense cold. If the pain returned, then the prospects of revisiting Antarctica were fading.

By the time we had finished our drinks that evening, Miles and I had agreed to run in Siberia; Jon had been enlisted in his absence, and Toby, the 14-year-old son of Miles's work colleague, Julia, was severely tempted but had a bit of work to do to persuade his parents.

Unlike the Sahara and China, when months of planning and training preceded the event, there were barely two months to prepare for the Siberia race, which was to be held in the city of Omsk, almost 1,400 miles east of Moscow.

The distance itself presented no great problem. Despite being called the Siberian Ice Marathon, the race was, in fact, a half-marathon, and 13.1 miles was a distance I could comfortably manage. What was less certain was coping with the weather. How to stop my eyes freezing? Ski goggles seemed obvious, but would they ice up? What would be the effect of breathing air that cold? If I covered my mouth to warm the incoming air, would it restrict the airflow? And what footwear would I need?

It was never going to be a vest and shorts race, but what clothing would be warm enough to survive in temperatures that might reach 40 degrees below, but yet still allow me to run? The range of technical clothing available was bewildering, but Jon and Miles were clearly a superb source of advice, given their polar experience. And then our itinerary meant we were going to spend a whole week in Russia. What clothing would I need for the many hours when we were not going to be running?

More advice arrived from a surprising source. As with my previous 'exotic' runs, I channelled my efforts into raising some cash for charity, and this time chose the Meningitis Trust in memory of a young girl from my home town of Redditch, whose sudden death from the disease on a family holiday had had a major impact on the local community.

Unlike the multiple-stage ultra-marathon races in the deserts of Morocco and China, I figured that a half-marathon, even in a place as inhospitable as Siberia, would be less newsworthy, and confined my press releases to local newspapers. But just like a rolling snowball, which I suppose is an apt metaphor, the news story gathered mass and pace and I was soon featured on several radio stations, BBC TV, the BBC News website, as well as regional and national press. Clearly anyone choosing to run in Siberia in January just had to be a little bit crazy. As a result of this unexpected publicity, I was contacted by a number of cross-country and marathon skiers, and given useful tips on how best to protect my eyes and mouth during the run.

Time flew by, and Christmas and New Year seemed particularly inappropriately placed in the calendar that year. Toby had got his parental go-ahead and our little group had also been augmented by the addition of Jeremy French, another Midlander, who in our first conversation together had confessed that he hated running but just needed a mid-life challenge! Jeremy worked tirelessly in organising our flights and visas and in being our source of contact with the race organisers in Omsk, itself a thankless task as many of our questions were left unanswered.

For a start, what had seemed to be relatively reasonable costs for the trip were constantly being inflated by extra fees being added for this and that, and, as an accountant, Jeremy was there to fight our corner. Three guys from East Anglia, veterans of the 2001 Marathon des Sables, were also flying out with us for the race. They ran their own outdoor pursuits company and were therefore able to negotiate discounts on the specialist clothing we required, the downside being that, because everything closed down over Christmas and New Year, we wouldn't get it until we all met up for the first time at Heathrow and so wouldn't get the chance to try anything out beforehand.

In those final days leading to departure, fate had dealt me two hands: one good and one bad. On the credit side, the weather had turned wintry; heavy snow had fallen and then frozen hard for days on end, offering an ideal chance to see how the trail running shoes performed on ice. They didn't, but what I did learn was that even the thinnest film of fresh snow on top of the ice offered up some grip. It was a valuable lesson.

On the downside, and just as had happened to me before the China trip, a hacking cough had surfaced and a last-minute dash to the pharmacy was required for throat lozenges and a couple of bottles of linctus. As long as it stayed away from my chest, I would be OK.

As so often happens on these frantic occasions, chaos slowly unravelled and everything fell into place at the last moment. The specialist clothing was collected at the airport and it all fitted perfectly. What had been even more unsettling was that we had all set out to Heathrow without our passports. Last-minute hitches with the documentation required for the visas had left Jeremy in the invidious position of having to sort it out for the whole group, and bring all passports and visas along to Heathrow. He didn't let us down. On 3 January 2002 the eight of us flew out together to Moscow.

*   *   *   *   *

It was dark when we landed. The flight deck had taken great pleasure in announcing to us that the ground temperature was 25 degrees below zero, and as the Aeroflot flight made its final approach, the airport lights illuminated what appeared to be a landing in an ice field. Our quiet relief at the perfect touchdown was in marked contrast to the Russian passengers' reaction; they greeted the landing with a spontaneous and boisterous round of applause as if this was clearly not the norm.

Immigration was not without incident either, particularly for me. After a never-ending delay in the slowest-moving queue ever, my turn to step forward to the booth eventually arrived and I handed my passport over to the stern young lady behind the desk. From his viewpoint in the queue behind me, Jon watched her scan my photograph and tap details from the passport on to the keyboard. The screen turned red with a large black cross. She reached below her desk and pressed a button. Within seconds I had been ushered away to a sparsely-furnished office by another mini-skirted official, curiously eating a banana, and my passport taken away for further scrutiny.

One by one, the others in our party were allowed through – no questions asked. After what seemed an interminable wait, my passport was returned to me and I was finally waved through. No questions, no inkling of what the problem might have been. Fortunately my colleagues had waited for me, although our East Anglian friends had already headed off to their city centre hotel.

In our desire to keep costs down, we had ended up with a less-than-salubrious hotel in the suburbs. We set off in an ageing minibus to our lodging. Despite the best efforts of the battered heating system, our view through the windows was blocked by ice on the outside, and soon our breath was freezing on the inside.

Worse was to come. On a stretch of motorway at the edge of the city, the driver, who could speak no English, pulled into the banks of snow to the side of the road as the engine spluttered and died. Would we end up walking? Thankfully, after ten long minutes of careful nurturing, the engine began to fire randomly again and we continued the journey, albeit at a snail's pace.

The hotel was what we expected – austere. But we only had to spend the one night there and at least the rooms were warm. Austerity we could live with, but when the management refused to re-open the bar, then our patience was being stretched. It had been a long, hard journey and we needed to finish it with a beer.

A tip-off that a tiny shop around the corner stayed open until 2am set us scurrying off into the frozen night and we returned with a veritable feast of salami, crisps and, most importantly, bottles of beer. Even the lack of a bottle-opener failed to dampen our spirits. A blind man needs to be resourceful and Miles had mastered the art of opening a beer bottle with another beer bottle, even having a technique for coping with the last one.

It wasn't the first time I'd made the journey from magazine article to distant hotel room before, and this had been more rushed and hazard-strewn than most, but now, sitting among like-minded adventurers supping our beers, I knew this was where I belonged and that we were about to have some fun.

We had just a few hours to gain an impression of Moscow. A hurried breakfast of Russian ham and eggs, and our guide and driver were there to whisk us out on a whistle-stop tour of the city. Where else could you start but Red Square and it didn't disappoint. With snow falling steadily, it was a picture postcard scene: the Kremlin, Lenin's mausoleum and the nine stunning turrets of the Cathedral of Saint Vasily the Blessed. We walked the banks of the frozen Moskva river, marvelled at the statue of Peter the Great, and wandered around the parks, art markets and the Olympic stadium. By mid-afternoon, darkness was already beginning to fall and it was time to head back to our hotel and begin the long journey to Omsk.

With our destination station kindly scribbled on a scrap of paper by our morning guide, we entered the unknowns of the Moscow Metro, thrusting the paper in front of anybody who looked as if they might know where they were going. The stations overflowed to bursting point, hardly surprising when five of us could travel as far as we liked for a total fare equivalent to 50 pence. Soon we were aboard the train and speeding along line nine, Jon explaining to a disbelieving English-speaking Russian lady that this motley selection of individuals really had come to Russia to run in Siberia. The alleged five-minute walk to our hotel at the other end took considerably longer, again largely as a result of our collective inability to understand directions.

Having retrieved our luggage, it was time to set off for the airport and this time we'd done a bit of wheeling and dealing. The driver who had picked us up from the airport the previous evening, and who had toured us around the city that morning, had quoted us what we considered to be an excessive price for the ride back to the airport, but he'd priced himself out of the market! The hotel owner had found us someone who would do the trip for less than half the price, but when we saw the van, we began to have misgivings.

If the previous one had been ageing, then this one was positively primeval. With our luggage heaped upon our laps, which at least gave us some protection from the draughty windows, and suffocating in the fug created by the chain-smoking driver, we set off in the driving snow for the airport. It was clear from the outset that the driver's movements of the steering wheel did not always coincide with the direction the van was taking. He was constantly fighting for control, and the rear end slewed wildly even at a speed that was, at best, sedentary. A traffic light changed to red 100 yards ahead and a touch on the brakes had us spinning and skidding wildly, bracing ourselves for the collision that never came.

Even more disconcerting was the view outside. Not the snow or the ice. Nothing was familiar from the previous evening's drive and we now seemed to be driving into open countryside. Was he even taking us to the right airport? Moscow has five! We asked the question. There was not a glimmer of understanding.

He shrugged his shoulders, gave a toothless grin, lit another cigarette, and continued on his leisurely, erratic way. Within the hour, we were at the airport and it was even the correct airport. Never had we doubted it!

*　*　*　*　*

It was 6am local time the following day when we finally touched down in Omsk; there was no round of applause this time. When you see the chaos a few centimetres of snow can cause to our British airports, it was a mystery how they had managed to keep that airport functional in those conditions. Fifteen-foot high mounds of snow and ice lined the runway, seemingly inches beyond the wing tips as we taxied to a halt.

The bus from the plane dumped us at a large iron gate, beyond which frozen faces peered through the railings: taxi drivers, friends and relatives. We walked through the gate and that was it, we were outside the airport. The wind was biting into my lips, aggravating the cough that still barked out at increasingly frequent intervals.

Inna was there to greet us. Inna Tchernoblavskaia was the race's director of external affairs, and was responsible for looking after all of the foreign entrants. Tall, slim, attractive, she was encased in fur from head to toe. Introductions were made as we waited for our luggage to be offloaded, and then we took a short minibus ride to our hotel, as heavy snow fell steadily all around us.

We yearned for sleep but there was barely time to check in to our rooms before we were escorted on foot to the race HQ. It was a perilous mile-long journey, slipping and sliding on the ice, and reinforcing our very worst fears of what the race conditions were likely to be.

Race registration was a shambles. Endless delays, nobody to answer our questions, hardly anyone appearing even to understand them. Tired tempers began to fray. It certainly wasn't the slick operation that you might expect at a big city marathon, but then this wasn't a big city marathon. We had come to Omsk to race, and when in Siberia, do as the Siberians do; we waited in a long, slow, tetchy queue.

Eventually, Helena came to our rescue. Helena was a middle-aged, immaculately dressed lady who had been allocated to the British runners by the race committee to act as our guide and interpreter. Helena stood no nonsense. Within minutes of her arrival, our race numbers had been issued and we were on our way for a spot of lunch and it was over this meal that Helena announced that we were scheduled for an afternoon of Christmas carols, followed by an ice hockey match in the evening.

Our jaws collectively dropped. We were exhausted. We'd had less than two hours of very broken sleep on the overnight plane to Omsk, and the race was now less than 24 hours away. As politely as we could do we declined Helena's invitation, and her disappointment was palpable, almost to the point of taking offence. We had come to enjoy the Siberian hospitality, and enjoy it we would, but for now we were in race mode, and carols and hockey had to come a poor second to much-needed sleep.

Race day dawned to sunshine and clear blue skies, although there had been further heavy overnight snowfall. Okay, it was around 20 degrees below zero, but that was still 20 degrees warmer, or should I say less cold, than the runners had endured during the previous year's race.

After a light breakfast we again trekked on foot to race HQ, and I was relieved to find that the fresh snow underfoot provided considerably more traction than we had had the previous day. It was on arrival at race HQ that things first began to go wrong – in my haste to leave, I had left my race number in the hotel room. Yes, a stupid and careless error, but surely no big deal. I knew what my number was, so they could either write out a duplicate, or even issue me with a new one, but no, I was sternly informed through Helena that no blank number sheets or spare numbers were available. If I wanted to run, I would have to get a taxi back to the hotel.

'Of course I want to run! I haven't come all the way to Siberia to watch a half-marathon,' I bellowed at Helena, who calmly translated my outburst to the race director, but he was unmoved, spreading his arms out wide with a laconic expression on his face. With less than an hour to the start, Helena called a taxi and we waited and waited and waited, and then just as desperation was setting in, an unused number was suddenly unearthed – number 444, and the problem was solved. The forgetful Englishman had been let off the hook!

If I have one golden rule in my race preparation, wherever I happen to be running, it is that I like to give myself plenty of time to prepare. I hate a last-minute rush. There was now no such luxury here, and a sense of panic began to rise within me as I rushed through my final preparations. Did I need goggles? We wouldn't be running in the eye-freezing conditions of the previous year, but the icy wind was strong, so I opted to carry them round my neck just in case I needed them later.

The ski mask was a definite yes, recommended to me by a cross-country skier as an essential aid to breathing the icy cold air. Even walking into the wind on the way to the race had been uncomfortable. The air seemed to freeze in my throat, further needling the cough. I stuffed a silk neck buff into my bum bag in case I needed that as well. It was a wise move.

I rummaged in my rucksack for the woolly hat and bulky pair of mittens. Helena was urging us to make our way to the start, but Miles was obligingly answering the questions being fired at him by the local media horde, and Jon was struggling manfully to get their protective clothing together.

'Please hurry, please hurry!' called Helena from the open doorway of the hall, the icy draught scything into the warm interior. The start was several hundred yards away so Miles politely excused himself from his media entourage and we left together, slipping wildly on the treacherous surface, with reporters and cameramen in hot pursuit. The faster I tried to move, the more I slithered and the slower I went. We reached an area where runners and spectators alike thronged together to keep warm.

On a wooden podium, speeches were being made, but we knew not what. Still Miles patiently answered the journalists' questions and the cameras continued to roll. Jeremy, Toby and I took photos of each other in our bizarre race attire; apparently I resembled a ninja.

'Where have the other runners gone?' Jon suddenly asked. We looked around to see only fur-laden spectators. In the distance a klaxon sounded. The race had started without us!

Pushing through crowds and past metal barriers, we caught sight of the back of the pack and set off in pursuit. The route had been well gritted, my trail shoes gripped firmly to the surface, and I started to build up to what, for me, was race speed.

'Are we still running together?' called out Miles.

'Doug just made a break for it but I think I've got him,' joked Jeremy.

Effortlessly he passed me again, with Toby just behind him. Tucking in behind them both, I sought shelter from the icy blast but, already, I was needing to work hard to keep up; the stubborn, nagging cough was taking its toll on my stamina.

Negative thoughts drifted into my psyche. I'd travelled thousands of miles to be at this race; surely it wasn't going to be one of those days.

A quick mental reality check was required. Never, ever in my life had I run in conditions as remotely cold and icy as these were, so I could hardly expect it to come easy, particularly as we'd had no chance beforehand to try out our equipment and clothing.

But there lay the problem. The ski mask just wasn't working – my face was warm enough, but I was blowing like a whale and I hadn't run half a mile yet. I pulled the mask down from my mouth and gulped in the icy air – it razored into the back of my throat. A few hundred yards further on we turned into the wind, and I had to pull the mask on again. Fine for a minute or two and then that suffocating feeling returned; I simply couldn't get enough air in through the grille at the front.

Jeremy had now pulled away but Toby had dropped behind me. I stumbled on, mask off, too cold, mask on, can't breathe. Heading out of the city centre and into open parkland, we followed a tree-lined path alongside a river that appeared more like a glacier.

To provide a half-marathon route that was possible to run on, Helena had briefed us just before the start that we would be running seven laps of three kilometres each. This was only the first lap, and the thought of heading down this icy trail six more times, fighting for breath but not wanting to freeze my throat, didn't bear thinking about. Something had to change, so I wrestled my ski mask off as I ran; no easy task with huge mittens on my hands.

I pulled a mitten off, tucking it under my arm, and rummaged through my bum-bag for my silk neck buff that I then pulled over my head to provide some protection to my mouth. Somebody was shouting something unintelligible from behind. I looked back; I'd dropped my mitten, not a good move as the tips of my fingers were already feeling numb from the cold. I ran back to retrieve it and then onwards again, battling to pull the mitten back on as I ran.

My ski mask, where was my ski mask? I'd tucked that under my arm as well while I'd grappled with buff and mittens. Again, I glanced back and could see it lying in the roadway, maybe a hundred yards behind. Cursing my clumsiness, I backtracked for the second time, stuffed the mask down the front of my top clothing, and set off after Toby who was by now some way in front.

Soon we were heading on snow-covered roads back towards Omsk city centre. Slipping, sliding, back to the start and what, in another six laps' time, would be the finish line. As I turned into lap two, a quick mental calculation of my lap time multiplied by seven produced a half-marathon time I really wasn't proud of, regardless of the horrendous conditions. I knew it had been slow, and on future laps I would hopefully not keep dropping things and having to backtrack, but this was proving far harder than I'd ever imagined. It was time to dig in.

One of the best ways to block out the negativity of what is going on inside your head is to take more notice of what is happening on the outside. I began to absorb the harsh beauty of my surroundings. The icicles hanging down from the tree branches, bushes glistening with permafrost diamonds, the river crushing tiny wooden rowing boats in its icy jaws.

When we turned into the wind I pulled the silk buff up over my nose and mouth. It worked for a while. but then my breath would freeze and the soft silk would harden like cardboard. I twisted it round a few degrees to an unfrozen segment, pulled the silk buff down when out of the wind; slowly I was getting on top of the breathing problem.

But now it was getting much trickier underfoot. The course had been well gritted beforehand but the surface was getting more and more polished, as a melee of running shoes compacted the snow into lethal ice. Turning the tight corners became a hazardous business; the proverbial turning around of an oil tanker sprang to mind. The second lap passed more quickly, my spirits were rising, and then, on the third lap, I received even more of a boost.

Helena was at the roadside to yell out that the race would be only six laps! Apparently the course measurer had lengthened each lap to three and a half kilometres, so now we would only have to run six of them – they'd just forgotten to tell us of the change at the start, or maybe that was what the incomprehensible pre-race speeches were about! Now the mental arithmetic was much more acceptable. I was almost halfway there, and started to go after those in front. Great, I was at last beginning to enjoy myself.

What happened next caught me totally unawares. After taking on and beating the demons of the Sahara and Gobi deserts, and as a veteran of 20 marathons, I was only too aware of the dangers of dehydration and how best to manage my fluid and salt intake during a long run. What I hadn't appreciated was that I could get just as dehydrated in these bitterly cold conditions. I'd decided not to carry a drink around with me as, in all likelihood, it would be frozen solid before I needed it. I assumed there might be drinks available on the route, in common with most other big city road races, but there were none, probably for the very same reason.

From the halfway point I developed a desperate thirst, as intense as any I have ever experienced. My lips were dry and cracked from the icy blast, and the cold sore on my upper lip that had started as a tingling sensation in Moscow, was now tugging painfully at the cracked and tender tissue surrounding it. My head was throbbing, and thick and sticky sputum coated the inside of my mouth like glue, making breathing even more difficult. I had to find a drink.

On one of the city sections I spotted a young lad in the crowd holding a bottle of water. Clasping my mittened palms together as if in prayer, I pointed to the bottle and with a grin to his parents, he offered it up to me. The water was nearly all frozen but I managed to get a few drops of precious liquid on to my lips, and struggled on. My pace was declining but I kept going, a curious mixture of sensations and emotions running through me – dizzy, irritable and confused but, at the same time, a part of me was enjoying this very surreal experience. An obscure and unidentified piece of fruit grabbed from a roadside table provided another brief respite from the thirst, but if some enterprising Russian had been selling hot tea at the roadside, he could have named his price!

And then it was the last lap. In the parks and along the riverbanks the crowds were somewhere between sparse and non-existent, save for a few frozen marshals and television cameramen, but in the city centre they lined the streets and cheered enthusiastically. I'm convinced the body must hold back a spare fuel tank for the latter stages of a gruelling race. Previously-leaden legs were suddenly rejuvenated, towering hills became slight inclines, and the world just seemed a rosier place. Now I was taking in all the sights and sounds of this once-feared city that had been all but closed to the outside world during the Soviet period. I rounded the final bend to come face to face with Father Christmas; our gloved hands slapped in friendship. No sign of Rudolph.

Jeremy was waiting to welcome me at the finish line and, despite the parched lips and the sensation of fragmented glass splinters in the back of my throat, that warm glow of achievement still managed to permeate the cloak of discomfort that seemed to be slowly engulfing me. We waited for the others; young Toby, who'd never run so far in his life in any conditions, let alone in a freezer, and Jon and Miles who finished to rapturous applause and who were then surrounded once again by the Omsk media pack. Sadly, the pain written across Miles's face signified the failure of his damaged fingers to cope with the extreme cold, and that his dream of a second attempt at the South Pole would now never be.

In time, we drifted back to race HQ, where hot tea and sandwiches awaited. I lay on the floor and, for the next hour or so, I felt as ill as I have ever been after any run in my life: nauseous, light-headed, my body and hands shaking violently. Despite the urgings of my compatriots to get up and return to our hotel, I just could not move. I think it was the fifth cup of hot tea that finally did the trick. Helping hands hauled me to my feet and, clutching my most incomprehensible finisher's certificate ever, we again confronted the icy route back to our rooms and a welcome siesta, if that is the correct word in such an icebound climate.

*   *   *   *   *

The post-race hospitality of our Siberian hosts was as warm as the weather was cold. We were treated to a couple of days deep in the Siberian wilderness, tobogganing down icy slopes, walking and skiing the forest trails, being hauled on horse-drawn sleighs and staying in rustic wooden cabins with spectacular ice sculptures adorning the gardens. A celebration fish and meat banquet, topped off with a magnificently decorated Siberian Ice Marathon cake, was laid on, accompanied by traditional Siberian music and dance, and, rather bizarrely, a Russian Punch and Judy puppet show.

'I'm so hungry, I could eat anything,' boasted Miles.

'We'll see about that,' chuckled Jon, mischievously placing the massive head of a freshwater perch on to his blind pal's plate.

The Russian beers and vodka flowed freely, which was probably a good thing as Inna and Helena had bought each of us a souvenir gift to take home with us. The catch was that we had to earn it by entertaining our somewhat inebriated international gathering with a short performance of some sort. Cue a succession of dodgy vocals, debatable musicianship and, in my own case, my first, and undoubtedly my last, performance as a stand-up comedian. As I said, it was a good job there was an endless supply of vodka available.

Hangovers were the order of the following morning but our hosts had even arranged a cure for that – a Russian bath! We were taken to a wooden cabin in the grounds of the complex, with smoke billowing from a large chimney. Inside was the hottest and steamiest sauna in the world. We were ordered to strip completely naked and then, once adequately cooked, were led, one by one, into an adjoining steam-filled room and invited to lay down on a couch.

Here, I was repeatedly thrashed with a large bunch of birch twigs, not sadly by a curvaceous Russian blonde but by a rather grisly and withered man, probably well into his 80s. Once the beating had brought blood streaming to my skin's surface, turning it to the colour of a beetroot, I was ordered to sprint into the forest outside, naked as the day I was born, and roll around in a snow-drift! Not a pretty sight but it was remarkably invigorating for the skin and, as a hangover cure, it had to be right up there with the best!

And so closed another chapter of my running journey. This wonderful planet of ours offers many climatic extremes and now I had had the opportunity to experience life and running at both ends of the temperature scale. Each had offered challenges that needed to be overcome but here, in Siberia, I had only run a single half-marathon stage, and the thought of running a multi-stage, ultra-marathon in conditions such as these just didn't bear thinking about.

12

Back from the brink

THE period following my Siberian adventure is not one I look back on with particularly fond memories. Chest infections seemed to crop up at regular intervals, raising the spectre of a return of either the tuberculosis or psittacosis, although X-rays eventually allayed those fears. Increasing pressures at work were once again winding up my stress levels and, recognising the return of that familiar slide in self-esteem, motivation and energy, I once again needed the support of antidepressants.

It wasn't all bad of course. For some time I had been in a new relationship but, as lovely a person as Nicky is, even this was producing its own stresses and strains. With us both having busy, time-consuming jobs that often extended into the evening hours, and living too far apart to meet up during the week, it was essentially a weekend-only relationship with me travelling to Nicky's house in Leamington, and then fretting about the neglect I was inflicting on my own pets and home. As with many couples that meet in later life, we both had grown-up families we wanted to share time with; Nicky had an elderly mother, and we both had siblings dotted liberally around the country. It was all added pressure to meet everybody's expectations.

Nicky is not a runner but was wonderfully supportive of my desire to fit at least one run into each weekend, and would often join me on the canal towpath on her bicycle or support me from the sidelines at local races. She was even there for me when, on a holiday break in Scotland, I entered my first – and only – fell run at the Newtonmore Highland Games.

From a competitive point of view it was a disaster as I finished very close to the back of the field but the novelty of two river crossings, clinging desperately to the rope that bridged the fast-flowing current, and the hands and knees crawling on the higher rocky slopes of a hill enshrouded in mist, made it an experience I will never forget.

The mad descent was crazy and I fell several times, jarring a knee, but the race ended in exhilarating fashion with a final lap of an athletics track to the sound of bagpipes, the dull thud of cabers being tossed, and the enthusiastic applause of the crowd.

Running in the months that followed was boosted by the news that I had been successful in the 2003 London Marathon ballot. Sticking to a training schedule is so much easier when there is a juicy goal at the end of it. However, it proved to be a false dawn. At the beginning of December, Nicky and I reluctantly parted. It had just not been possible to fit all the pieces of a very complex jigsaw together to everybody's satisfaction so we went our separate ways.

My gloom returned, and even deepened, and with it went my appetite to run. In my mind the periods of depression that have occasionally punctuated my life are U-shaped journeys. On the downslope, an overwhelming sense of apathy swamps my desire and motivation to undertake anything, no matter how pleasurable that activity usually is.

After bumping along the bottom for a variable period, something would prompt a change in direction. It may have been a particular event, or even a subliminal trigger, but whatever it was, it was akin to beginning to regain control of a runaway car. Little by little, I would begin to haul myself back up that slope, and it was on this part of the journey that running, and the clarity of thought that comes with it, provided the greatest benefit. That's how it works for me, at least.

On this occasion the downward slide had lasted for three months, and that had put paid to any hope of my being in shape to take my place in the 2003 London Marathon. I deferred my entry for a year and, for a whole month, I took the first tentative steps on my journey back to running fitness – that was until it nearly ended altogether.

Maybe I am what is dismissively referred to as an 'anorak', but, from the very beginning, I have always maintained a record of just about every run I have ever done, initially in a notebook, and then in later years in a spreadsheet.

Run number 1,171 in my logbook was an unremarkable training run of six and a half miles of canal towpath on a warm spring evening, but it could so easily have been my last. Less than 24 hours later my training and racing plans had been thrown into disarray by a painful back injury. I was very lucky. As it happened, it cost me many months of running and burnt a giant hole in my pocket with physiotherapy fees. It could have cost so much more.

As I have mentioned before, I am a supporter of Brighton and Hove Albion Football Club – the Seagulls. Although many decades have passed, I can still remember clearly the first match my father took me to at the age of seven – a 1-1 draw between Brighton and Chelsea reserves. Roman Abramovich had not even been born then.

By this point the Seagulls were facing a crucial test. After the euphoria of two successive championships, the final day of that season saw us facing relegation from the First Division. A simple equation: we had to win at Grimsby, and Stoke City had to lose at home to Crystal Palace. Having failed to get a ticket to see the match, I set off for my brother's house in Bristol to take advantage of his satellite TV facilities. It wasn't to be. We could only draw, although Stoke beating Palace sealed our fate anyway.

A family meal followed, some wine, and a further few drinks of commiseration, interleaved with loud music from our youth, and then it was bedtime. A small suitcase in one hand, a drink of water in the other to combat the likely dehydration, and I climbed the stairs. Or rather, I didn't.

To this day, I don't know exactly what happened. Okay, I'd been drinking, but not enough to make a flight of stairs insurmountable. There was no trip, no stumble, just a misplaced footstep, a frame-by-frame sensation of toppling backwards, a swift realisation that, with both hands occupied, I wasn't going to arrest it by grabbing the handrail, and then the inevitability of impact.

I landed on my back, juddering head-first and backwards down the final few stairs, before my head struck a wall at the bottom, bringing me to a standstill. I was winded, I was shocked but knew immediately the impact had been on my spine. I wiggled my fingers and toes. They wiggled. Phew! Ten minutes later I made it up the stairs at the second attempt, my brother adopting the sensible precaution of walking up behind me.

It was the next morning that reality dawned. An early attempt to get to the bathroom on my own was futile. Sitting up on the bed was just about possible. Getting to my feet unaided was completely out of the question.

Eventually an ambulance was summoned but the news from the casualty officer was good. No damage to the spine, just badly torn muscles and ligaments. She even backed up my guarded defence that alcohol hadn't been a major contributory factor. If

I'd have been truly inebriated, she declared, I'd have been loose and relaxed when I landed! I knew I should have had another drink.

In the days that followed, every shuffled footstep and movement was agony. There was no way I could drive back to the Midlands in my own car so I had to wait a week until my son, Chris, could get some time off work with the RAF to come and collect me. When the sun shone, I tiptoed tentatively around my brother's garden, and when he returned from work and helped me bathe, he remarked that he'd rather hoped it might be many more years before he'd have to undertake this task.

It was a visit to my GP on returning home that truly put me on to the long road to recovery. No, there was no miracle medical intervention – he just waved a red rag to a bull! Having repeatedly advised me in the past to curtail my 'risky' running sorties because of borderline blood pressure readings, he now proclaimed, 'At least this back injury will put paid to your marathons!'

What an incentive! Having just deferred my 2003 London Marathon entry, and with the rules guaranteeing me a place the following year, I had 11 months to prove him wrong.

There were many milestones on that journey. My first, shuffling, walk to the local shop and back. Normally five minutes at the very most, this half-hour epic was as satisfying as many of my long-distance triumphs. Several times a week the physiotherapists manipulated, stretched and massaged my back. At work every day I locked my office door to sit on cushions on the floor, and work my way through a rigorous exercise programme. Little by little, a range of movement was coaxed back.

And then, after four gruelling months, my physio gave me the go-ahead; I could jog for one minute, walk for one minute, but no more than ten minutes in total. It felt great, and not without its amusing moments. 'Why does that runner keep stopping to walk?' asked a young boy as I circled the footpath skirting our local lake. 'It's because he's old and not very good,' replied his mother.

Gradually the total time and the proportion of running to walking were tweaked upwards. By November, I jogged every step of a local five-kilometre race in a time I'd have been ashamed of a year earlier. My eyes were moist as I crossed the line and it wasn't from back pain; I knew I was on the way back. I continued to squeeze more miles out, but it wasn't all plain sailing. Three times I set out on a local, hilly eight-and-a-half-miler, and three times I ground to a halt. The back was still a little sore, but there were gremlins to defeat in my head as well.

Races provided stepping stones – a half-marathon, a 15-mile run. Times were sluggish but the stopwatch was irrelevant. I now knew with absolute certainty that I would never again achieve the times I had before the injury. What had previously been a comfortable jogging pace, now had me gasping for breath. I would have to readjust to new targets and goals, but at least I was still running!

Maybe the London Marathon arrived a month or two earlier than I'd have wished, and I'd be made to pay for the lack of long training runs, but, as I lined up on Blackheath Common under battleship grey skies for my 27th marathon, there was apprehension and excitement within me that I hadn't felt since my first.

Less than five hours later, as I rounded the final bend into The Mall, and glimpsed the finish line ahead, I offered up a mental toast to my GP who had inadvertently launched me on this road to recovery. Sometimes, it is only when something is nearly snatched away from you that you truly appreciate the joys it can bring.

* * * * *

It was a time to reassess. I was now entering the second half of my sixth decade on this wonderful planet and, notwithstanding the back injury, age was beginning to creep up on me. However, although I would never get back the pace of my younger years, the fact that I had just successfully completed another marathon still showed that there was plenty of endurance in those ageing legs.

Conversation with a runner of any standard will inevitably lead to talk of personal bests (PBs), or personal records (PRs) if they happen to be an American. Now I have never been a particularly competitive person, but my lifetime PBs at various race distances, and even those on training routes that I have run on countless occasions, remain warmly and indelibly etched into my memory.

Does the prospect of knowing that you will never, ever again scale those heights mean that the remainder of your running life will just be a slow meaningless decline until the day you finally grind to a halt? Not a bit of it. As each birthday passes, so the PBs can be reset, and the satisfaction of running a time that you haven't achieved for two or three years is every bit as great as those lifetime PBs, even if it is many minutes slower.

* * * * *

Once again the lure of running in foreign climes was drawing me in, and once more it was Jean-Claude and Dominique Le Cornec at SDPO who offered up just what I was looking for. Building on the hugely successful Les Foulées de la Soie series of runs around China, the organisation had been spreading its wings further afield and, in 2004, had successfully launched a new multi-stage event on the island of Sri Lanka. In February of 2005, a return visit was scheduled, and the draw of the 'Pearl of the Indian Ocean' was strong. I had never set foot on the Indian sub-continent but had heard nothing but good about the country from my son, Chris, who had only recently holidayed on the island with his girlfriend.

To further whet my appetite, I was collaborating closely with a clinical colleague, Mike, from Sri Lanka as part of my ongoing research at the university, and he almost exploded with enthusiasm when I showed him the planned itinerary.

A brief exchange of emails revealed that once again I was likely to be the only British runner. Entente cordiale? Perhaps it was the fear of spending many days in a largely French-speaking community, but I really couldn't understand why there were not more British runners signing up for SDPO running tours, with no similar offerings available on the UK market. With the knowledge that my pidgin French would see me handle the basic pleasantries of communicating with my Gallic colleagues, and knowing that most native Sri Lankans were far more likely to speak English than they were to speak French, I signed on the dotted line.

Once again, the autumn months were filled with training runs and races as I gradually built up a level of fitness that I trusted would cope with the challenges that lay ahead. After the icy blasts of Siberia, it was once again a question of coping with extreme heat, but not the dry heat I had faced in the deserts of Africa and China; this time the debilitating combination of heat and extreme humidity would add an extra dimension.

There was one extra factor in the equation, and one that my colleague Mike constantly reminded me of; more people die of snakebite in Sri Lanka each year than in any other country. Knowing the kind of terrain that we ran on in China with SDPO, reptile encounters were not out of the question, and Mike offered helpful advice on how best to avoid them and, if the worst was to happen, how to deal with a bite before help arrives. This could only be good knowledge to store in the bank – after all, it wouldn't be the first time a snake and I had crossed paths! Allow me to digress a little.

As a teenager I had managed to persuade my initially reluctant parents to allow me to keep a snake as a pet, by employing the classic tactics of suggesting my father might not have the carpentry skills required to build a vivarium. Like me, dad couldn't resist a challenge and about a month later, he finally unveiled his masterpiece, much to mum's despair. I drove off to the pet shop with £8 in my pocket, and returned with an 18-inch-long boa constrictor who I named Jeffrey, although I have no idea why. Jeffrey soon became a star attraction to anyone who visited our home, but his fame spread wider than that.

I was on a day release course at the local technical college and my classmates were constantly inquiring about him so, one day, I took him to college with me. As he had to be kept warm he lived in a little cloth bag which I kept inside my shirt until it was time to pass him round my colleagues, most of whom had never handled a snake before. Jeffrey even made it to a couple of late-night student parties, again revelling in the attention he was getting, and always being impeccably behaved, but perhaps his greatest achievement was to allow my nan, on my mum's side, to overcome her fear of snakes.

Nan was a tiny but gritty character who feared nothing – except snakes. It was a genuine phobia – even the sight of a snake on a TV programme would lead to the set being turned off instantly, whoever was watching it. When nan heard I had a snake at home, she vowed she would never, ever visit our house again. Of course, that didn't happen, although we had to keep a blanket over the front of the vivarium to spare her having to come face to face with the beast. Eventually she was persuaded to take a peep and, within weeks, the magic moment arrived when nan finally held Jeffrey in her own hands, and a photograph of that occasion sat beside her chair at her home until she left us.

I kept Jeffrey for over four years. In his early days he would be fed with thawed-out frozen mice and, as he grew, he moved on to eating thawed-out rats. A good meal would last him anything from a week up to a month or more and this meant that Jeffrey very rarely went to the toilet. However, when he did, you very soon knew about it, and it was this that led to the day that Jeffrey blotted his copybook.

I was sitting on the sofa watching the television and mum was doing the ironing in the middle of the room. A sudden, truly vile smell drifted into the air and I leapt to my feet to collect the tools for removing the offending material from the gravel. As mum continued ironing, wafting away the odour at the same time, I lifted the lid of the vivarium, and with a trowel and plastic bag, began the removal process. It was then that Jeffrey struck.

With a loud yelp, I snatched my left hand back out of the vivarium with a four-and-a-half-foot snake attached to the flap of skin between my thumb and forefinger. My mum screamed but, admirably, managed to avoid fainting or dropping the iron. I managed to prise Jeffrey's jaws apart and dropped him back down into his tank. There was no bleeding from the wound, just four neat rows of pinpricks from the needle-sharp teeth of the upper jaw, and two on the other side of my hand from the lower jaw.

It was so out of character but I knew instantly the mistake I had made. Every two months or so Jeffrey would shed his skin and, during this process, his eyes would go opaque, restricting his vision. He almost certainly saw the movement of my hand and thought it was mealtime!

Although there was no real physical damage to my hand, I had been bitten by a large tropical snake carrying goodness-knows-what germs in its mouth, and it seemed wise to have it checked out by a doctor. Accompanied by brother, Dave, I wrapped my hand in a makeshift bandage and drove off to the local A&E department.

'And what is the problem?' asked the receptionist as I checked in.

'I've been bitten by a boa constrictor,' I replied, in my most matter-of-fact voice.

'Now look here,' she retorted sternly, 'I really don't have the time for stupid games – have you been drinking?'

'No really, I have been bitten by a boa constrictor,' I insisted, peeling off the bandage and revealing the multiple rows of seeping toothmarks on my hand.

'Oh my, I'm sorry,' she responded. 'Was it poisonous?'

'No, they normally crush you but I persuaded him not to,' was the wittiest reply I could come up with at the time.

I was eventually seen by the casualty officer. As he opened my notes there were five giant words written in block capitals covering a whole page – 'BITTEN BY A BOA CONSTRICTOR'! The wound was cleaned up and then it was a case of 'drop your trousers and we'll give you an anti-tetanus'. There were no further consequences to the bite.

Although I kept Jeffrey for a couple more months, I always wore heavy gloves when handling him after that. My confidence had gone, and with that the rather special magic that had existed between us. Jeffrey was now outgrowing his accommodation anyway, so when the offer of a place in a London zoo arrived it was time to bid farewell. It was an experience that left me with a healthy respect for scaly serpents.

*   *   *   *   *

Anyway, to return to my running story, Chris spent his Christmas leave from the RAF at my house in Redditch that year, and it was on the morning of Boxing Day that news first came through of the massive earthquake and resulting tsunami that devastated so many countries surrounding the Indian Ocean, including Sri Lanka.

As the days passed, and the total death toll in the region climbed towards a quarter of a million, including over 35,000 in Sri Lanka alone, it was clear that there had to be serious doubt as to whether the run could take place. Was it right that an international touring running event could take place so soon after not only the devastating loss of life but also the loss of whole villages and communities?

Sri Lanka was reeling from what had happened, but, at the same time, the last thing it needed was for other parts of the world to turn their back on it in its hour of need. Tourism remained key to the Sri Lankan economy.

Early in the new year, the news came through that the tour would go ahead. Most of the race stages were inland and therefore not affected by the devastation caused by the tsunami. Jean-Claude, and other key members of SDPO, would arrive in Sri Lanka a few days earlier than anticipated, to visit the areas most affected and to deliver aid donated by the organisation and other French authorities. As competitors, we were invited to bring along anything we could squeeze into our luggage that might just help someone somewhere and the new motto of the race series became 'Courir Pour Reconstruire' – run to rebuild. Just eight weeks after one of the world's worst natural disasters, we flew from a snowy Charles de Gaulle Airport in Paris to a steamy and humid Colombo.

With most of the key members of the organisation already in Colombo, it was reassuring to recognise a few friendly faces on the plane; faces familiar from the dunes and mountain paths of China and Tibet. Indeed, I was sitting next to a non-English-speaking couple who greeted me as a long-lost friend before slightly spoiling the moment by pointing at my midriff and implying, in the nicest possible way, that I had put on a noticeable amount of weight since our paths last crossed four and a half years earlier.

Sleeping on a long-haul flight is not a skill I have ever been able to master so I was feeling pretty frazzled when we eventually arrived in Colombo just after dawn. Jean-Claude and Dominique were there to greet us, and embraced me warmly, although worryingly they too seemed preoccupied by the size of my midriff! Had I really put on that much weight? As we boarded the coach to our city-centre hotel, we were each presented with an orchid garland of welcome by the local organising committee; a nice touch given the heartache the country was still going through.

Once again I was fortunate enough to be roomed with somebody who could speak excellent English – this time it was Bruno, not a runner, but a French film cameraman who was there to record the whole visit, including the earlier relief visit to the devastated south coast of the island. He had tears in his eyes when he described to me what he had seen.

An early lunch, a brief period of relaxation around the hotel pool and a chance to get to know some of the other runners, and then we were off on a whistle-stop tour of Colombo. There would be no prologue stage this time; the running competition proper started early the next morning, so there was very little time to acclimatise to the steamy humidity.

Whether it's the sudden change of climate, the water, or the food, I seem to have a digestive system that wastes very little time in letting me know that I am in unfamiliar surroundings. Even as we boarded the coach to tour the city, the initial rumblings of discontent had me reaching for the loperamide tablets that are one of the first items on my packing list for any foreign running trip. I sat behind Philippe and Corinne, a Swiss married couple who were a cardiologist and paediatrician respectively, and who both spoke perfect English. Now, if we ran out of conversation about running and travel, we could even talk shop if the need arose!

We toured the city, visiting ornate Hindu temples covered with hundreds, if not thousands, of stone carved figures. We visited the parks, where I came across my first sight of a cobra, although this one was being charmed out of a wicker basket, swaying to the tones of its owner's pungi. Barefooted, we tiptoed around the scented Buddhist temple at nearby Kelaniya but, as magnificent as these sights were, my focus was on the increasing turmoil inside my stomach, and a longing for a good night's sleep before an early start the next morning.

A further dose of loperamide was employed to try and settle the first problem, but I was to endure my second sleepless night in succession as a faulty air-conditioning system blasted our room with icy-cold air throughout the night. Neither Bruno nor I were able to switch the damned system off, reception were unable to get in touch with an engineer until the morning, so we resorted to donning layer after layer of extra clothing in order to try and get warm enough to sleep. This was not what we were expecting to do in humid Sri Lanka. It was not the best of starts to what promised to be a challenging series of trail runs, but my little streak of bad luck was about to get worse.

It was 6.15am when we left our hotel to drive the two and a half hours to the start of the first stage, a 17-kilometre run from Sisira to Metiyagane. The outskirts of Colombo were a complete contrast to the almost salubrious buildings we had visited the day before, with mile after mile of what can only be described as shanty towns. The good news was that the diarrhoea at last seemed to be settling; less positive was the fatigue induced by 48 hours of insomnia.

However, my mood was soon lifted when we arrived at the start and were treated to the warmest of welcomes from children at the local schools. As the girls in their pristine white dresses sat on the grass, busily plaiting together palm leaves to build shelters from the sun, the boys, all immaculately dressed in white shirts and royal blue shorts, lined up behind a wire fence and cheered and chanted with massive enthusiasm. Just as in China, there was music as well, as a troupe of red-and-white-costumed dancers and drummers entertained us just before the start. It couldn't be anything but uplifiting and, after a slightly dispiriting first day in Colombo, my running mojo was definitely on an upward curve.

Once again, as in China, we were joined by several of the older schoolchildren for the run itself. This boosted the field quite significantly as, unlike China where there were just over

100 SDPO competitors, there were only 39 of us here in Sri Lanka. Given the very wide range of running abilities this spanned, we could expect to spend a great deal of time on each stage running on our own, or at least in the company of some of the local athletes.

Under an increasingly hot sun, a blaring hooter sounded to mark the start of another international leg of my running journey. First, two laps of the school playing fields and then we headed out into the Sri Lankan countryside along rocky and dusty trails.

It all started so well, despite the scorching heat, and I soon settled into a steady rhythm which had me passing many of those who had started at a slightly too enthusiastic pace. We sped through isolated villages and the warmth of the welcome we received seemed to vindicate Jean-Claude's decision to go ahead with the race; these people were genuinely pleased to see us.

And then, at four kilometres, everything changed. My toe struck a large, loose rock on the trail and before I could react, I was sliding face down through a dusty, gritty surface. The right-hand side of my ribcage had landed on another heap of rubble and the pain of the impact shot through me. Gingerly, I picked myself up and brushed the worst of the dirt off my arms and legs. Blood was running from scrapes on my face, my left elbow, my right hand and my right knee but at least there didn't seem to be any deep abrasions that might need stitching.

Immediately I was surrounded by concerned villagers and a young lad, who had been following the runners along the trail on his moped, sped off and returned with a bucket of water to help clean me up. Maybe the water was as contaminated as the grime now embedded into the cuts and abrasions, but it looked unsoiled and I was happy to use it to bathe the wounds, with plenty of help from my little team of anxious carers. These people were truly wonderful.

Several runners stopped by but I urged them to carry on as I was being well looked after and just needed a few moments to get cleaned up and regain my composure. And indeed that is exactly what happened, although the remainder of that stage was anything but comfortable. The heat and humidity were becoming truly oppressive and I'd made a stupid mistake at the outset when I had only half-filled my Camelbak drinking system in an effort to reduce the amount of electrolyte drink I would have to carry. I wouldn't be repeating that error on future stages, as you needed every precious drop of liquid available in those sultry conditions.

I also felt far more fatigued than I should have been, given the relatively short distance I had already covered. Was it the lack of sleep, the after-effects of the diarrhoea, or was I still suffering from the fall? My ribs jarred with pain with every footfall but I was at least able to get some painkillers at the next aid station, although I did have to endure a stern reprimand from the doctor for setting off without enough liquid on board to sustain me. For the remainder of the tour, my drinking system would be checked at every single aid station to make sure that I didn't become a repeat offender.

And that wasn't the end of my problems! As I trotted sluggishly through yet another remote village, with sweat dripping from every piece of exposed skin, a young lad decided to help me keep cool by emptying a very large pail of water all over me. I have no doubt that this was done with the best of intentions, rather than as a wanton act of vandalism, but this single act was to have long-lasting effects that would endure for the remainder of my race series.

On the physical side I ran the rest of that stage with soaking wet shoes and socks on hot, dusty and uneven surfaces, and finished with three of the largest and most painful blisters I have ever had, and these were to plague me for the remainder of the trip. On a more materialistic note, the deluge of water penetrated the bum-bag I carried around my waist, causing dire, and potentially terminal, damage to both my mobile phone and the small digital camera I carried with me to record the highlights of my journey.

I meandered on to the end of the stage with runner after runner passing me, and when I finally did reach the finish line there were only seven of my fellow competitors still behind me. I felt exhausted, emotionally drained, unsteady on my feet, and the medics quickly ushered me to the first-aid tent where I was laid down on a bed and given a quick once-over check – temperature, blood pressure, heartsounds. I was given the all-clear, my wounds from the fall were cleaned up and dressed, aseptically this time and, after about 20 minutes, I was able to rejoin my colleagues.

The aches and pains I knew would heal; I had overcome far worse injuries in past events and been able to run again the next day, but the damage to my camera and phone was a cause for concern. Okay, it wouldn't be the end of the world if I returned home without any photographs of my time in Sri Lanka, other than those I'd already taken in Colombo, and that was assuming that they could be recovered from the soggy memory card, but holiday photographs are such a powerful way of rekindling wonderful memories many years down the line.

Even more concerning was my phone which stubbornly refused to show any sign of life. This was my only link with my family back home, and indeed held all their telephone numbers. I'd promised to update them regularly with text messages of my progress, and knew they would become concerned if they didn't hear from me. All I could do was wait until we reached our new hotel that evening, take both phone and camera apart, and pray that I could dry them out sufficiently to coax them back to life. As the first day of a new running adventure, this one couldn't have gone much worse.

13

Waves of emotion

ELEPHANTS. It was with elephants that I began this tale, and in an almost surreal fashion these gigantic mammals seem to have developed a habit of wanting to poke their noses, or rather their trunks, into this story as it unfolds.

After a rejuvenating post-race lunch we had paused our northbound coach journey at the Pinnawala Elephant Orphanage. Now this was one part of Sri Lanka that I did have some knowledge of despite never having visited before. As I mentioned earlier, my son Chris and his girlfriend had recently holidayed on the island and had recounted how they had been forced to seek shelter in a shop on the village high street when a belligerent captive elephant decided to go on the rampage.

There was no such drama this time from the handful of shackled jumbos that ambled through the village, under the watchful eye of their private owners, but the major attraction of the visit was to stand on the riverbank and to watch the herd of many dozen Indian elephants, many of them orphans, bathing and playing in the river below. It was a scene that begged for a few photographs and it was frustrating to have to leave that to others.

Our next destination was, for an inveterate nature lover like me, a magical place – Habarana. The whole place teemed with wildlife. Lumbering monitor lizards ambled across the grounds surrounding our chalet rooms. The tree trunks were alive with numerous smaller species of lizard, although my lack of Attenborough skills prevents me from naming them. Indian palm squirrels occupied the lower branches of the trees, and high above our heads, many varieties of monkey squealed and hurled themselves around in the treetops. And then there were the birds, of every size, sound and plumage colour imaginable. Extraordinary.

Habarana boasted an exotic lake as well. Twisted branches and tree trunks curled upward out of the waters, natural display pedestals for the rich variety of birdlife that perched upon them; crocodiles lurked in its shallows, and we were assured that, at first light, herds of wild elephants would drink from its waters, although our schedule never allowed us to view this.

It was an early start again the next morning for a stage of just over 15 kilometres. The cuts and grazes were no issue, the rib pain subsided under hefty doses of ibuprofen, but the blisters on my feet were a real problem and I rose especially early that morning to tape them up as best I could. They would certainly need to be dealt with in a more professional manner once I had a chance.

It never ceases to amaze me how, on some days, your mind and body are primed to want to run and run and run, while on others all sorts of mental alarm bells are ringing in your head, begging you to adopt a much more sedate approach to life. This day dawned in the former category and, as we lined up on the start line with around 80 young Sri Lankan runners, the majority of them in bare feet, I was once again feeling the love for my hobby.

We set off on tarmacked roads, stony trails and sand-covered tracks. I ran steadily for the first five kilometres with other runners who had finished comfortably ahead of me on the previous day. Even when I was forced to walk for a while to climb a steep and uneven hill trail, I was relieved to find others around me doing the same.

Of course, the faster runners had long since disappeared into the distance, but I was coping so much better with the heat and humidity and, when you are less focused on your inner pains, you have more time to take in your surroundings. We passed through remote villages that had almost certainly never seen a tourist before, young children drawing water from a well, and the slightly chilling sight of a line of various animal skulls, each perched on top of a stake hammered into the ground at the side of the track. I had no idea what the significance of these was.

On a couple of occasions the marked route took us along the narrow gravel path that ran alongside a railway line but happily no trains passed that might have sent us diving for cover.

As the heat intensified in the final third of the stage, we began to climb on a sandy track that took us over the top of a long-extinct volcano, and there below was the welcome sight of Habarana Lodge and the finish line.

As we descended we ran past more shackled elephants, working in the fields with their masters. I really hoped that these magnificent creatures were well cared for but the regular proddings they received from hefty wooden staffs seemed to suggest that that might not always be the case.

As I crossed the line there was undoubtedly a greater spring in my step than the day before. A few places higher up in the rankings, a time I was quite pleased with given the terrain and humidity – yes, the smug satisfaction of a job well done. Finishing at our lodge also gave me the rare opportunity of a post-race shower before we moved on to another phase of sightseeing. Oh my, those feet were a real mess and would need to be looked at again later, but I was suddenly distracted by shouts of anguish from the cabin next door.

I hastily pulled on some clothes and dashed outside, just in time to see a pair of monkeys disappearing off into the tree-tops with my neighbour's running vest and shorts. We had been warned not to dry our race clothing by hanging it on the balcony – now somebody had learned their lesson the hard way!

Lunch not only brought good food to replace the calories we had burned, but also a conversation that even today brings a smile to my face.

Waiter, 'Can I get you a drink with your meal, sir?'

Me: ponders a moment, and reflects on the fact that there is no more running to do until the following day, 'Yes please, I will have a glass of beer.'

Waiter, 'I am really sorry, sir. Today is a national holiday in Sri Lanka and I am afraid I am not permitted to serve you with a glass of beer.'

A little wave of disappointment swept through me as that momentary vision of ice-cold beer on my sore and parched lips began to fade.

'However,' the waiter continued, 'if sir doesn't mind taking his drink in a cup and saucer rather than a glass, then we could allow that.'

My cold beer duly arrived in a cup and saucer, with the remainder of the bottle's contents hidden in a teapot!

* * * * *

The next stop was Sigiriya and this visit once again illustrated that the many running friends I have made, both at home and on my travels, are just the nicest and most supportive people you could hope to meet. Before travelling to Sri Lanka, I had studied the guidebooks of the places we were scheduled to visit and Sigiriya qualified as a must-see, while also triggering that 'cold-sweat' feeling linked to that old chink in my armour: my fear of heights.

The red stone rock at Sigiriya towers 600 feet above the forest below it, resembling the silhouette of a lion from a distance. On its flattened top lie the ruins of a fifth-century palace but the walls of the rock were nearly vertical and the only access to the palace was via a series of twisting and precarious stairs and ladders, for me the stuff of nightmares.

I feel embarrassed by my phobia. Running for miles across hostile deserts holds no fears for me, but lift me more than 15 feet off the ground with an unprotected drop below and my legs turn to jelly. As our coach approached the foot of the rock, I revealed my fears to those sitting near me. Here I was at Sigiriya rock; I could see it, touch it – I could tick it off on my list of places I had visited during my lifetime. I didn't actually need to climb it, did I?

Rather than dismissing me as a lightweight, my colleagues rallied around in heart-warming fashion. In particular, Philippe, Corinne and a young lady called Florence agreed to stay with me all the way to the top, one in front and two behind. We began the climb, initially on stone steps although the lack of a handrail still made some sections a little uncomfortable. We arrived at the Lion's Platform where the remnants of two gigantic stone lion paws are all that remain of the beast that gave the rock its name. A brief respite as we admired the astonishing wall paintings of the Ladies of Sigiriya, perfectly conserved in a protected crack in the rock and then, passing between the giant paws, we began the ladder climb towards the summit. Hammered into the side of the rock, the seemingly flimsy steel staircase wound backwards and forwards up the sheer walls.

As I edged upwards my gaze was glued firmly to the rock face – I did not dare to look downwards as in all likelihood this would cause me to freeze completely. Step by step, and with encouragement from in front and behind, I was guided to the very plateau, the ancient remains of the palace and a breathtaking view of the jungle below, although I steered well clear of the edges where braver souls ventured. Of course, I still had to get back down again, but adopting the same approach of staring fixedly at the rock, I slowly but steadily returned to ground level. Now, not only had I seen and touched the world-famous rock at Sigiriya, I had also climbed it. This day was getting better and better.

There was more good news when we eventually returned to my room at the lodge; a combination of being dismantled, the hot sun and the sporadic use of a borrowed hairdryer had restored life and function to my mobile phone and I was at last able to get a reassuring message back to my family at home. Sadly, the same treatment had failed miserably to reawaken my camera and the realisation that the damage was quite likely permanent began to dawn.

Dinner, and a late visit to Francoise the nurse, who again patiently blitzed the festering blisters on my feet, ended a largely rewarding day, although the way she kept drawing in deep breaths and shaking her head in dismay did not fill me with much confidence for the future.

Run three, and our final race in the Habarana region – 15 steamy kilometres and this time finishing at the foot of Sigiriya rock that I had conquered the day before. It was an inauspicious start to the day with more tummy turmoil meaning I could only manage a very small breakfast. I wasn't the only runner suffering. Corinne arrived at the breakfast table to announce that Philippe was running a high fever and would be missing from that day's stage at the very least.

Once again Sophie from the SDPO team translated the pre-race briefing to me and, this time, some of the content was rather disconcerting and, for me, highly prophetic, although I would have to wait several years for that prophecy to come true.

Crocodiles. For part of that day's route we would be running alongside a lake. Crocodiles had been known to bask in the sunshine on the bank, but would probably slip off into the water once they heard the runners coming. Probably! I would have liked a little more comforting reassurance than that and, for once, was grateful for the fact that I wouldn't be among the leading group of runners to arrive there. And then it was elephants. Today we would be running in a region where wild elephants lived, not the captive, shackled animals we had encountered so far, or even the confined, semi-liberated elephants that had entertained us in the river at Pinnawala.

The instructions were clear. If confronted by a wild elephant showing aggressive intent, then stand still and face it down, staring it directly in the eyes! To run away would be the worst thing to do as it would only encourage the elephant to chase and they could comfortably outpace a fleeing man. I just hoped we wouldn't have to put that theory to the test.

The start was delayed while some logistics were sorted out on the route, and as we baked under the sun we were once again entertained by our resident songstress. Marie-Francoise was a wonderful middle-aged lady, happy to jog along at the rear of the field and to regale those around her with a seemingly endless collection of French folk songs. Every day was a joy for Marie-Francoise and, as much as she took her running very seriously, and was to complete every step of this particular journey, she also wanted to record and document every memory of the tour and would stop every few minutes to take photographs and diligently record details of them in her notebook.

For me this turned out to be a lifesaver. On my eventual return to the UK, I corresponded at length with Marie-Francoise, and eventually became the grateful owner of a wonderful set of photographic memories to replace the ones I was never able to take myself.

We eventually set off along a wide, sandy trail with overhanging palm trees providing intermittent shelter from the sun, and began a 16-kilometre stage that offered the very best of the country's outstanding natural beauty. An exquisitely beautiful lake and sections of jungle where the trees overhead all but blotted out the sunlight and the screaming and screeching of the birds and monkeys had to be heard to be believed. Apart from our usual companion runners from the local region who would complete the whole stage, we were also occasionally joined by tiny children from the villages who would run barefoot with us for a few hundred yards, their little faces alive with joy.

In time the rock at Sigiriya came into view and this time, rather than climbing it, we ran a complete loop around its base, seeing this unique monolithic structure from every possible viewpoint. Although emboldened monkeys scampered to within inches of my feet as I ran, the elephants that roamed these parts never showed themselves, much to my relief. Out of the jungle, and along a long straight trail, and there was the finish line.

Once again the heat and humidity had left me feeling utterly exhausted and I found a large rock, with a surprisingly cool surface, to stretch out on while we waited for the slower runners to come in. Nearby, a large pile of discarded water bottles was being systematically searched by a group of our monkey friends, each one being checked in turn for any remaining liquid. There was one saving grace to that day's running – for the first time I had kept my feet dry and this could only be good news for the deteriorating blisters on my feet.

Any hope of a post-run recovery snooze was dashed by the relentless schedule, but then we had come to Sri Lanka to see Sri Lanka, and not to sleep. An outdoor lunch in the gardens of Habarana and then a tour of the monuments of Polonnaruwa, the former capital of Sri Lanka in medieval times. Although as many as 900 years old, the Hindu-inspired architecture and monuments of this ancient city were in astonishingly impressive condition and the few hours available to us were nowhere near long enough to do justice to the many sites of interest.

If there had been one stabilising factor on this trip that distinguished it from the SDPO trip around China, it was that we had been based in the one hotel in Habarana for several nights and that avoided the constant packing and repacking of suitcases and bags, often with soggy contents. That was about to change.

When I recall the individual legs of the multi-stage events I have run in Morocco, China and now in Sri Lanka, there is almost always one event during each stage that defines that day in my mind. The fourth stage, 14 kilometres along the Dambulla trail, was defined by Elizabeth. Elizabeth was 12 and led a very hard life for a child of her age.

It was a relatively short stage as we had a lot of travelling to do after it, and it had been a very early start as we had to pack and load our bags for our onward journey. As ever, the heat and humidity sucked the energy out of me, but there were additional warnings at the pre-race briefing that, once again, Sophie had kindly jotted down on notepaper for me. Unlike the previous day when the canopy of jungle and forest had sheltered us from the worst of the sun, today's race was entirely out in the open, included some very steep climbs in the later stages, and would be by far the hardest we had encountered so far.

It was about two miles into the race, as I ran along a riverbank, that I caught up with a slim young girl, wearing the obligatory but ludicrously large SDPO T-shirt that fitted her more as a dress. Her long hair held in place by a vividly bright red and white headband, she turned as she heard me running up alongside her.

'Bonjour,' she greeted me with an already weary-looking smile.

'Good morning,' I replied absent-mindedly, and her face lit up like a beacon.

'You can speak English?' she exclaimed.

'I am English,' I replied, and her grin grew ever wider.

She held out her hand to introduce herself. 'My name is Elizabeth. I thought everybody in this race was French and I

218

don't learn French at school, but we do learn English. Do you mind if we run together for a while so that I can practise my English?'

'Of course not,' I replied, 'although from what you've said already, it seems to me that your English is very, very good.' She grinned.

I commented on the fact that she was wearing a really smart pair of running shoes.

'I love my running shoes,' she smiled. 'They are the best thing I have ever owned.

'Sport and running are my favourite subjects at school, but it is very hard to get proper running shoes in this country, so I had to get a job.'

'You have a job?' I enquired quizzically.

'Yes,' she smiled, 'but it is on my uncle's farm. I work for three or four hours each morning before I go to school.'

'Before you go to school?' I replied, scarcely being able to disguise the disbelief in my voice. 'What time do you get up in the morning?'

'Four o'clock,' Elizabeth replied nonchalantly. 'School starts at half past eight, so I have time for breakfast as well. My mother and father could not afford to buy me my running shoes.'

This was true dedication to her sport and I felt humbled, considering how much most of us take for granted when purchasing our running kit.

Elizabeth stopped to walk for a while and urged me to carry on without her. She still managed to complete the stage as the third girl of the local runners and had tears in her eyes as she collected the trophy that she had worked so hard for.

The winning girl, who had finished far ahead of me, had apparently collapsed with heat exhaustion as she had crossed the finish line and, even an hour later, had to be supported by two of her friends as she stood on top of the rostrum – yet another example of the enormous dedication that these local youngsters put into what was probably the highlight of their athletic career to date. For a country that was suffering so badly, it bodes well for the future if these young people are shining examples of future generations.

The remainder of my run had been both picturesque and quaintly memorable. 'Come on, come on, grandfather,' yelled a tiny child as I plodded through a remote village. A young lad, who proudly announced his name was Jack, hurled a bucketful of water over me that he had just drawn from a deep well with a cast-iron hand-pump. I had learned my lesson from the first stage and carried no electronic equipment with me, but once again my shoes and socks were drenched and I knew this would only be bad news for my fast-deteriorating feet.

We crossed fields of long grass with a barely visible trodden-down path indicating the 'safe' route across. This was snake country. We'd been warned that morning not to wander off into the undergrowth should we need a call of nature and my feet deliberately pounded into the ground like jackhammers in the hope of scaring away any reptile that might be lying in wait ahead. As it happened, and despite all my fears and forebodings, I never did encounter a wild snake in my travels around Sri Lanka.

This had probably been the strongest stage that I ran in the whole series and, although I felt physically drained as I finally crossed the finish line, the beauty of the hills and lakes, the friendliness of the villagers, and the inspiration I had drawn from my conversation with young Elizabeth, had left me with that warm inner glow that marks out a hard run as very special, and one that will live long in the memory.

It is a fact that an SDPO day seems to contain many more hours than any normal day! After the race presentations, there was time for a leisurely visit to the magnificent cave temples of Dambulla, a splendid lunch and then a visit to a spice garden that boasted miracle cures for just about every medical ailment known to man. Laden with remedies for my tummy, aching muscles and sore gums, and refreshed by a free back massage, we were ushered along to a demonstration of batik art, where I made another purchase to hang on my wall of running memorabilia at home. We then began the coach journey south to Sri Lanka's second city, Kandy.

High in the hills of the central plateau, and surrounded by tropical plantations – mainly of tea bushes – Kandy offered an altogether more sedate and arresting ambience compared to the hustle and bustle of Colombo, although the city's roads were pretty chaotic. Looking down upon a huge lake from the beautiful gardens of our hotel, we enjoyed a late evening outdoor meal of the most succulent, and certainly the largest, shrimps I have ever eaten in my life. One of those culinary moments that lives with you forever.

Our day concluded with an evening of Kandyan dance, music and fire, with barefooted performers gliding across hot coals, which served as a timely reminder to me that my own feet, that were metaphorically on fire, needed more repair and attention before I could get any sleep.

And sleep was not to come easily. I now had a change of room companion: André was a large, affable Frenchman whose knowledge of the English language was even less than my scanty knowledge of his native tongue. Hand signals got us through the niceties of settling into our room and preparing for a few hours of much-needed sleep, but there was a degree of tension in the morning after a largely sleepless night. André was one of the world's loudest snorers and, almost as a deliberate act of retribution, my mobile phone interrupted what little sleep we were getting by singing its happy tune at 3am. It was my very forgetful brother enquiring as to what day I would be flying out to Sri Lanka!

*　*　*　*　*

Stage five was in the time trial format that I had really enjoyed in China. Knowing that all runners starting after you were faster, and all those in front were potentially catchable, provided a double incentive to push hard. Although a comparatively short route of around six miles, this was very different terrain to the relatively moderate hills we had run in the Habarana region.

Our transport had taken us up into the mountains that towered over Kandy and the trails were steep, narrow and littered with ankle-turning loose rock. On the plus side, the greater altitude bought cooler temperatures and some relief from the suffocating humidity we had endured in the lower tropical regions.

For three kilometres I free-wheeled downhill, each twist and turn in the track opening up new viewpoints of the spectacular surroundings below. For most of that time I was accompanied by two of the local young lads running in bare feet. The soles of their feet must have been made of rhinoceros hide – I could just not envisage how it was humanly possible to run on that jagged surface without shoes.

I passed two of the French runners on this descent but in the certain knowledge that we would soon have to reclaim the altitude we had lost to get back to our start point and the pain I was getting from the big toe on my left foot was now becoming a significant concern. Sure enough, the winding climb back up round the back of the mountain tested my staying power to its very limits and my two French colleagues passed me again, along with a few of the faster runners who had started well behind me.

But pain is temporary, and when I reached the brow of a fearsomely steep section to look down at the finish line a few hundred yards below me, my torment was washed away in an instant as I skipped happily downwards to the applause of the waiting throng. Another stage in the bag, the negative demons in my head had been beaten once again and there were just two more stages to run.

A post-run visit to the renowned and astonishing Botanical Gardens at Peradinaya, where clouds of thousands of bats swirled and squealed among the tallest trees, and a single Javan fig tree covered an area of 1,600 square metres. And then on to Kandy's most celebrated Buddhist temple and UNESCO world heritage site, the Temple of the Tooth, housing the very well-guarded relic of the tooth of Buddha. There was something very appealing about this ancient city and its surroundings that made me wanted to stay longer but, once again, it would be time to move on in the morning.

It was a very early start. Not only did we have to have our bags packed for our onward journey, but I knew I needed to spend a lengthy period of time to prepare my feet for even more running. Three toenails were now hanging on by a thread. The heat, humidity and regular drenchings with water of doubtful origin had taken their toll, and there was growing evidence of infection despite the antibiotic powder the nurse had given me to dust on to the open wounds. To cap it all, the penultimate stage was to be the longest of the whole series, at around 12 miles, and carried with it the rather foreboding title of the Hellbode Climb. As ever, Sophie passed me her hand-written translation of the pre-race briefing. At the bottom she had added in red ink, 'Be careful, this is a difficult race.'

I had worn open-toed sandals to the start of the run, to take the pressure from my throbbing feet but also to let the air get at the wounds. Now, as we sat beneath the shade of a few scattered trees waiting for the start, it was time to squeeze those feet back into a pair of trainers. It was a painful process but, as any distance runner will testify, it never ceases to amaze how quickly those feet adapt to their new cramped conditions and, as soon as the running restarts, the pain slowly ebbs away.

Most of the stage was to be on smooth tarmac-covered roads that at least offered some respite from the ankle-twisting surfaces we had endured on the previous day's time trial. But, as the name of the stage strongly hinted, the first six miles wound steadily uphill at a gradient of around five per cent. The hill ahead of us, filling the whole horizon, was a vast expanse of tea plantations. The road climbed to the right edge of the hillside, twisted around a tight hairpin bend, and then continued to rise towards the opposite end of the hill, zig-zagging repeatedly in this way up to the very summit. A one in 20 hill is a serious challenge.

Six continuous miles of this gradient, with virtually no shelter from the sun, was more than I could manage and after two hard miles I slowed to a walk. Still the top of the hill seemed no closer but, as difficult as this challenge was, the beauty of my surroundings buffered the pain and exertion, and I was once again entering that semi-hypnotic zone that carries you through the tough times.

We runners were not alone up on the estate. Scores of young women, in long dresses and encased in colourful head scarves to protect them from the sun, were expertly plucking the most aromatic tea leaves from the bushes and tossing them over their shoulders into the large open sack they each carried on their back. Some were barely into their teens, but mechanical tea-picking had certainly not reached this part of Sri Lanka.

The young ladies waved cheerily as I struggled on upwards, forcing myself into a routine of five minutes running, five minutes walking. Backwards and forwards the road swept, occasionally passing the same tea-worker twice, once on the slopes up above me, and then on the return leg, they would be below.

'Hello again Mister,' they would grin mischievously.

Finally the summit came into sight and, unbeknown to me at the time, I was about to experience one of the most remarkable few minutes of my running career. I am occasionally asked to pick out the single most memorable moment from my adventures and, from an athletic point of view, I am pretty certain that nothing will ever come close to the euphoria I felt as I crossed the finish line of the Marathon des Sables. But my love of running goes much deeper than that. The raw beauty of the wilderness, the human spirit triumphing over adversity, unexpected interactions with people of an entirely different culture – all of these can transform a simple moment of running into a memory that will last forever.

As I came over the brow of the hill, I looked down into the deep valley below on to the brushwood rooftops of tiny villages. What goes up must come down and it was a massive relief, both to my mind and to my feet, that the remaining six miles of this stage would be downhill.

Six children sat at the roadside, maybe seven to eight years old. They were brightly dressed in shirts, shorts and frocks of every colour of the rainbow, although the colour co-ordination left a little to be desired. They grinned widely as I came into view, revealing large gaps in their teeth, with other teeth protruding outwards at crazy angles. No orthodontic service up here. There were no other runners in sight, either in front of or behind me.

'Bonjour,' called out the boldest lad.

'Hello,' I replied, and once again there was a buzz of excitement as they realised I could speak English.

'Can we run down the hill with you, grandfather?' asked the same young boy.

'Of course,' I replied, and immediately two of the young girls ran across and held my hands. I started jogging slowly and the children joined hands so that we stretched across the entire width of the roadway.

'We can go faster if you like, Mister,' called out one of the girls.

I increased my pace and started to chant, 'Come on, come on!' My new friends joined in. As we rounded one of the hairpin bends, there were more children at the roadside and, not needing an invitation, they joined our running cavalcade.

Soon there must have been 20 of them and the chanting changed to, 'Run, run, as fast as you can, you can't catch me I'm the gingerbread man!'

They bickered gently among themselves to take turns at holding my hands but that hillside rocked with their laughter. Down and down we ran and sang, until we came across some of the primitive dwellings in the village below. Many of the adults, having heard the noise echoing down from above, had come out into the street and roared with laughter as my Pied Piper procession came into view. People came over to shake my hand, high-five me or pat me on the back.

The children, again reunited with their parents, talked excitedly of the fun we had all just had. I dallied a short while but I still had a race to run, so waved them all goodbye and carried on alone. I felt a million dollars. Sore feet, what sore feet?

The remainder of that stage was as easy as any run I have done in my life. Yes, it was all downhill, but my spirits had been lifted to an altogether different level. I could still hear the sound of the children singing in my head, I could feel their clammy palms gripping my hands, and a smile was permanently etched on my face as I ran those final few miles.

As I gingerly removed my trainers while we waited for the final few runners to come in, my feet exploded to a larger size, rather like one of those shrink-wrapped temporary plastic raincoats that expand massively when you remove them from the packaging and you know you'll never ever be able to pack it so small again. Thank goodness I still had my sandals in my bag.

Those feet had just about reached the point at which they would no longer be able to carry me onwards but there were two pieces of good news that allowed me to dismiss any fears of not finishing. The first was that there was only one more stage to run, and that was along a beach, and the second was that the following day was a rest day. I now had nearly 36 hours to work on and patch up those septic toes and blisters for one final effort.

Our journey now took us on to Nuwara Eliya, the highest city in Sri Lanka, and overlooked by the country's highest mountain, Pidurutalagala. This was the capital of the tea industry and our dwelling, aptly named the Grand Hotel, was a classic remnant of the British colonial rule that had governed the island until its independence in 1948. With the end of the running now in sight, we enjoyed a great dinner that evening with two of our group celebrating birthdays, live jazz music and, while my feet weren't up to an evening on the dance floor, they did manage to shuffle around with our joyous hokey-cokey sauntering between the dining tables.

But then came an unexpected linguistic challenge. Before we dispersed to our rooms for the night, the programme for the following day was to be announced, and guess who had been nominated to deliver it – in French. Sophie handed me a piece of paper with times and a few brief headings in English and I spoke to the gathered masses in French – not particularly well I must admit, but well enough to warrant a round of applause for my efforts.

Afterwards, I spent a little time alone outside in the beautiful gardens where the air was refreshingly cool, and even late in the evening, the chatter of wildlife mingled with the calls to prayer that echoed back from the mountainside above. I felt serenely calm.

The following day, after a rare and delicious cooked breakfast (my stomach would not have tolerated such a feast if I had had to run shortly afterwards), we set off to our final destination – Negombo, on the west coast of the island.

Although this side of the island had been spared the very worst of the tsunami, this was the very same Indian Ocean that now lapped gently on to the shoreline. It was time to stand there and look out as the tiny waves rolled in – and contemplate.

The final race was two circuits, each of seven kilometres, and held entirely on the beach. It was hot, almost unbearably hot.

After a few days in the highlands we had become accustomed to the slightly cooler temperatures and the sudden return to scorching conditions was hard to deal with, particularly once the running started. The golden sand was soft, it was powdery and it was very deep, making the mechanics of running a near-impossible feat.

The most densely-packed sand was at the water's edge but the camber was quite steep and difficult to adjust to, and the occasional larger wave would inevitably swallow everything from your lower calves downwards.

For me, Sri Lanka and wet feet will forever be inextricably linked. A gentle run on a sunny, tropical beach may seem like an idyllic way to end a race series, but this was tough, and there were more 'did not finish' competitors on that day than on any previous stage of the series.

However, I did make it to the end. The 'Arrivée' banner strung between the masts of two beached fishing boats may not have had the majestic impact of finishing on the Great Wall of China, but it marked the end of almost 100 miles of hot and sweaty racing in a week and the completion of yet another memorable chapter in my worldwide running travails.

* * * * *

The sporting endeavour may have been over but we had one more task to fulfil, albeit voluntarily, and that was a visit to a local orphanage. We were guests on an island that, only weeks before, had experienced a natural catastrophe of gargantuan proportions, and yet the people had been so warm and welcoming everywhere we had visited – no hint of resentment that we were visiting them at such a difficult time. There had been massive loss of life and the country's orphanages were struggling to cope with the sudden influx of children who had lost their parents.

Once Jean-Claude had made it known that the event would still go ahead, the possibility of a visit to an orphanage had been mooted and we had been asked to bring along clothing and other gifts if we could squeeze them into our luggage.

It was to be one of the most moving two hours of my life. We were welcomed with open arms and treated to a show of music, song and dance by around 30 of the youngsters. Several of the instruments on which they played their tunes had been built from debris washed ashore by the tsunami. They mimicked the sounds of wind and water. There were sad songs of lives lost but also uplifting songs of a new life beginning, and even an opportunity for Marie-Francoise to sing one of her French folk songs to the children, as they sat cross-legged on the wooden floor. There was barely a dry eye in the hall as we stood en masse and applauded at the end of their show but, for me at least, the most emotional part of the visit was still to come.

Like most people around the world, I had watched endless hours of television news coverage depicting the tragic scenes as the huge waves struck the coastlines of so many countries around the Indian Ocean but nothing, and I really mean nothing, came close to the impact made on me by viewing the children's drawings of what they had been through. Upturned cars floating past their houses, household pets being washed out of their grasp, dead bodies floating face down in the water. It was part of the healing process for them to try and rationalise what they had experienced, but this exhibition of almost 100 drawings and paintings, every one by a child, simply took my breath away. I have marvelled at old masters' paintings in big city art galleries, but no collection of art has ever driven its message home so forcibly.

Our visit to Sri Lanka finished with a traditional celebration lobster dinner, this time out on the beach, and the beers and local coconut arrack cocktails flowed freely. I even received a trophy for coming second in my age category; definitely the first and quite probably the last award I shall ever get for athletic prowess. The hotel cat curled up in my lap in a final act of friendship as a spectacular fireworks display lit up the night sky.

We landed back in Paris the following evening and, would you believe – it was still snowing.

14

Peaks, troughs then Petra

O NE thing you learn as a recreational runner of modest talent is that no matter how great the personal triumphs, there is always a slump lying just around the corner. That final run along the sands of Negombo beach took place on the very first day of March in 2005. It proved to be the final highlight of my running in that particular year.

Problem number one was to recover my health after the debilitating conditions I had endured in Sri Lanka, and it was only after I arrived home that I truly appreciated just how bad those had been. I can still remember the tiny, pale green, winged insect that nipped me on the chest in Dambulla. What, at the time, had been a minor irritation that I could ease with antihistamine cream turned into a huge, festering, pus-filled blister within days of my return, that required twice-daily visits for over a week to my health centre, to have it drained and dressed.

And then my poor feet! These had plagued me from the moment that young lad had drenched me with a pail of dirty water on the very first run, but I never expected that I would have to endure weeks of multiple antibiotic treatment to clear up the infections that had spread right through to the nail beds. In the end I was to lose six of my toenails completely, although I was relieved to find this was nowhere near as uncomfortable as I had imagined. It was over 12 weeks before I pulled on my running shoes again. Even then, I still had some toenails hanging on by a thread, and so what running I could manage tended to be very short distances and very slow.

There were increased pressures at work as well. Nothing that risked the return of the dark clouds of depression but I had taken on the task of editing a new textbook about the brain, and there simply weren't enough hours in the working day to fit this in on top of all my other duties. This meant weekend working and, for most of that summer, a seven-day week in front of my office computer was the norm.

Maybe once a week I could fit in an after-work run along the canal towpath with some of my colleagues, but even that option disappeared once the evenings started to draw in, as there was no lighting down there. At the end of October I finally packed my running shoes away, and it would be another four months before they would see the light of day again.

If 2005 had been a bad year then 2006 was little better. I hadn't lost my love for running entirely, and continued the fairly regular after-work canal runs. We all ran at different paces, so would stagger our starts to create hare and hound situations, which added interest and a touch of competitive edge.

I even meandered around a springtime ten-kilometre race and then took the plunge, entering an autumn half-marathon. It was not to be – I upped my training mileage too quickly, pulled a thigh muscle, and had to miss out. When the darker nights came round again, the running shoes went back into the cupboard.

In 2007 the pattern continued – sporadic running at best, but there were two tiny sparks that year that were to eventually lead to the re-ignition of my enthusiasm. In May I went on a week's holiday with my sister, Lin, to Malta. All-inclusive, lots of food, wine and beer, but I did pack my trainers and went on just the one four-mile run along the seafront. I jogged along gently as it was pretty hot, aware that once again I was running abroad, and the time passed quickly as I recalled the foreign running adventures that I had so enjoyed in the past. Why stop now? All I needed was a target, a goal to aim for, and by the time I got back to my hotel room, candidate destinations were being listed inside my head.

The second spark came from my obsession with recording all of my runs. I was now approaching a total of 10,000 miles and, when the moment finally arrived, I was joined on the canal towpath by several work friends, some of whom hadn't even run before, and we shared a glass of bubbly once the milestone had been passed.

'So what is your next target?' asked one. It was that word again. Target. That's what I needed – I needed a target.

In fact, I set two; one for mileage and one for destination. The next mileage goal to aim for would be 12,436 miles – a bit arbitrary you might think, but this was the distance between the North and the South poles, and it meant I had nearly 2,500 miles still to cover. After 30 months of relative lethargy, I needed to get my finger out!

The destination target I set myself was to complete a run, of at least half-marathon distance, on every one of the planet's seven continents. So far, I could tick off Europe, North America, Asia and Africa. That left me with Australia, South America and Antarctica, although the latter would require investment beyond my means, and some sort of sponsorship deal. It was South America that leapt out of that list – the comeback was on, and the objective was to find a suitable event on the largely sub-equatorial continent – my first running venture in the Southern hemisphere.

With the wonders of the internet I soon came across a company that offered exactly what I was looking for: the California-based Andes Adventures. In fact, they offered too much; I was spoilt for choice, and had to be careful about which challenge I took on. I was lurching towards my 60th birthday and, as much as one doesn't like to admit it, age does creep up on you and I needed to stay realistic about what I was still capable of. One voice in my head was telling me that if I was prepared to spend money to travel halfway round the world, then it would hardly be worthwhile to enter just a single run. The voice in the opposite corner was questioning whether I could still cope with the multi-day race format.

What had been hard but just about doable in the Sahara was noticeably more difficult in China, and in Sri Lanka, the toll of running successive days, in hostile conditions and on injured feet, had very nearly become a step too far. In the end I narrowed down my choices to two. The one-off race would be the classic Inca Trail Marathon to Machu Picchu, the sternest of tests with high altitude and thousands of feet of climbing, but with a magical conclusion that I had long yearned to see with my own eyes. The multi-day alternative was named the Andean Triangle adventure and featured runs in Chile, Bolivia and Peru, including a full marathon in the Atacama Desert. It was the draw of perhaps one, final long desert run, my favourite environment, that drew me towards the latter, but could my body handle it?

One thing was for sure – after over two years of just ticking over with my running, the answer to that question was a definite 'no'. Before signing up for anything I needed to prove to myself that I still had what it takes in me. Once again, I felt that little tingle of excitement you get when you fill in a race entry form. Some ten-kilometre runs, an eight-miler, a ten-miler, and some multi-terrain races to once again get used to running on all sorts of surfaces. Some races went really well, others less so, but each was a step along the way to keep me motivated and, as the months ticked by, so my optimism increased that I could still take on another big running challenge.

Crunch-time arrived in the spring of 2008. I had entered two half-marathons and vowed that if I could complete those in respectable times I would sign on the dotted line for the Andean Triangle running adventure at the end of June.

In March I ran the first of those half-marathons on the Silverstone Grand Prix track, finishing just a few seconds outside of the two-hour mark, and a month later I took five minutes off of that time on a much hillier circuit around Stratford-upon-Avon. I was back. I was back doing what I loved. I signed up for the Andes, booked my flights for Santiago, and drew up an intensive preparation plan for the final few weeks of training, allowing a few 'rest' days around the time of my 60th birthday at the end of May.

The best laid plans! The life of a long-distance runner never flows smoothly. My natural style of running involves a low foot-lift that I am told, by those in the know, is very economical in terms of efficient use of energy. The downside is that it does leave you rather prone to tripping if you haven't got your wits about you, and there have probably been a dozen occasions in my running career when I have had to pick myself up off a pavement or canal towpath and head off home to treat cuts and grazes on my knees, elbows and hands.

This time, on a pacy, solo after-work run around the streets of Birmingham, my toe caught a raised piece of paving and I performed a manoeuvre that I am reliably informed is called a face-plant. If I lost consciousness, it was only for a few seconds. There was a lot of blood from a cut on my forehead, but someone up there was looking out for me. At the very moment of my tumble, a doctor happened to be driving past and saw the whole incident. He kindly stopped, dressed the wound and assessed me for signs of concussion (happily absent), and then another passer-by gave me a lift back to work. Sporting a massive black eye, I then had to convince my fund-raising supporters in the following days that, although I struggled to run safely around the streets of Birmingham, I would be just fine in the Andes.

Another 12-mile training run was ended prematurely by the recurrence of a thigh strain that had plagued me previously. It was manageable, not ideal, but I was confident a combination of rest, ice and anti-inflammatories would allow me to be back running within a few days.

However it was the dreaded medical form that delivered the final *coup de grace* to my South American ambitions. This particular form had to be completed by my GP no more than two weeks before departure, and with my previous bad experiences of pre-race medicals I entered his surgery with a degree of trepidation. It was not unfounded – my blood pressure, that for some years had hovered around the limits at which something more than lifestyle changes might be needed to address it, was now through the roof.

I'd been here before.

'It's white-coat hypertension,' I bleated. 'I'm just stressed from being in a doctor's surgery after what happened to me previously, plus I'm excited about the challenges ahead.'

To be fair, my GP didn't pull the plug on me immediately. He suggested I go away, purchase a reliable blood pressure monitoring machine myself, take readings every few hours for the next few days, and then come back.

I did exactly that, and very soon knew that the game was up. My blood pressure really was dangerously high and to subject myself to over 100 miles of running in the Andes, with only limited medical support, was a foolhardy risk I wasn't prepared to take for my family's sake.

At the end of the day, I didn't even have to take the decision myself; my GP did it for me. Yes, there were treatments available that could bring my blood pressure back under control, and that I would probably have to take for the rest of my life, but they would take some weeks to become effective. To run at high altitude with uncontrolled hypertension carried with it a very high risk of stroke that he wasn't prepared to condone. He refused to sign my medical form, which in turn invalidated my insurance. Just four days before departure, my South American dream was over.

Of course I was bitterly disappointed having devoted so much time in preparation for the trip, but the financial consequences of the late cancellation were largely covered by travel insurance and there was always the thought in the back of my mind that I could get my blood pressure back under control, and re-book on the same trip the following summer.

The most difficult task was to contact individually each of the people who had pledged money to my chosen charity for the trip, CLIC Sargent, and explain that I would no longer be able to take part. To their massive credit, not one person asked for a refund of their donation and my disappointment was at least partly lessened by the charity being nearly £700 better off.

There was, however, a curious aftermath to this unhappy episode. As the actual date of each race stage arrived, I would look longingly at my map to see where I should have been at that time and wonder how my fellow runners were faring. There were three other competitors from the UK, all related to one another, and I'd been in touch with them several times by email in the run-up to the event, although we had never actually met. Indeed we had booked adjacent seats on the flight from Madrid to Santiago to get to know each other.

Once I knew they were back home, and had had a few days to recover, I contacted them by email to find out how the trip had gone and to share my plan of re-booking for the following year. The response took me aback: they were absolutely scathing about the organisation and safety of the whole trip.

'I hate to say it but the best advice I can give you is – DON'T GO. It was an unmitigated disaster from start to finish.'

One of the group had previously travelled with Andes Adventures on the Inca Trail Marathon, and had a wonderful time, so I presumed the problems were specific to this particular event. I canvassed the opinion of several of the other US-based runners and the vast majority thought the trip was a fantastic experience, although there had been several enforced changes to the original itinerary which, to an extent, was inevitable on such an unpredictable adventure. Managing your expectations and a willingness to be flexible are essential requirements on trips such as these.

Confusion reigned. In the end there was no need to make an immediate decision about re-booking – I had some health issues to sort out first.

I was lucky. The first medication I was prescribed was effective in bringing down my blood pressure, despite some initial problems with swollen ankles and feet, and it seemed to have very little effect on my training. However, routine blood tests also revealed that my cholesterol level was unacceptably high, despite my best efforts at sticking to a healthy diet.

My background in medical science and pharmacology meant that I knew a lot more about cholesterol metabolism than the average patient and, without getting too technical, I knew that there were two forms of cholesterol circulating in the bloodstream – 'good' and 'bad' cholesterol. Thanks in part to my fitness and healthy diet, I had a lot of the 'good' form pumping round me, but the total level was still high enough for my doctor to advise that I should consider starting to take statins, the wonder drug of modern medicine (according to some).

As you will appreciate from previous chapters, I have had to take a variety of medicines at different periods in my lifetime – some on a temporary basis, others long-term. The first thing

I want to know when faced with taking a new drug is, 'Will it affect my ability to run?' If the answer is 'yes' but it's a short-term measure, then okay, I can put up with it for a short while. If the answer is 'yes' and we're talking prolonged medication, then I will seek an alternative. To me, running has become essential for my physical and mental well-being, and to lose that as a result of side-effects of a drug that is possibly protecting my health, is an equation that just doesn't balance. My journey with statins was a case in point.

I began to take the tablet prescribed by my doctor and within days I noticed excessive muscle tiredness after even the shortest runs. Perhaps this would wear off after a short period, but no, for week after week it persisted. In the springtime of 2009, I entered a local half-marathon that I had also run the previous year. Before I reached the halfway point I was reduced to walking by intense muscle soreness and, although I eventually finished, it had taken me over 30 minutes longer than it had done the year before.

Once again I could arm myself with medical knowledge not available to every patient. There were many different varieties of statin on the market, and pronounced muscle pain and weakness after exercise was a known side-effect of only some of them. Armed with a scientific paper comparing the different varieties, and highlighting one particular statin with minimal muscular side-effects, I went back to my doctor. I was fortunate; as with many health centres these days, you cannot see the same doctor every time, and some are more conservative than others. This one, now sadly retired, was willing to offer me a challenge.

'The statin you've been prescribed is the one we are instructed to use.' I think this is code for 'it is the cheapest'. 'I can only change the prescription,' he continued, 'if you can provide convincing evidence that it is harming your running. What I suggest is that you stop taking the statin for a month – this won't have any long-term consequences on your cholesterol level – and then enter another half-marathon, and come back and tell me how it went.'

I did precisely that. I bettered my previous half-marathon time by over 20 minutes, and was rewarded with a prescription for the statin that I had proposed. I have had no muscular side-effects since.

After the disappointment of missing out on South America, and the subsequent medical glitches, it was now time to re-evaluate where I was heading with my running career. I was now into my seventh decade, with two medical issues that would likely require medication for the rest of my life and that might impact on my getting the necessary medical go-ahead to enter future adventure races. On the other hand, neither of these medical issues had caused me any symptoms or illness whatsoever.

I was still running several times a week, and any occasional downtime from running was either from drug side-effects or the usual aches and pains encountered by any runner at any age.

Yes, I was getting older, I was getting slower and my endurance, particularly over successive days, was not what it used to be. Two or three rest days every week had now become an essential part of my training programme.

I was now resigned to the fact that multi-day events, running long distances on consecutive days for a week or more, were almost certainly in the past. Reluctantly, this meant abandoning plans to have another go at the Andean Triangle adventure. However, the urge to travel and run was still as strong as ever and, in the summer of 2009, I considered a more realistic goal, just three months ahead.

You may remember that after my personal triumph in the Marathon des Sables, I had considered entering the Jordan Desert Cup the following year, although that race was eventually removed from the calendar because of the ongoing hostilities in neighbouring Iraq. One of the great draws of the race had been the finish, in front of the Treasury in the ancient lost city of Petra. Now, a Danish travel company, Adventure Marathons, was offering a single race in the city, with a marathon and what was described as an ultra-half-marathon option, being about a mile longer than the standard 13.1-mile distance; an opportunity too good to turn down.

There was a seven-hour time limit on the full marathon and, knowing how difficult it was to run in desert conditions, notwithstanding my relatively poor level of fitness, I leant towards the shorter distance, arguing that it would be more satisfying completing that rather than being pulled out of the full marathon if I couldn't make it in time. Ultimately, that turned out to be a wise decision.

Of course, this race wasn't going to advance my ambition to run on the seven continents, but after the setbacks of the previous few years, and an extended period of, what was for me, relative inertia, this target was both achievable and a chance once again to experience the joys of desert running.

There were only a few weeks to prepare but, in the knowledge that it was 'only' going to be a half-marathon, I convinced myself that it was a physically attainable target within the time frame available. There were other doubts, however. Jordan was in the heart of the Middle East, a region I had never visited, but also a deeply troubled part of the world. Even though we were now into the post-Saddam era, the Iraqi border was not too many miles away from where we would be running. Advice from the Foreign Office stated that most visits to Jordan were trouble-free, but also spoke of a general threat from terrorism, indiscriminate attacks on foreign travellers and heightened tensions following a recent Israeli incursion into Gaza.

How vulnerable might I be running out there in the Jordanian desert, quite probably alone at times, as this was not a race that would attract massive numbers? I sought reassurances from the race organisers, which they were happy to provide, and in the end signed on the dotted line. Nothing in life is without risk.

So, three months later, I flew into Amman Airport to be greeted by local guides and to meet, for the first time, Richard, who had just flown in from Gatwick, and who I would end up sharing a room with for the duration of the visit. Richard was a London bobby, probably 20 years my junior but with over 100 marathons under his belt. He was also a gifted amateur footballer and a Spurs fan so we were never short of conversation.

Indeed, when chatter with other runners over breakfast revealed our respective occupations, it was a source of some amusement that a 'London copper' was sharing a room with a bloke who was 'into drugs'!

We stayed just one night in Amman – the fortification, airport-like security and armed guards at the hotel, a stark reminder of the doubts that had troubled me before booking the trip. The following morning we headed south, along the biblically-historical Kings Highway, through barren but scenic landscapes and into the Jordanian desert.

Although the majority of the 100-plus race entrants were from the race organisation's own country of Denmark, there was a strong international feel about the field, with runners from as far afield as Mexico, Australia, Ukraine and the USA, among many others. Along with many of the international runners, we were taken to a hotel high above Wadi Musa, the nearest town to the ancient heritage site, and with amazing views over the Great Rift Valley.

Pre-race day opened with an information briefing at the Petra Visitor Centre but this carried with it somewhat disappointing news with a late change of route. The original plan had been to start the race at the centre and to run through the 1.2-kilometre narrow gorge, known as the Siq. Anyone who has seen the closing scenes of *Indiana Jones and the Last Crusade* will know this route only too well, and be familiar with the breathtaking climax as the world-famous Treasury, Al-Kazneh, gradually becomes visible through the shaft of daylight ahead. Sadly, a new crack in the rock surface inside the Siq, and a resulting rock fall, led to those responsible for the preservation of the site requesting that we should not run through the gorge for fear of causing further damage. Given the fragility of such a unique archaeological site, no doubt a wise decision although, rather incongruously, they were still happy to allow horse-drawn carriages to rattle noisily down the Siq, carrying fee-paying tourists.

The briefing launched a day of mixed emotions. A leisurely stroll to the securely-guarded entrance to the site, a ride by horseback to the beginning of the Siq, and then a slow walk though the narrow canyon, just a few metres wide, marvelling at the carvings and the astonishing engineering skills of the ancient Nabataeans who had controlled the erratic natural water supply, and allowed the ancient city to flourish even during long periods of drought. And then came that moment. As you rounded a slight bend in the narrow path, that first glimpse of the Treasury, basking in golden sunlight. Not built on the sandstone, but actually carved into the red sandstone mountain – truly one of the Wonders of the World.

Al-Kazneh is undoubtedly the jewel of Petra but is by no means the only highlight. The amphitheatre, the Street of Facades, tombs, caves and monasteries, all carved out into the mountainside, were all around as we gradually descended through the sprawling city. And there lay a problem: the mercury in the thermometer was creeping up above 30 degrees, we'd been on our feet for a couple of hours, and we still hadn't reached the far end of the city where lunch awaited.

For those who were looking to run a good time in the race, a few grumbles began to break out, questioning the scheduling of what was turning out to be a strenuous little trek. However, the majority of us were in awe of our surroundings and the aesthetic value of the experience far outweighed any resulting time deficit in the following day's race.

Lunch finally provided both much-needed sustenance and shelter from the sun, and then it was time for the return journey, only this time it was uphill. With the sun gaining in strength with every minute, a few broke into their wallets and hired a camel for the return journey, but most walked and it was a very tired band of athletes who finally trudged into their hotel rooms. It had been a unique preparation for the day before a long-distance race, but then this was a unique race.

When race day dawned we had already been awake for several hours. With the start scheduled for 6am in order to avoid the worst of the midday heat, we had been woken in the early hours for a very light breakfast and transported to the centre. With the last-minute change of route the start was now to be in front of the Treasury itself – surely the most spectacular race start in the world. Extra distance had been added to the route later on to make up for the loss of the section through the Siq but, of course, we still had to walk through the Siq to reach the start.

At 5.30am, we left the centre in pitch darkness and began the 25-minute walk, under strict instructions that anyone seen to be running inside the Siq would be instantly disqualified. Even when the sun was at its highest it was gloomy within the Siq. In those final minutes before the sun came up, it was so dark that it was difficult to pick out even who was walking alongside you and, with some sections being very uneven underfoot, people were stumbling and tripping as they edged their way forward through the black canyon. How would the race have unfolded if we had stuck to the original plan and run through the Siq in such darkness? Carnage was a distinct possibility.

As we finally emerged in front of the Treasury, dawn was beginning to break and a warm red glow blanketed the entire scene. I had recently become the proud owner of my first GPS running watch so I wandered up and down, desperately trying to find a spot where the watch could pick up enough satellite signals in the tiny sliver of sky visible above, in order to locate my position. I failed, so close and towering were the walls of the gorge.

I drifted in and among the other runners waiting for the call to start, and came across a familiar face. Surely not! Our eyes met and there was instant recognition. It was Stefan Schlett, the ultra-distance-running German I had shared rooms with as we had travelled around China and Tibet. It's a small world as they say, and we embraced warmly as a loudhailer called us towards the start banner. A brief countdown and we were on our way; I saw very little of Stefan after that as he sped off with the leading group of runners.

I settled towards the rear of the field, the route gently descending through the ancient city, retracing the footsteps we had taken the day before, only this time the searing heat had been replaced by a slightly chilly dawn breeze.

As the surrounding mountains opened out, and more of the sky became visible, my watch suddenly sparked into life and I was able to press the button that would record my journey for posterity. There was an air of jollity among the slower runners: nobody was there to break any personal records – we were there to share a once-in-a-lifetime experience and to soak up our unique surroundings. We paused briefly to take photographs of one another, but then the road began to climb steeply and the level of conversation dropped as we began to appreciate the challenges that lay ahead.

A few more steep road climbs, skirting the perimeter of a tented Bedouin village, and then the fun really began as the clearly marked route directed us out into open desert. I was back in an environment with which I was all too familiar and, as I jogged gently along, great memories of the Sahara and the Gobi deserts were rekindled. To be fair, this was on an altogether different scale in terms of the size of the dunes, and the steepness of the climbs and descents. Nevertheless, the heat from the sun was now increasing in its intensity and the difficulties of trying to run in soft sand were as familiar as ever.

Ten years had passed since I had been in the Sahara, ten years of ageing, but, yes, I still had it in me to race in the desert, albeit over short distances and without having to carry my home on my back. In fact, the organisational support on this trip was exemplary, with water available every five kilometres and medical advice at strategic points.

I paused briefly at the ten-kilometre point to top up the water bladder I carried on my back and to give my desert hat and neck buff a good soaking to keep my head cool. Of course, in no time, they would be dry again but it provided a few minutes of relief from the growing heat. The full marathon runners had had to endure an extra loop around the Al Musihr mountain and so having set off ahead of me, they were now coming through again from behind, offering a brief chance to exchange pleasantries and progress reports.

The desert running continued and I was loving every minute but after skirting around the perimeter of the site of Little Petra, about eight miles north of its more famous counterpart, we returned once again to track and then to road running. At this point, the full marathon runners turned off on a long, but relatively flat, out-and-back road loop. I did not envy them, but for us a huge mountainside loomed ahead with the tarmac road meandering towards the summit.

Of course the marathoners would have to tackle this later in the day but, for now, it seemed that for the next hour, it was those running the half that would be facing the greater challenge. After passing by a small village and a Bedouin school, the road began to climb and continued doing so for the next four miles. Although the surface was well maintained, I do not recall a single vehicle passing by as I climbed.

The sun was now beating down fiercely, radiating off the road surface, baking me from above and below. In the distance ahead, and also far behind, I could just pick out through the heat haze the small figures of other runners toiling in the blazing sunshine. As much as the desert phases of this race had been so uplifting, this was purgatory. On a regular basis, my gentle plodding was replaced by walking, and several times I ground to a halt altogether, bent over, hands on knees, the silence of the surroundings being broken by rasping intakes of breath.

On and on the road climbed, and the temperature climbed with it, and my mind, struggling to find something to occupy itself other than pain and discomfort, went back over a decade and recalled the words of Graham Taylor, the former England football manager, speaking to the masses before the start of the Watford half-marathon.

'Remember, every hill has a top to it!'

And he was right. This heat-baked climb did indeed have a summit, and even better, there were drinks and bananas available to restock my depleted energy banks. From here the route went off-road again for a while, although now we were really high on the mountainside and could look down on the stunning desert vistas below us.

Once again, limbs that could barely manage a step forward 30 minutes before were now reinvigorated and a combination of a downhill gradient and spectacular surroundings lifted my spirits immeasurably.

Even then my performance would be put into perspective as the lead two runners in the full marathon, both Jordanians, came hurtling past me. They had run a good 12 miles further than me in the same time and looked as fresh as daisies.

Back on to the road and we entered the outskirts of Wadi Musa and the winding, steep descent to the Petra Visitor Centre where the finish line beckoned. The local people were out in force in the streets, yelling what I took to be words of encouragement, and my pace quickened to a rate I had not reached during the whole race. The final corner, first sight of the finish banner and a final sprint to an excited throng of well-wishers; a medal being hung around my neck as I fought to recover my breath.

In terms of time for the distance I had covered, it was possibly one of my slowest races ever. But it mattered not. I was back: running in hostile conditions in a spectacular setting that few people will ever get to experience. After the challenges and setbacks of the previous few years, I had proved, predominantly to myself, that despite a few health issues and the passage of time, I could still get out there and do it.

The following day, after a final and more leisurely amble through the remains of the ancient city, the tour would come to an end with a celebration meal in the evening. We were taken by coach back out into the desert to the site of Little Petra that we had skirted around during the run itself. In the black darkness of the desert night, we were led along a candle-lit trail to the short, but very high, gorge lined with its carved facades, houses and temples. Tables and chairs were laid out in the narrow gap between the steep walls, and a veritable feast of Jordanian food was served, interspersed with song and dance from local entertainers. The beer and wine flowed and, before the evening was out, almost all of the runners were dancing around a campfire, despite the foot blisters from the day before.

It was a fitting end to a wonderful event that had dovetailed neatly with my refined running priorities. No longer could I manage the sheer barbarism of the Marathon des Sables, or even the relentless itinerary of a ten-day or more SDPO event, but here was a company that specialised in running adventures in exotic locations that were still within my capabilities. There had been some gentle pressure at the meal to join them at an event on the Great Wall of China, but this was a box I had already ticked, and I preferred to look to pastures new. I vowed to run again with Adventure Marathons some day.

15

When in Rome…

AFTER returning from Jordan, I completed my local half-marathon in Birmingham just two weeks later and at a pace a good five minutes per mile faster than I had managed out in the heat of the desert.

At least this time there had been no long-lasting consequence from my foreign escapade. With my desire to travel and run re-invigorated, I perused the other events offered by Adventure Marathons and almost immediately found what I was looking for: the Big Five Marathon.

I had long been an avid fan of TV nature documentaries, and the prospect of running in a South African game reserve was just so tempting. The website spoke of 'no fences or rivers separating the runners from the wildlife' and 'the start time being dependent on the position of the local pride of lions' but the event had been running for several years and an internet search revealed no mention of anyone being eaten, although some of the route marshals did appear to be heavily armed.

There were no places available for the 2010 race, so I pencilled in June 2011 as my next foreign travel adventure and focused on a variety of domestic races until that time. I also asked Angela, my daughter, if she would like to come with me.

Angela, who was living alone at the time, was not a runner: full stop! She had once managed to jog a lap of my local lake with me, but that experience had not awakened the running genes that I had passed on to my son, Chris.

However, Angela was a lover of all things related to wildlife, especially African wildlife, and the prospect of a safari holiday was one she couldn't resist. We agreed to sign up for the 2011 event as soon as the entries opened, with Angela as a non-running supporter.

I was also reaching something of a crossroads in my academic career – statutory retirement was looming. For a few years I had been trying to get funding for an expensive piece of equipment I needed to take our successful research project into liver transplantation further. It was the all-too-familiar routine of months spent writing and polishing the grant application, and then receiving a letter saying that although the project was innovative and well-presented, there simply weren't the funds available to support all good research ideas. And then the cycle would begin again.

Now there was an added pressure. Even if my next grant application was successful, would there be enough time to complete the study before I retired? I did have the option of spending my remaining years teaching but it was the clinical research side of my job that gave me the most satisfaction. Gradually, the pressures on my time were increasing, and with it my anxiety but, as ever, running was helping me to keep this under control.

At the end of 2010 the pot came to the boil. I had finally booked the Big Five Marathon trip for Angela and myself for the following summer, when I received the worrying news that she had fainted at the wheel of her car on her way home from work one evening. Fortunately, when she realised what was happening, she had the presence of mind to pull over to the roadside.

Further fainting episodes occurred over the next few days and a series of hospital stays and investigations began. Some of the scenarios being considered by the medical team were quite scary, and I was allowed time off work to stay down in Sussex for a while to be near her. This worry further impacted on my own health and, once again, the dreaded anxiety and depression returned and, as a result, I spent several weeks on sick leave.

The good news that came out of the unhappy episode was that no serious pathology was ever found that might have caused Angela's symptoms, although she had suffered a severe episode of nervous exhaustion of unknown cause that would take some months to recover from before she would be able to work again. What she didn't need at the time was the worry of whether she would be able to cope with an international flight to South Africa a few months ahead and so, once again, the safari run was postponed for a further year until 2012.

For me, the consequences of that period were also to be life-changing. During the darkest days I didn't have the energy for running although, once again, it was of immense benefit as I slowly emerged from the gloom. I returned to work at the start of 2011, feeling better but far from fully recovered. As was normal practice after a prolonged period of absence, I was summoned to meetings with an occupational health adviser and the human resources department. To cut a long story short, the university made me an offer to retire at the end of September 2011 – about 18 months before my scheduled date.

I had been thinking ahead as to what I would be doing with my life once retirement came but suddenly it was potentially just months away. Given a period of a few weeks to think about their offer, the greatest clarity of thought usually came to me when I was out running and this is where I weighed up the pros and cons.

From a financial point of view I would be just as well off if I accepted the university's offer as I would have been by continuing to work until I was 65. No-brainer you may think: 18 months of doing what I pleased as opposed to 18 months of doing what I was told! Of course, this would signal the end of my research plans, although there were other aspects of my job I could comfortably live without.

Perhaps my greatest concern was what I would do with my time if I did retire. With my son and daughter living some distance from me, my social life largely revolved around work and work colleagues with weekends reserved for those boring house- and garden-related jobs that I never had time for during the working week. Other than immediate neighbours, I knew very few people in the wider Redditch community and would have to make a really positive effort to turn this around.

Of course I discussed my future with family and friends but, deep down, I think I had made my decision fairly early on. The fact was that for a few years I had not been particularly happy with several aspects of my job and this had been having an increasingly adverse effect on my health. I accepted the university's offer. Major changes were afoot.

I didn't want my retirement to just be a chance to put my feet up after a long working career. It had to be an opportunity to explore new avenues and pursue new hobbies that I hadn't had time for previously.

There would also be changes in my passion for running. At that time, most of my training was done on the canal towpaths around the university with a group of colleagues who helped to motivate each other. Once retirement arrived, I would be much more dependent on self-motivation. I considered joining a club but, for me, my local club was a little too elitist and didn't have so much time for recreational runners like me. Other more suitable clubs were rather too far away to travel to on a regular basis.

And I would have to find some new routes nearer to home. Yes, I had a few key road routes in and around my home town and surrounding villages, but Redditch has a massive area of lakes and parkland running right through its centre, and a veritable treasure chest of footpaths and cycle paths that I had never really had the time to explore to see how they all linked up. Now was the time.

Once the decision to take early retirement had been made, it felt as if a huge weight had been lifted from my shoulders and, with Angela making a slow but steady recovery down in Sussex, life was much rosier again. There was even an unexpected breakthrough on the research front when the company who I was hoping to buy the equipment from agreed to loan it to me for a period of a few weeks.

I spent much of my final working summer in the laboratory environment that I enjoyed so much, seven days a week, accumulating a huge amount of research data that I planned to continue to analyse and publish, even after I had retired.

At the end of September 2011, my retirement from work was marked by an emotional barbecue among some great and loyal friends. It was the end of a very significant chapter of my life but as one door closes, another opens.

*   *   *   *   *

My son, Chris, his wife Lynne, and my granddaughter Holly had moved to Germany with the RAF in December of 2008. There were of course far more dangerous places to be posted, but it did mean seeing rather less of them than I had become used to with them living just an hour down the road in Oxfordshire.

Nevertheless, the regular location moves were customary for military life and, of course, Germany was just a short flight away. Several times a year I would make the journey to Düsseldorf and sample the delights of the villages and towns around the Rheindahlen base, the German Christmas markets and even an opportunity to watch Liverpool, Lynne's hometown team, play Borussia Mönchengladbach in a pre-season friendly game.

The countryside around the base was heavily wooded and pancake-flat, and over a period of several visits I had developed several new training routes, running sometimes with Chris, and sometimes on my own when he was away. It was early October in 2011, very soon after my retirement, when, in a routine weekend phone call, Chris told me that he and two of his RAF regiment colleagues, Kevin and Tonto, were going to enter the Rome Marathon the following spring to raise funds for the Royal Air Forces Association.

Chris had suffered a serious hamstring injury just a few months previously, while on a promotion course, and had been advised to use distance running to aid his recovery. Almost as an afterthought, he dropped a tiny hand-grenade into the conversation.

'I don't suppose you'd like to join us, would you, mate?' he enquired.

The line fell silent as the cog-wheels started to turn in my brain. My last full marathon had been London over seven years previously. I had entered that race to prove to myself that I could still complete a marathon after recovering from my back injury, and I achieved that goal, although with some difficulty. I had nothing left to prove in terms of marathon running, and had just about reached an inner agreement with myself that, in the future, I would focus my running on shorter distances of up to half-marathon. They were, after all, much more enjoyable, which was the fundamental reason that I run anyway, and avoided the physiological meltdown that usually accompanies the final few miles of a full marathon.

Chris prodded further, 'I just thought that it would be great if my first marathon coincided with what could be your last marathon. There is a seven-hour time limit, but I'm sure you can manage that.'

The wheels continued to turn. It wasn't just the 26 miles of the race – it was the miles and miles of training I would have to put in over the winter to get myself in shape for it, and the time schedule was pretty tight. There was no way I could replicate my marathon times of the past but I calculated that if I could at least run to halfway, and then power-walk most of the rest of it, I could probably finish within six hours.

I took a deep breath, 'OK Chris, I'll give it a go!'

'Ha ha ha ha ha!' he roared down the phone line. 'I just knew you wouldn't be able to resist the challenge. You've got the breaking strain of a Kit-Kat!'

*　*　*　*　*

Entries had now re-opened for the 2012 Big Five Marathon and it was just a matter of confirming the places that had been held for Angela and myself. However, Angela's personal situation was now very different from what it had been 12 months previously. In the early weeks of her recovery, she had received comforting moral support from a friend, Ben, and shortly afterwards they started going out together.

Now, in just a few months, they were planning to live under the same roof, and Angela's life had taken a massive turn for the better. Ben's work commitments meant he was not in a position to join us in South Africa but he was happy for Angela to go, knowing how much she had been looking forward to her safari holiday after the disappointment of the previous year.

Spending Christmas 2011 in Germany allowed me the chance to do some training with Chris, Kevin and Tonto, although I wasn't up to running great distances as I was just recovering from a fairly nasty chest infection. Unfortunately, Tonto had had to withdraw from the Rome Marathon as he was shortly due to be posted out to Afghanistan and would be away on pre-deployment training. I'd been offered, and accepted, his place in the fund-raising trio, and the four of us (plus two eager dogs) managed a couple of enjoyable runs together through the wintry German woodlands.

So 2012 dawned. Other than in the immediate aftermath of Angela's illness, I had maintained a reasonable mileage throughout the preceding two years and had completed a number of races, up to half-marathon distance. I was, however, missing my adventures overseas and now the new year was offering up two considerable challenges: my first full marathon for eight years and then, just three months later, a half-marathon surrounded by African wildlife.

Even had I been 20 years younger I could not have properly prepared myself to run a full marathon at a reasonable pace by mid-March. The best I could hope for was to run a steady first half and then, as the language of the day said, 'wing it' for the remainder. I set the pacer on my watch for a relatively tardy six-hour finish, knowing this was still an hour inside the official time limit, and hoped for the best.

I met Chris, Lynne and Holly at Rome's Fiumicino Airport; the trio having flown in from Düsseldorf, and I from Gatwick. A bus ride through congested streets took us to our cosy but super-friendly little B&B that Chris had discovered online. This was my first visit to Rome, although Chris had been a couple of times so knew his way round a little better. Having settled into our room it was time for a meal, and what better city in the world for pasta loading can there be than Rome? We searched, we found and we loaded.

We had two clear days before the marathon, so the plan was simple. On day one we would cram in as much sightseeing as we possibly could before race registration in the late afternoon. Eager not to repeat the experience of Petra by spending most of pre-marathon day on my feet, we elected to visit the Colosseum on day two, which was just a short walk from our little residence.

In warm sunshine we ambled around St Peter's Square and the Vatican, and enjoyed a tasty outdoor lunch in Piazza Navona, before moving on to the Pantheon, Trevi Fountain and the Spanish Steps, pausing for a cooling ice cream. It was then time to head out of the city by Metro, and a rather long walk to the Palazzo del Congresse, to pick up race numbers, kit bag and to visit the Expo. By the time we returned to our lodging, we were very grateful for the extra day ahead, before heading off to carbo load once again.

Day two and the nerves were beginning to bite. I had been in this situation so many times before but I had never been so ill-prepared to run a full marathon. Pre-race nerves were normal for me, and quite probably beneficial. In fact I even have a few butterflies before a longish training run, but this feeling was different. It was bordering on fear, which was ridiculous given what I had overcome in the past. I gave myself a good talking-to and we set off for the Colosseum, sticking to our intention of making the day as easy on our feet as possible. One final, huge evening pasta meal, a last-minute check to make sure I had remembered all my race kit, and then a fitful night's sleep.

Race day dawned. I was edgy. Chris and Lynne recognised this but sensibly left me to get on with it. A very light breakfast, and then a leisurely stroll to the start area that was in the shadow of the Colosseum. The early morning sunshine was already beginning to feel quite warm. Kevin, Chris and I dropped our bags off at the baggage buses and then bade farewell to Lynne and Holly who would be taking part in a four-kilometre fun run, before waiting for us at the finish.

After what we hoped were last-minute visits to the portaloos, we nervously entered the fenced-off start area. Chris and Kevin were expecting to run a faster time than me (they were a lot younger after all!), so we wished each other good luck and they edged their way further forward.

The nerves were still jangling. Around my waist I wore a belt with six energy gel sachets tucked into it. I'd already taken one before handing my bag in, and the plan was to take another at four miles, and then every four miles after that, up until 24 miles. The belt was uncomfortable and the foil sachets kept catching on my bare arms. What I didn't appreciate at the time was the key psychological boost that gel belt would give me as the race unfolded.

As we waited for the off, another British guy started to chat with me and, if I thought I had had problems leading up to the race, then I was about to be trumped. This poor chap had turned up at the airport the day before only to find that his luggage, containing all his running gear, had been loaded on to the wrong plane.

He had spent a frantic few hours in the running shops of Rome re-equipping himself, although it is never a good idea running a marathon in a brand new pair of shoes. One of my unbreakable rules of running abroad is to always pack my race trainers in my hand luggage.

Our conversation was interrupted by a crescendo of noise up ahead – the race was under way. If you've ever watched a big city marathon start on the television you know the routine. At first you stand stock-still. Then very, very slowly, you edge forward a step at a time. You bump into the person in front, and then edge forward a little more. As you approach the start line, those in front of you break into the gentlest of jogs. Then it's over the timing mats, your chip is activated and you are on your way.

The weather was warm and sunny as we set off and I had a clearly-defined first goal in my head. My longest non-stop run during my limited training had lasted around 90 minutes. I knew I had that in me so that was the initial target.

After less than half a mile I ground to a halt. It wasn't an embarrassing lack of fitness, but a sharp left turn and a narrowing of the route that had created a major bottleneck.

Some impatient multilingual mutterings from those around and then we were off again, initially heading towards the southern suburbs of the city.

I was feeling good although the weather was considerably warmer than anything I had encountered during my training. As I approached the first water station at around three miles, I caught sight of two familiar, pale-blue RAFA running vests up ahead – it was Chris and Kevin! How could I be so close behind them? Even as I tried to close the gap to talk to them, they moved swiftly away and that would be the last time I saw them during the race. I was later to learn that they had been forced to join the queue for an emergency toilet stop!

After four miles I took on the first of my gels; all was good but the heat was increasing. As we headed back north again, running long sections alongside the Tiber river, and eventually crossing it by bridge at the ten-kilometre point, the first signs of fatigue were beginning to surface, and I still had 20 miles to run. But then cloud cover started to creep in and suddenly everything became a whole lot more comfortable.

I did manage to achieve my target of running for the first 90 minutes, other than that first little hiccup, but then I began to introduce a few, very short, walking phases – no more than a minute at a time. I know that for some marathon runners, including myself in earlier years, this is considered unforgivable, but you do use different muscle sets for walking and running and the brief respite was welcome, especially as much of the route was on hard, unyielding cobbles.

Ten miles in and we were passing through massive crowds in St Peter's Square – they had one eye on the marathon, the other on the balcony where the Pope would shortly be making his weekly address. The weather was much more comfortable now and I was feeling good. The RAF roundel on my vest was attracting a good deal of attention, with shouts of support from the sidelines and the sparking of conversation with fellow competitors. I ran for a mile with a US Air Force veteran and compared tales of air shows we had visited. It all helped pass the time and take the mind off the pain.

I passed under the decorated arch that marked the halfway point and suddenly realised I had become so engrossed by my surroundings that I had forgotten to have my 12-mile gel. I quickly dispatched it, leaving only three gels left in my belt and I was less than three miles from consuming the next one. Suddenly, in my mind, those gel sachets became crucial symbols of my relentless progress towards the finish line.

I ran for a while with an emotional British man who had only recently lost his father to Alzheimer's disease and who spoke so proudly of him. It was his first marathon and he was raising funds for research into dementia. I ran with a group of boisterous British Army wives and they marked my presence in their midst by chanting the *Dambusters* theme music. Fatigue does not dampen a marathon runner's sense of humour.

We passed by the Olympic Stadium and the former Olympic village in the northern part of the city and the route began to climb. A bit more walking but I was comfortably inside my six-hour schedule. We headed south once more towards the city centre. At 20 miles I devoured another gel – just one left in my belt; I was just one gel away from finishing!

And then a surreal moment. We ran through Piazza Navona, where we had all enjoyed a lovely outdoor lunch just two days earlier. The diners urged us on and I looked longingly at the jugs of cold beer that sat on their tables. A young male runner came up alongside me.

'Can I just thank you for running for such a magnificent cause?' he said, pointing to my RAFA running vest.

'No problem,' I replied. 'I'm proud to help out.'

'Are you in the RAF?' I asked, as we ran along together.

'Yes, I'm a PT instructor currently working down in Naples,' he replied. 'A group of us have come up for the marathon.'

I didn't like to ask, but assumed that not all of his group were PT instructors, and perhaps they were running together for most of the race. Why else would a military PT instructor only be catching up with me 20 miles into the run?

'Are you ex-RAF?' my friend inquired.

'No, not me, but my son is a Corporal in the RAF Regiment. He's in this race as well, but some way ahead,' I responded.

'What's his name?'

'Chris Richards.'

'Chris! Corporal Chris Richards! I know Chris. He's been down to Naples a few times to do some of our training!'

It's a small world as they say! My friend ran on, but our chance conversation had given me another mental boost at that most painful stage of a marathon, with just a few miles to go.

Once again the route cruelly turned away from the city centre as we headed up narrow, shop-lined streets, with enthusiastic support being only an arm's length away. It really helped and I was feeling as good as I have ever felt this close to the end of a marathon. In fact my mind was telling me that I could probably have run on further if I had to.

A loop then came around the large, open Piazza del Popolo and then back towards the centre, but for the final time. At 24 miles I swallowed that final gel – the belt around my waist was empty at last – and the positive vibe I took from that carried me towards the final hill as we took a large loop around the Colosseum.

That hill seemed unreasonably steep, although I suspect it wouldn't have been if it had occurred during the first few miles of the race. I ran most of it but excruciating cramps were gripping my calves and I had to pause occasionally to massage life back into them. Any thought now of running one step further than the mandatory 26 miles, 385 yards was firmly dismissed.

As is always the case, that hill also had a top to it. We looped round three sides of the Colosseum and then the finish line came into view. The calf pain was agony but there was no stopping me now. With a style not dissimilar to a newly-born giraffe, I made it across the line and glanced down at my watch. Five hours and 27 minutes; by some way my slowest road marathon, but still over 30 minutes inside my target time. A marathon finish is a marathon finish, and this was my first one for eight years! I couldn't have felt prouder.

Reunited once again, Chris, Kevin and I posed for a few post-run photographs, proudly brandishing our hard-earned medals. They had run together for most of the race before Kevin pulled away in the latter stages, finishing in four hours and 23 minutes with Chris just 12 minutes behind. With Lynne and Holly, who had successfully completed their own fun run, we were three happy marathoners who hobbled towards a nearby restaurant for a major refuelling exercise, including one of those large jugs of cold beer that I had so enviously eyed as we ran through Piazza Navona.

It was on my flight home to London the following day that I reflected on what I had achieved. One of my favourite running mantras my blind friend Miles was always quoting was, 'The only limits on what you can achieve are those that you impose on yourself.' Was I guilty of imposing a marathon embargo on myself, just because I felt I was getting older and slower? Had it taken Chris's challenge to prove that I still had it in me to run another one? It was food for thought, but it could wait for now. In three months' time I would be running with lions!

16

A hasty retreat

'It has always seemed miraculous to me that these colossal animals can move noiselessly through the bush, and are thus able to surround one without warning.'

A quote from *Born Free* by Joy Adamson regarding the African elephant.

IT was never going to be just a routine trip from the moment I woke on the day of departure and read Angela's Facebook status that read, 'Angela Richards thinks she may have tonsillitis. Epic timing as I fly to South Africa today!'

I was due to drive down to Sussex to pick her up so rang and asked if there was any chance she could make it to her GP while I was on my way from the Midlands. Angela, having only recently moved in with Ben, was still in the process of registering with the local GP practice. However, they were kind enough to give her an emergency appointment and, on my journey down, I received a text to say that although the GP thought the infection was likely to be viral, she had been given a course of penicillin as she was travelling to a remote area.

Once safely through check-in and security at Heathrow, we relaxed with a coffee. Angela was clearly struggling with the sore throat and loss of voice but we had both looked forward to this trip for so long and, after so may false starts, we collectively crossed fingers that she would shake the infection off sooner rather than later.

We managed a few hours of broken sleep on the long flight and, once on the ground in Johannesburg, we soon found our contact and waited for the remaining runners from other flights who would be joining us on the 10am shuttle bus to our destination, the Entabeni game reserve.

The minibus journey to Entabeni, scheduled to last for about four hours, was not without incident. Just over an hour into the journey our driver was pulled over by the police and asked to produce his driving licence. He didn't have it on him! After several radio calls to check his identity, and an extensive search of our luggage trailer, we were eventually allowed to continue on our way.

The landscape became increasingly mountainous. Not once, not twice, but three times our driver took a wrong turning, and had to perform difficult U-turns on a narrow road with a trailer attached. Soon the tarmac-covered road turned into a sandy and bumpy dirt-track, with passing vehicles throwing clouds of red dust into the air. For mile after mile we followed this track until we reached the right turn that would lead us up to the main entrance of the game reserve. We were greeted by a picket line!

Workers on the estate were clearly unhappy with their rates of pay and had blocked the entrance with ropes and placards. It was hard not to feel some sympathy for them as they were clearly very poor people, and they stared and gesticulated angrily at us in the minibus as if we were another life form. Eventually, a senior figure of the group was summoned and after a conversation with our driver, the rope was pulled aside and we were allowed to proceed up to the main gate.

The accommodation at Entabeni was spread across a number of different locations, but Ravineside Lodge, our chosen destination, was the first stop, just five kilometres away. The roads and tracks inside the reserve were of even poorer quality, and our minibus and trailer were now beginning seriously to struggle to make any progress, but then a single- storey cluster of buildings came into view, and we spotted rhino and ostrich in the grounds. Our long outward journey was complete.

Outside the entrance to reception we were greeted by our tour guide, Jonatan, a large, affable, ponytailed Dane with, we were to learn later, an encyclopaedic knowledge of the natural world. Two others in our minibus were also staying there. Judy and Brita were from Virginia in the USA, and Jonatan took us all to the dining area for lunch where we were introduced to the remainder of the Ravineside Lodge group. Andrew, a New Zealand sheep farmer, was the only non-runner in the group and was supporting his wife, Jan. Jan's friend, Linda, was from the same running club in Invercargill and was a librarian. Also from New Zealand was Lesley, a teacher from the Bay of Plenty, and an experienced trail marathon runner and triathlete. Finally our group was completed by a brother and sister from the USA; Rahool, a cardiologist from Phoenix, and Ketaki, a veterinary radiologist from Los Angeles, who would be running her very first half-marathon.

From the very beginning, and despite the range of ages and job backgrounds, the shared objective of running in the African wilderness brought a closeness to our group that would only tighten as the days passed.

Over lunch, the organisation of Ravineside was explained to us. Our rooms, which as the name suggests were built on wooden structures overhanging the edge of a deep ravine, were some half a mile from the central reception/dining area.

However, as the African wildlife could roam freely between the two sites, we were required to be transported by jeep driven by the rangers at all times. The accommodation was split into seven blocks, each consisting of four individual cabins (bedroom and bathroom) and each block had its own communal area. The blocks were accessed by steep wooden and rock staircases, leading precariously down from the rim of the ravine; our party had been allocated to blocks three and five.

There was no time to rest after our long journey; our first safari drive was scheduled for 4pm. On our arrival at Ravineside the weather had been pleasantly warm and sunny but this was the South African winter. We had had plenty of warnings about how the temperature plummets once the sun sets at around 6pm, so we were prepared with warm hats and gloves. Our party was split between two open-sided vehicles, our own being driven by Sander, the other by Marco, Ravineside's two resident rangers. Sander gave us a brief warning that we should remain seated at all times so as not to disturb the animals, and handed us sheets, prepared by Jonatan, that would help us identify and record the wildlife we came across. Then we were on our way.

I had never been on a game drive before and had no idea what to expect. I had read of the rangers' legendary ability to spot animals that were all but invisible to the untrained eye, so I expected to be watching the African wildlife from some distance away.

The first game drive soon changed that expectation. Within minutes we were in among rhinos with young, sharing the sparse winter vegetation with warthogs. Sander's knowledge of all aspects of the animals' behaviour and habits was fascinating, and soon camera shutters were clicking frantically.

Some time later, as the light was beginning to fade, we came across a scene on a rocky plateau that took my breath away. It was as if Noah had emptied his ark in one place. Just yards from our vehicle, rhino, zebra, giraffe, kudu, warthogs and various bird species jostled each other. On the hillside above, a group of elephants was slowly descending to join them. This far, far exceeded all my expectations and we stayed there hypnotised by the beauty of the scene until it was almost too dark to see.

Once darkness fell we drove on along narrow tracks, Sander turning on a handheld spotlight, sweeping its beam all around the vehicle looking for the tell-tale reflections from the eyes that peered at us from the bush. It was almost time to return to the lodge for dinner when Sander received a radio call from Marco to say he had a sighting of a leopard in a tree. It was some distance from where we were, and the leopard was unlikely to hang around for long, but Sander asked if we were happy to race there as quickly as possible to see if we could catch sight of it. We agreed!

What had previously been fairly gentle progress, along albeit bumpy and rocky tracks, turned into something akin to a white-knuckle fairground ride with everybody hanging on for dear life to the handrails. For Angela this was particularly difficult. She had been able to protect her sore throat to some extent by keeping a hand over her mouth but darkness had fallen, temperatures had plummeted and both hands were required to stay in the vehicle, so her throat was cruelly exposed to the icy cold wind.

Eventually we arrived at the scene where Marco was parked up. He could still see the reflection of the leopard's eyes but it was very well concealed within the tree and in no mood to expose itself further. Sander skilfully manoeuvred our jeep into increasingly inaccessible positions to try and get a better view, but to no avail, and eventually we gave up and returned to the lodge for dinner, sighting hyenas and jackal on the way.

After 36 hours with very little sleep it was a real effort to force down some dinner and then we were driven back to our room in Cuckoo Lodge. Having only the energy to find our bedclothes and a toothbrush, we fell into our beds hoping for several hours of solid sleep at last. It was not to be; Angela's sore throat and nagging cough gave her very little respite.

Barely able to utter single words before exploding into another fit of coughing, Angela decided to skip breakfast the following morning. With nothing on the agenda until after lunch she took the opportunity to try and catch up on lost sleep, while Linda, who was in the adjacent cabin, and I stood outside in the warm sunshine, photographing our precarious lodging and the views into the ravine below.

Soon we spotted groups of small furry mammals squabbling among the trees. Although appearing to be large rodents, and being rather short-legged and chubby, they had an extraordinary ability to climb to the very tops of trees in search of fresh leaves to eat. I had no idea what they were but Sander later identified them as rock hyrax.

For lunch, the tables had been set up outside in the garden area of the dining complex, with fantastic views across the open plains. Angela was feeling a little better and was able to join us, although she was pretty much unable to engage in any conversation. The ten of us were really beginning to gel and to share details of our different lives in various corners of the world. Our friends in block five had spotted a green snake beneath their lodgings. This was rather disconcerting, as Sander had already assured us that the weather was too cold for snakes, and rekindled my latent fear of the deadly and aggressive black mamba which apparently was prevalent within the reserve!

Our afternoon/evening game drive was to take us on to the lower escarpment of Entabeni for the first time. Let me take a little bit of time to paint a picture of the geography of the reserve to put this into perspective. Covering an area of 85 square miles, Entabeni means 'place of the mountain' and the whole area was at considerable altitude. On the upper escarpment, where Ravineside and some of the other lodges were situated, the landscape was dominated by the Entabeni mountain, rising alone from in among rolling plains and rocky outcrops, not unlike the Sigiriya rock I had climbed in Sri Lanka.

The altitude was over 5,700 feet above sea level. In contrast, the relatively flat lower escarpment was at around 3,700 feet and the only connection between the two was a narrow road, less than a mile and a half long, cutting through Yellow Wood Valley. It doesn't take a great mathematician to work out that this road was massively steep, and was only accessible to just a few of the four-wheel-drive vehicles on the reserve, and then never in wet weather. Before beginning our game drive down below, Sander, Marco and Jonatan bore the most sadistic of grins as they explained that we would all be running both down and then back up this hill, whether we were doing the half or the full marathon!

As we began the descent a mood of black humour took over the group. Yes, the views both to the rocky side of the valley and to the plateau far below were breathtaking, but the prospect of running or even walking this hill seemed laughable. The engine roared as it tried to brake the jeep's descent, the exhaust intermittently exploding like rifle fire and the prop shaft groaning and wailing as the vehicle inched its way down the steepest sections. We were pitched forward in our seats, clinging on as you would on a rollercoaster.

Once we had reached the lower escarpment, the road levelled out and we drove around various small lakes, passing herds of skittish zebra before Sander suddenly spotted a huge crocodile lying motionless in the grass. Again, he manoeuvred the vehicle to within a few feet of the creature, which was around seven to eight feet in length. Yet another unforgettable experience to be so close to a wild crocodile.

As the light started to fade, Sander and Marco stopped the jeeps in a clearing where they considered it safe for us to step out of the vehicles. The back of Sander's jeep was suddenly transformed into a snack buffet and bar. We were stood among friends in the African bush, me enjoying a beer and Angela a glass of red wine, so we all raised our glasses to Sander and Marco – and it wouldn't be for the last time!

After a nervous and extremely watchful natural toilet break we climbed back on board the jeeps and were on the way again, with the spotlights now picking out jackal scampering past as darkness descended. We were in lion country. Soon we spotted a lioness leading her four cubs down a sandy track, the youngsters playfully jumping on each other's backs as they walked. For a while we followed them, Sander's spotlight picking them out in the gloom. We turned off the track, sped along another road, and were then in position to see them coming towards us before the lioness led her young family into the bush, turning to look back over her shoulder to make sure we wouldn't follow. Another epic memory, although the fact that the track they were travelling on was already being marked out as part of the run route was a little disconcerting.

For me there was an unfortunate ending to what had been a wonderful evening. On the fast and bumpy drive back to Ravineside, my telephoto zoom lens flew out of my jacket pocket and smashed to pieces on the ground. After my bucket of water episode in Sri Lanka, cameras and running trips have proved not to be a good mix. Why hadn't I secured it properly? Hindsight is an exact science. Yes, it would affect my photographic ambitions during the trip, but I still had a working lens, and insurance would cover the cost of a replacement. It was plastic, glass and metal that was broken, not bones and flesh – much, much worse could have happened.

The schedule planned for day three looked particularly busy, and Angela and I were both concerned about whether she was well enough to get through it all. After a morning game drive, an early lunch was to be followed by a bush walk and then a trip down to Lakeside Lodge for a boat trip where we hoped to see hippos.

Again, Angela had slept poorly with constant bouts of coughing and real difficulty catching her breath, but there was a new factor in the equation. After two days of quiet sunshine we had both been kept awake in the early hours of the morning by a howling wind that penetrated the thatched roof of our cabin. When the 5.30am alarm call came I peered outside and could see the ravine shrouded in mist and cloud, the trees bending in the gale.

We agreed that she would give the early game drive a go, as at least she would be seated in the jeep, but that, if conditions proved to be too much for her, she would skip the bush walk. In fact there was little new to see on that game drive, the wildlife appearing to be as reluctant as we were to expose itself to the fearsome wind, and it was now obvious that Angela was not going to be able to complete the full programme for that day, so she decided to skip the bush walk after lunch. As it turned out this was probably one of the best decisions she would make in her life. I also spoke to Jonatan about my concern that she was getting no better despite the antibiotics her GP had prescribed, and he kindly arranged for the race medical team to visit her while the rest of us were out in the bush.

After lunch I waited with the other eight members of our group outside the main entrance of Ravineside for the bush walk to begin. Eventually Sander arrived, armed with a rifle. He grinned, explaining that it was a necessary precaution but that in over five years of bush walks he had never had to fire a shot in anger.

He issued a thorough safety briefing, emphasising the need to stay in single file, with him at the front and Marco at the back. We could rotate within our single file, giving everybody a chance to be near the front, but conversation should be kept to a minimum. We would not be sticking to paths but crossing open bushland and we should always follow the route he was taking, even if it seemed there was an easier alternative available. All instructions from the rangers were to be obeyed; these would normally be by hand signal or whistle, and if a situation did arise, we should not stop to take photographs. Thoroughly briefed, we set out on our way.

What was to follow was probably the scariest moment of my life! It started pleasantly enough on relatively easy terrain and we stopped occasionally while Sander whispered descriptions of animal tracks and droppings, and what information could be gleaned from them. It was clear that there had been recent elephant activity in the area as there was still damp urine in some of the tracks despite it still being so windy. Sander noted the tracks had turned down into a deep wooded ravine – the slightly rounded front part of the footprint indicating which direction the elephants were moving.

We climbed part of the way down to a large flat rock known locally as 'The Lookout', and we were hoisted on to it by the rangers to see if we could spot the elephants. We saw nothing, Sander concluded that they had probably continued to the bottom of the valley, and as we had now been out for some time, we decided to return to the lodge and started to climb back out of the ravine.

At this point I was following immediately behind Sander when a large elephant suddenly emerged from the trees above us, maybe 50 yards away. My immediate and thoroughly naïve reaction was, 'Wow, we have found an elephant!' but the urgency of Sander's reaction left me in no doubt that this was not a good situation. In fact we were in mortal danger.

The lead elephant immediately began to react aggressively and Sander signalled us to descend into the ravine as quickly as we could. It was steep terrain littered with trees, bushes and boulders and I was now at the back of the party with just Sander behind me. He was yelling, screaming and waving his arms at the matriarch female who had now been joined by five others. Marco was bellowing instructions to try and keep us together and not to isolate ourselves. I was focused on leaping from boulder to boulder but could hear the elephants were getting closer as they ripped out small trees and bushes in their path.

My overriding memory will always be the noise, with continuous piercing trumpeting and deafening roars. At one point I stumbled briefly and fell, twisting the back of my knee and, glancing back, I saw the lead elephant no more than 20 yards behind us, huge ears outspread and tusks waving wildly. Sander was even closer than that, still screaming and shouting at them, and as I picked myself up, I heard him fire a warning shot into the air from his rifle. This seemed to make the elephants bellow even louder and so he fired a second warning shot. Thankfully, this slowed their charge, and we were eventually able to make our escape to the bottom of the ravine, and then to climb up the other side to a track where a vehicle could come and rescue us.

Back at Cuckoo Lodge, Angela was lying on her bed, texting Ben, when she heard the gunfire and commotion. Even though she was almost a mile away it sounded to her as if the elephants were right outside the lodge and she was too afraid to step outside on to the balcony to see what was going on. Of course, at this stage, she had no idea that it was our bush walk caught up in the situation, and she thought that maybe poachers were after the elephants.

'I think we pissed them off,' was Sander's classic understatement as we gathered together to await rescue. There was more black humour now we knew we were safe but I have no doubt that our lives had been saved by the professionalism and training of Sander and Marco and it was no bad thing that, with the exception of Andrew who was after all a hill farmer, we were all marathon runners.

Once back at Ravineside, and with the adrenaline levels now subsiding, my left knee was beginning to feel quite uncomfortable with pain at the back radiating down into the upper calf. While others opted for a strong cup of coffee, or something even more potent from the bar, I armed myself with a large bag of ice and hitched a ride back to Cuckoo Lodge.

Angela was looking a lot better for her restful afternoon. She told me how the doctor had given her a stronger antibiotic and also some codeine to suppress the coughing fits. I then related the events of our bush walk to her. As I did so my hands started to shake more and more violently. It was as if talking about it was releasing all the pent-up emotion that I had, up to then, held in, and I began to feel quite emotional.

I then started to unburden myself of thoughts that had entered my head in the rescue jeep. As much as Angela had suffered and had her holiday partially spoilt by this miserable infection, it may well have been the best thing that could have happened to her. Angela, by her own admission, was no athlete, and even had she been in full health, which clearly she wasn't, she would very likely have struggled to escape from the elephant charge, although one can never discount the amazing effects of an adrenaline surge. I would of course not have left her, and nor I'm sure would Sander, but there might have been a very different outcome, to either us or indeed the elephants, if Angela had been in our party.

Dinner that night was a celebratory occasion – there was only one topic of conversation. The glue that had held our group together before the elephant incident had now turned into concrete. There was much hugging, and an ever-growing realisation of just how much we all owed Sander and Marco. We named ourselves the 'Elephant Ten' – Angela was granted full membership as although she had not experienced the chase, she had had a full rendition of the sound effects! It was also agreed that 21 June would for evermore be celebrated as 'Elephant Day'.

With a race recce drive scheduled for the following morning, we all headed off back to our cabins. However that extraordinary day had yet another sting in the tail.

As we prepared for bed, Angela showed me what appeared to be a conjunctivitis-like infection in her eyes with her eyelids already beginning to swell and stick together. Whatever next! I took more painkillers for my leg but I was concerned about how well I would sleep, as I was still feeling really stressed and shaken.

Lights out. Just after midnight, Angela called out to me that her throat was swelling up and that she was finding it difficult to breathe. Lights back on again, and I could see that she was now more distressed than she had been at any stage of this holiday so far. Her eyes were now very swollen and puffy; it seemed that she was experiencing some sort of allergic reaction, perhaps to her new medication.

We had to get the doctor back. I rang Jonatan's room and he answered sleepily. He immediately became concerned and said he would get straight in touch with the husband and wife medical team. They were based at a lodge some three miles away but both agreed to come over just as soon as they could find a ranger to drive them.

Within an hour they were knocking at the door. Although Angela's throat was considerably swollen and constricted there was still a clear airway, and her oxygen levels were good. They identified the codeine as the most likely cause of the reaction, so took those pills away and started her on a course of steroids to suppress the immune reaction.

I was also emotional. I was cross with myself for not holding it together as well as my colleagues, but the combination of the elephant incident, and now having to deal with a family medical emergency in the middle of the night, was just a step too far. While his wife was dealing with Angela, Klaus, the male doctor, took the trouble to assess my leg injury even at that unearthly hour and reassuringly confirmed that there was no damage to the knee joint itself, but probably a sprain of the calf muscle.

Eventually they left, warning us that we were unlikely to get any sleep that night. Angela was to sit upright to aid her breathing and in those first few hours the deep inspirations between coughing fits were whooping cough-like, which she found very distressing, but as the night wore on, these seemed to ease a little. I dozed fitfully, but my bladder had gone into overdrive – I must have visited the bathroom at least a dozen times that night. Where was it all coming from?

Morning came and Klaus rang for an update. He was pleased to hear of Angela's improvement and said his wife would be across as soon as she could get transport. I spoke to Linda next door to explain the night's events. The rest of the group were off for breakfast and then down to race HQ at the Lakeside Lodge for a safety briefing and the route recce. I hoped to catch up with them later. A short while later Klaus's wife arrived. She examined Angela and confirmed that the allergic response was now subsiding and Angela, who had been very frightened during the night, was now beginning to feel a lot brighter and sounding much more like her normal self.

The doctor turned to me and asked what I planned to do about the race. It had been a hugely difficult 24 hours and I was still a little tearful. I described my frequent visits to the bathroom overnight and she put that down to huge levels of circulating stress hormones. My inner feeling was that I could probably manage the physical pain in my leg, but I was mentally fragile as well. How, for example, would I react if I encountered an elephant during the race? She reassured me that my fears were perfectly natural after what had happened and she offered me a couple of days of diazepam to settle my nerves. The anti-doping authorities might not have been impressed but I was happy to lean on that crutch.

While I was free to make a final decision about running the race until the very last minute, it was essential I went on the route recce and attended the safety briefing so I travelled with the doctor on her journey back to Lakeside while Angela caught up on some much-needed sleep.

When we arrived a few of our group were in the entrance foyer picking up their race packs. Again I was a little emotional as I described the overnight events but there were lots of warm hugs and everybody seemed relieved that Angela now seemed to be on the mend. The doctor returned with yet another ice pack and suggested I strap this to my calf during the route drive. In that instant I knew that, with so much support around me from so many new friends, I was destined to compete in the half-marathon that I had travelled so far to take part in.

* * * * *

Race day. A 5am alarm call, a light breakfast at 5.30am and an hour later we were being driven down to Lakeside. Mercifully the strong winds of the previous day had subsided, and the weather forecast for the race was good with plenty of warm sunshine.

The full marathon runners set off at 8am. They had an extended uphill section on the upper escarpment taking them out to the Hanglip viewing point. They would turn and retrace their steps back to the plains. Crucially, at the turning point, they would be given a plastic wristband to wear, and this was their proof that they had run the whole distance. Without a wristband at the end they would be disqualified.

As I waited in the roadway for our 8.15am start I remarked to Angela how calm I was feeling. Even in the most mundane ten-kilometre road race at home there are usually butterflies in my tummy – but not this time. The diazepam was definitely working its magic. A couple of start-line photographs and then we too were on our way. A gentle downhill start and then soon we were climbing the first of many hills.

I ran alongside Ketaki for a while but she pulled away from me after the first long uphill section. Brita and Judy were behind me in the early stages but they later passed me as we began the descent of Yellow Wood Valley and I would not see them again until the end.

As the plains opened out I ran for a while with Bernard, a South African runner of similar age to me. We paused to take photos of a mother and baby rhino grazing not 50 yards from the track on which we were running. Reassuringly, a nearby ranger sat quietly in his vehicle keeping an eye on the pair. Bernard, it turned out, was a Royal Air Force enthusiast and was keen to find out where he could buy a running vest like the one I was wearing. This was from the Royal Air Forces Association, the charity for which I was running the race. We spoke of my son, Chris, and I told Bernard of the Rome Marathon which I had run with Chris just a couple of months previously.

Our conversation was suddenly and unexpectedly interrupted by large numbers of full marathon runners being among us; much, much sooner than expected. Confusion seemed to reign. Some ran past us, turned, and then ran towards us again. Eventually a consensus seemed to have been reached and the full and half-marathoners were running together towards the top of the Yellow Wood Valley road.

It later emerged that the reason for this confusion was our friends, the elephants. The group that had pursued us two days earlier had congregated on the narrow track to the Hanglip viewing point and the organisers, not wanting to risk yet another incident, had closed the track and turned the runners around.

For the marathon runners, this created a problem. The kilometre markers they were passing were now wildly inaccurate and much more optimistic than the distance they had actually covered. It was a headache for the organisers as well. Even as the race was unfolding, they were calculating two extra loops on the upper escarpment later in the run to make up the full marathon distance. Furthermore the point at which the confirmation wrist bracelets were handed out now had to be relocated.

As we started the deep descent down the valley I ran for a while with Linda and Jan, and Lesley also sped by. They were all running the full distance. Running down a long hill may sound like nirvana but this was so steep that the brakes had to be constantly applied to avoid you going out of control and crashing into the huge fallen boulders that littered either side of the road. For the first time I felt the pain in the back of my leg as I tensed my thigh and calf muscles to maintain control. At times the gradient eased a little and it was possible to free-wheel for a short period, but always in the knowledge that the anchors might suddenly have to be re-applied as we rounded a sharp bend.

At the foot of the hill was an aid station where I gratefully grabbed some more water in sealed plastic bags. With practice you could tear off one corner with your teeth, drink what you needed and then carry the rest, sealing the hole between thumb and forefinger – a lot easier than carrying a bottle or trying to drink from a cup. Our lady doctor was also manning this aid station and I was delighted to report that I was going well, without too much discomfort.

We now entered a flat lap around the crocodile lake that had looked so appealing from the comfort of the recce jeep just a day earlier. This was lion country, although we had been assured at the briefing that the pride had been under constant surveillance for over 24 hours. I was still very watchful. The sand on the track was a lot deeper than it had looked from the jeep and I was quickly reminded of just how difficult it is to run in deep sand, lessons learnt from many past desert races. However, that section wasn't too long and soon I was back on a firmer surface, passing a ranger's jeep with a large sign on the back stating 'Africa is not for wusses'!

Now I was back at the foot of Yellow Wood Valley and the long steep climb began. It was relentless; some sections required your hands to be clamped to the fronts of your thighs to give you extra stability and power, others actually required both hands and feet to be on the road. Rahool, running the full marathon, passed me partway up the hill and boosted my confidence by saying how fresh I was looking. I wasn't feeling it!

I would set small targets maybe 50 yards ahead – a boulder, a bush or a tree – drive myself towards it and then take a few seconds' breather while I looked ahead to pick out the next target. Some people seemed better able to cope with the incline; others sat motionless at the side of the road, almost in tears. One person was running some of the steeper sections by zig-zagging backwards and forwards across the road, reducing the gradient but increasing the distance.

There was a welcome drink stop halfway up, and then the relentless climb continued. I rounded a bend and there was a lady with a video camera urging me to run. I managed maybe ten paces before my legs once again turned to blancmange.

Finally the height of the ravine walls began to lessen, the gradient started to ease and we were back on the open plains of the upper escarpment. A figure ran towards me – it was Klaus, the doctor. 'Are you alright, are you alright?' he shouted. I didn't have the breath to answer but gave him a double thumbs-up and we slapped palms in a high five as I again broke into a slow trot.

The next few miles were relatively flat by comparison and I was able to run long sections. Herds of wildebeest were galloping across the wide plains and it was indescribably awesome and an absolute privilege to be racing in such a spectacular setting. At the next water stop a band of African drummers and dancers beat out a rhythm for us to run to. Again, I came across Bernard, my South African friend, and we ran and walked together for quite some time, relishing the fact that, despite our advancing years, we were still able to enjoy such an experience.

In the final few kilometres the track became steeper with much more loose rock underfoot. Nobody wanted to fall or twist an ankle at this stage so we slowed. We came across a dead wildebeest by the roadside – it seemed to be a natural death as opposed to being the victim of a predator. A ranger stood nearby to discourage scavenging hyenas from congregating near the running route. I took a photograph of the animal and then the ranger offered to take a photograph of me with it. I knelt beside the unfortunate creature, taking its horn into my fingers and offered a silent prayer for the old fellow.

Then we could see the lake below us. Bernard wanted to stop for a breather so I ran on and completed the last couple of kilometres by myself. As I approached the final bend, a small truck by the roadside was relaying my running number to the finish so when I turned and saw the finish banner less than 100 yards away, I heard my name being called out over the tannoy, and could hear Brita and Judy shouting me home.

A large man came out from the crowd and high-fived me. I crossed the line, my arms outspread. Somebody, I don't remember who, put a medal round my neck and then Jonatan was there. He gave me a great Danish bear-hug. 'You did it, you did it – after everything, you did it.' He urged me to get a drink and a banana but I had no idea where from.

I was looking around for Angela and then spotted her standing near the finish line, waving. She had been trying to get photos of me finishing but the large man who had high-fived me had stepped in her way. Apparently he was a little the worse for wear from drink! Then Jonatan was back beside us, with a cup of water and a banana for me. I thanked him, and Angela and I sat on the wall beside the finish straight as I recovered my breath.

We shared hugs with Ketaki, Brita and Judy. Ketaki, who had never run the half-marathon distance before, and had trained on the flat Los Angeles coastline, cooled by Pacific breezes, had completed this most difficult of runs in under three hours and was understandably delighted. I had taken just over three and a half hours, with Brita and Judy finishing together around ten minutes in front of me. We each wore our medals with pride.

The half-cut man stopped by again with a large coolbox. 'Would you like a fruit juice or a cold beer?' he asked. I settled for the latter.

While some of us waited for Jan, Linda, Lesley and Rahool to complete their full marathons, Judy and Brita set off back to Ravineside a little earlier and were to be eternally grateful that they did. On being dropped off at block five they noticed smoke coming from the chimney above the communal area. Had someone lit a fire? Once they got inside, they realised the surroundings of the fireplace were on fire.

Judy raced back to her room to call reception. No answer! Brita was filling her cupped hands with water from a sink to try and quench the flames. Eventually they found a coffee pot to fill and this proved rather more practical. Finally, the fire was put out and they managed to get a call through to a security number. Two members of staff arrived. Did they have any firefighting equipment such as an extinguisher? Oh no. They surveyed the scene, made a few notes, thanked the girls for their efforts, and departed.

How had the fire started? On the evening before the race, our friends in block five had enjoyed a cosy chat around an open fire. Before retiring for bed they had made sure the fire was out. Once we had all left for the race, the housekeeping staff had put fresh logs on the fire but there must have been some heat remaining. The fire re-ignited, one of the logs rolled out and set fire to the surroundings and, in the nick of time, Brita and Judy arrived back. Had they been just ten minutes later the fire would have been much more established. With wooden cabins and thatched roofs, the consequences could well have been catastrophic. It was a lucky escape; another lucky escape. This trip was gaining a reputation for lucky escapes.

You might think that after such a strenuous and draining marathon day, the organisers would have arranged a bit of a lie-in the next morning. But no, Jonatan grinned as he announced another 5.30am wake-up call. Once again the benefits of witnessing extraordinary wildlife in their natural surroundings at sunrise far outweighed any fatigue.

In the afternoon, Angela and I visited the hippo lake, a trip we had missed as a result of the events of Elephant Day and then, as had happened in Petra, the evening was set aside for a spectacular celebration meal featuring a huge bonfire, mountains of food, beer and red wine, and the African percussion band. We danced like we had never danced before, despite the lactic acid in our muscles, and when Lars Fyhr, the head of Adventure Marathons, made a short speech congratulating everybody on their achievement and describing the difficulties the organisers had faced in re-routing the full marathon as a result of elephant activity, there was a particularly raucous reception from the Elephant Ten table.

So we came to the final day that our group would be together before returning to our homes around the world. One week ago we hadn't known each other at all. Now, thanks to our shared love of running, we were destined to be friends for life. In the same way that the challenges of the Sahara had knitted together the occupants of 'Tent 40', so our elephant adventure was the glue that would link us long into the future.

A late-afternoon safari drive, and we came across the very group of elephants that had pursued us just days before. As we stopped close by, Sander, at the wheel of our jeep, said in his finest and most informative ranger voice, 'African elephant – a truly placid animal!' We watched them for quite some time as they showered themselves in dust baths whipped up from the sandy surface by their trunks. From the safety of the jeeps, it was actually quite therapeutic to meet this group of elephants again in better circumstances than in our previous engagement.

After descending to the lower escarpment, we were once again invited to get out to stretch our legs as the back of the jeeps was transformed into a snack bar, and beer and wine appeared as if by magic. Lesley read out a poem she had written about our elephant experience and then Jonatan offered a few words, saying that he had been a natural world guide for over five years but had never before developed such a strong bond with a group as he had with ours. We could tell from the emotive way he spoke the words, that he really meant it.

Darkness was falling and soon we were on our way again in the search for lions. The one sight we were still all longing to see was the reserve's magnificent male lion. The two vehicles took different routes to double the chances of a sighting. Sander stopped our jeep, turning off the engine, and we sat in silence as he scanned the surrounding area with his spotlight, looking for the tell-tale reflections from the lion's eyes. Nothing. He turned the key to move on; the engine turned and turned and turned but did not fire.

You know that frustrating feeling when your car just won't start. The difference this time was that the bush around us was alive with the sound of lions roaring. He left it a good minute to let the carburettor drain and tried again. Nothing. Four or five times he tried to restart the jeep, but still the engine wouldn't burst into action, and in the silences in between we could still hear the lions nearby.

Once again, we quietly joked about our predicament. Sander radioed Marco and requested assistance and soon the other jeep was alongside. Between them they eventually coaxed the engine back to life, and another 'tricky moment' had passed. Within minutes we came across two beautiful lionesses lying side by side in the grass before they gracefully moved away into the darkness, but the male remained elusive, although Sander could recognise his roar reverberating around us.

The stalled engine had left us running a little late so there was no time to prolong the search, and we set off in convoy up the long, steep road back to the upper escarpment. Jonatan had promised us one final surprise that evening and had insisted we all dressed as warmly as we could. Our vehicles came to a halt towards the top of the Yellow Wood Valley road and we were led down a steep rocky staircase by torchlight to an area perched on the side of the ravine that, in the summer, was sometimes used as a picnic spot.

But we were possibly the first party to use it in the winter. We sat around a large table laid out for dinner, with a fabric awning above us, and a blanket over our knees being the only protection from the cold winter chill. This was an exclusive dinner for Elephant Ten members only.

Soon the wine was flowing again and, despite the cold, we enjoyed a warming bowl of soup followed by a spicy chicken dinner. Although Sander and Marco were strictly speaking members of staff, and not guests, we insisted that they join us at dinner and gratefully toasted the two men without whom some of us might not have been present around that table.

There was another moving moment too. We had collected some money between us for the staff and rangers of Ravineside Lodge, that Jonatan had promised to distribute. Just how much do you tip somebody who has probably saved your life? As a group we had also wanted to show our gratitude to Jonatan for the enormous efforts he had put into co-ordinating the whole experience, and for solving so patiently the many problems that had arisen. Jonatan seemed almost overwhelmed by this and said he would spend the money not on himself, but on his one-year-old little boy at home. He toasted the 'coolest and craziest' party he had ever led.

Time to return to the jeeps, but this was not the end of the celebrations. Brita and Judy had decided that we would hold a final ESP (Elephant Survival Party) on our final night together. The lodge's chef had baked us a special chocolate cake, and Jonatan had brought along a bottle of Amarula, a South African cream liqueur made from the marula fruit, a great favourite of elephants! We congregated in the communal area of block five, the fire surround still showing the scars of the flames extinguished by Brita and Judy just two days previously.

And yes, even at this late hour there was time for one more drama. Our celebrations were suddenly interrupted by a male voice outside shouting frantically for help. Sander and Marco raced outside – rangers are never off-duty. It later emerged that a Brazilian guest, staying in an adjacent cabin, had emerged from his bathroom after a shower to find a large dog-like grey animal in his bedroom. The animal, possibly a jackal or a hyena, had already run off but in his panic the gentleman had managed to get outside of his room and to lock himself out. Rangers to the rescue once again.

As Angela and I were not due to leave Entabeni until 2pm, Jonatan had arranged one final morning game drive for us, along with Lesley, Rahool and Ketaki. With Marco at the wheel we headed for the lower escarpment again; one final attempt at finding the elusive male lion. There was a radio message of a cheetah sighting down near a perimeter fence. It was some distance away and it was 'hold on tight' time again as we sped along bumpy tracks.

Once again we were unlucky. The cheetah had concealed itself in long grass and we never caught a glimpse. We passed the reserve's ranger-training school, and spotted the largest rhinoceros I have ever seen, before it disappeared off into thick woodland. At the very least it was double the size of any of the adult rhinos we had seen on the upper escarpment.

And then, another radio call. The male lion was nearby. In a minute we were there and the scene was stunning. Just 20 feet from our open jeep was the young male lion with its magnificent mane, and between its jaws were the remains of an unfortunate antelope. Marco pointed out the size of the lion's massive paws and told us that the tongue had a serrated surface that could remove the skin layer of a human being with just three licks. And yet it looked almost cuddly! It was the 'cherry on the cake' moment, and the only pity was that not all of the Elephant Ten were there to see it.

Seven days in South Africa came to an end, and I doubt whether any other seven-day period of my life has ever been so crammed full of beauty, drama and incident. Once again a running adventure trip had turned up trumps. Happily, all of the outcomes were positive and it was a relieved Ben who greeted Angela back at Heathrow the following morning. She had a few tales to tell.

17

Never too old
to learn

NOT unexpectedly, there was a fair degree of media interest once I got back from Africa. Not so much for my performance in the half-marathon but more for the elephant escapade. Headlines like 'Redditch Granddad Forced to Flee South African Elephant Stampede' sell more newspapers than 'Redditch Granddad Completes Half-Marathon in Africa'. However, it was another running-related story in my local paper that caught my eye just a week or two after I returned; our local council had launched a parkrun at our beautiful Arrow Valley lake.

I was vaguely aware of the growing parkrun (always spelt with a lower-case 'p') movement. Every Saturday, at 9am, a timed five-kilometre run in a local park, and free to enter to boot. All you had to do was register online, print off your personal barcode and remember to take it along with you each time you ran.

One of my work colleagues had run a few in Birmingham's Cannon Hill Park and had encouraged me to give it a try. I'm slightly ashamed of my reason for never having got round to it. At the time, I was finding getting through the working week a pretty stressful process and Friday evenings were 'let my hair down time', inevitably involving a few glasses of wine. The prospect of getting up early on a Saturday morning, a little hungover, and repeating that tedious drive back into Birmingham on a day off, just didn't appeal. Neither did the distance; five kilometres was a bit on the short side for me and to make it more satisfying, I would need to find some pace in my legs that I guessed wasn't there anymore.

But now there was a parkrun available just a five-minute drive, or 15-minute run, from home. Why not at least give it a try? Just four weeks after returning from Africa I went along to my first parkrun, clutching my plastic-coated barcode. It was a move that was to re-invigorate my running career in a way that I would never have thought possible.

So what benefits could parkrun possibly bring to me that I hadn't already learned or experienced in a running career that now spanned over 30 years? Well, since retirement, the great majority of my training runs had been solo and at a steady, comfortable pace that allowed me to take in my surroundings. With parkrun, at the very least, I could run with others and, for once a week at least, inject a little bit of pace over the shorter distance if, that is, it was there any more.

As the weeks unfolded so my passion for parkrun grew. Familiar faces became good friends and, for the first time in many years, a competitive streak inside me slowly emerged. You began to know those who ran at around the same pace as you, and if you spotted someone in front who you would normally beat, then the urge to chase them down was irresistible. Of course it was friendly rivalry; that is the very essence of parkrun, whatever speed you run or walk at.

Dogs on leads, infants in pushchairs, children of all ages and adults young and old trailing in the wake of the elite runners at the front, but all sharing an invigorating start to each and every weekend.

The competitive animal within me came to life. I wanted to get faster. I would never again replicate the pace I had achieved in my earliest running years but there was no reason I couldn't still improve my current times. After every parkrun you receive a text message giving you your official placing and time and whenever it finished with, 'Well done on your new pb' there was a whoop of delight and that weekend became a whole lot brighter.

A couple of months after my first parkrun, Chris and his family were visiting; they had moved back from Germany and were living in Telford. Having listened to me constantly eulogise about its benefits, Chris dipped his toes into our Arrow Valley parkrun pool. He was hooked.

Chris is a single-minded and determined individual. He was saddened to find that not only did Telford not have a parkrun, but that there was not one in the whole county of Shropshire. Despite being a newcomer to the area he set about establishing a core team and raising the necessary funding from the local council. Just 133 days after his Arrow Valley run, Chris, as event director, and in the presence of his local MP, mayor and several councillors, launched the first Telford parkrun, and one very proud dad was among the 178 runners.

Parkrun for me does not end on a Saturday morning. We occasionally socialise together, travel to other local running events as a team, hold summer midweek handicap races and, every Tuesday evening, all year round, a group of us meet at the lake for a training session with Ernie, one of our own, a former Scots Guard and also a qualified athletics coach.

My weekly training regime includes hill sessions, sprints, tempo runs and *fartlek*, not to mention a variety of warm-up and warm-down exercises and stretches. The result? Even as a pensioner I am still improving my run times. I will never repeat the times of my earlier running days but I am a much better runner now than I was five years ago. You are never too old to learn!

Inevitably there are highlights and lowlights of the parkrun year – two runs in blizzard conditions particularly stand out, where only a hardy few were able to make the start line because of impassable roads; I live close enough to be able to run to the park. And then there was our first anniversary run in fancy dress where I ran as a clown and Ernie ran in a lime green ball gown and still managed to run five kilometres in a little over 22 minutes.

On the downside, one of our regular runners was brought down by a stray dog, dislocating his shoulder in the process, and then there was the infamous 'fisherman incident'. An angler felt that one of our runners had disrespected him on the first lap of our two-lap course so lay in wait for him to come round again. Unfortunately the fisherman's memory was even shorter than his temper and he waylaid and attacked the wrong person.

And for me there is one golden parkrun moment that is right up there in my list of top, lifetime running memories. It was Telford parkrun's first anniversary and I ran the whole five kilometres with my lovely seven-year-old granddaughter, Holly. I was dressed as Prince Charming, with Holly as Cinderella, and it was such a privilege to be able to run together with her. I just cannot envisage having 'gone for a run' with my own grandparents, and hopefully one day I will be able to repeat the experience with my other granddaughter, Josie, although at just one year old that may be a few years away yet.

As much as I love my running, and as much as it has enriched my life so far, I still get almost as much satisfaction from seeing others set out on their own particular journey. A case in point is Chris's wife, Lynne. She was wholeheartedly by Chris's side as he made the often difficult and occasionally emotional journey towards the launch of Telford parkrun.

Every Saturday morning she would fulfil various roles, usually timekeeping, to ensure the whole event ran smoothly, but when asked if she would ever consider taking part, she would simply reply that she wasn't built for running. Eventually, on a family trip down to Sussex, Lynne took the plunge and entered a local parkrun. One year later Lynne improved her time by a massive 11 minutes and completed a half-marathon in her home city of Liverpool: so much for not being built for running.

Nearer home, I've been helping out at our local Couch to 5k programmes. Over a structured nine-week schedule, it is so satisfying seeing the smile on people's faces as they progress from not being able to run for one minute to being able to complete a five-kilometre run. What is even better is hearing them say that their achievement is only the beginning of a new, healthier lifestyle as they plan new and longer races in the future.

So parkrun, and its various offshoots, have given a whole new impetus to my running, both for myself and in the helping of others to get started. I would love to give a personal shout-out to all the fabulous new friends I have made since I first printed off my barcode but inevitably I would leave someone out, so here is a collective thank you to you all. You know who you are.

* * * * *

But old habits die hard. Whoops, there goes another cliché. As much as parkrun had brought a new perspective into my running life, the desire to run and travel was as strong as ever, and a new challenge was already looming. It was time to return to the cold. One of the most painful and difficult races I had ever run was the half-marathon in Siberia, and I had learned many lessons about running in sub-zero temperatures, particularly with regard to hydration.

This was the time to put that knowledge into practice and once again I turned to Adventure Marathons. They offered a full or half-marathon in Greenland, within the Arctic Circle, with part of the route on the polar ice-cap itself. As I had in Jordan and in Africa I opted for the half-marathon, not being confident I could complete a full marathon in such conditions within the seven-hour time limit.

At least I wouldn't encounter any elephants in Greenland, although a Google search for Kangerlussuaq, the town where we would be staying, revealed a photo of a polar bear strolling down the main road!

It was the year of my 65th birthday and Chris had asked me for gift suggestions. He was most amused when I asked for some crampon-like attachments that I could fit on to my running shoes to keep me upright on the polar ice, and questioned how common a present that was for people in their mid-60s.

I already possessed a good variety of clothing that I judged would protect me against whatever weather Greenland had in store, so I set about putting in the miles over the summer months with a series of half-marathon races. All was on track and then, just two weeks before departure, and I can pinpoint the day it happened, I felt suddenly overwhelmed by a sense of panic and anxiety. The old demon had returned, but why?

The preparation had been uneventful, everything was in place for a great trip, but I just could not shake that feeling off. I considered a trip to the doctor but knowing the likely outcome would be advice to call the trip off, I put that on the back burner, gritted my teeth and soldiered on.

Through social media, I had been in touch with a British runner who had run the race the year before. He had questioned whether I might find that the extra weight of my rather bulky shoe crampons would hamper my progress. It was a trade-off: stability on solid ice against cramp-inducing extra weight to carry on your feet. I needed to feel what it felt like to run with them on, but, even with our unpredictable British weather, Redditch was not renowned for snow and ice in October. A couple of miles round a local muddy field and the decision was made; stability on the ice was more important than any lack of pace.

Those final few days before departure were very difficult, constantly trying to outwit my inner doubts, but I completed the first leg of my trip to Copenhagen and was soon in the company of some new friends as we took a running tour of a city I had never visited before.

The next day, our flight from Copenhagen landed in Kangerlussuaq, our home town in Greenland, before 10am. It was cold but not really any worse than a bitter January morning in the Midlands. Although we had flown over the frozen wasteland of Greenland's interior, the town itself was relatively free of lying snow, although the mountains surrounding the airport were topped with it.

With a population of just 500, including 78 children, Kangerlussuaq was a tiny community divided into two by the long runway and airfield, built by the Americans during the Second World War. Far inland from the sea, at the beginning of the Sondre Songström fjord, the town had been chosen for the island's main airport because of its stable and dry climate. The nearest town was 140 kilometres away on the coast, with no connection by road. Isolated barely does justice to where we had landed.

That afternoon, several of us took a truck journey north along Greenland's longest road, which actually led to nowhere in particular, but was to form part of the marathon route. The gravel-filled, rutted surface had been built by the Americans as a test track for their four-wheeled-drive vehicles. We passed a stone quarry and Adam, our Inuit tour guide driver, joked that this was the beginning of their new Metro system.

A few miles out of Kangerlussuaq, we drove past an 18-hole golf course, the most northerly golf course in the world – the Greenlanders certainly have a sense of humour. In among the frozen and ice-filled landscape, little flags fluttered in the light winds. The clubhouse was an isolated, tiny wooden cabin, standing alone and deserted. No one was on the course and you certainly wouldn't want to play it with a white golf ball.

Further up the road, and lying within metres of its edge, was the wreckage of an American Lockheed T33 military trainer jet that had crashed in 1968. Eight of them had been on exercise when a sudden blizzard had cut electricity supplies to the airfield, blocking all communication. Five of the jets were eventually talked down safely but the remaining three ran out of fuel and crashed to the ground, although all crew ejected and were eventually rescued. This roadside wreckage had remained untouched for 45 years. Yes, this was Greenland.

The mood at dinner that night, as I tucked into my musk-ox burger in the airport café, was tinged with disappointment. Where was the snow? We had travelled all this way to run in extreme winter conditions and that part of the route we had already viewed, which would form most of the second half of the full marathon, was almost devoid of the white stuff. We joked about having to Photoshop our photographs to add whiteness to the landscape, but beneath the humour was a genuine feeling of letdown.

This unexpectedly created an extra pressure on me. I had signed up for the half-marathon, knowing that I could confidently expect to finish that within the four-hour time limit, but my three much younger dinner colleagues, Nottingham Dave, Melbourne Rob, and my young London room-mate, Antony, had all signed up for the full marathon. Having talked about some of my previous running exploits, including multi-day events in hostile deserts, they gently reminded me that it was not too late to upgrade to the full marathon, particularly as the most demanding sections of this race were in the first ten miles, and the second half of the route did not seem to be excessively onerous.

I slept little that night, my anxiety levels still being a lot higher than I would have liked. Could I run the full marathon after all? Almost certainly, this was the one and only time in my life that I would visit Greenland. Would I harbour regrets if I only completed half of the course, knowing that I could have made the full journey?

As dawn broke after a night of tossing and turning, I had made my final decision – I would stick with my original plan and run the half-marathon. Two reasons. One, I had only trained for a half-marathon and had done no runs longer than that distance. For my second reason I used a football analogy when explaining my decision to Antony. A player taking a penalty who changes his mind about where he will place the ball at the very last moment, is so often doomed to failure.

I opened the curtains of our room as I crawled out of bed early that morning, and looked out upon the airfield. Even in the darkness, I could see that snow was tumbling from the sky. My decision had been vindicated.

*   *   *   *   *

It was a somewhat comical start to the race. Adam, our guide, pointed his long rifle into the air and fired a single shot. Not one of the 98 runners from 24 different countries moved. Had he spotted his lunch flying overhead, or was he just testing his weapon?

There had been no countdown to the start, no announcement that the race would begin with a rifle shot. We just stared as a group at Adam and he stared disbelievingly back at us as we stood motionless. It was only when he started to wave his arms frantically that the penny dropped – we were on our way. Another crazy adventure run had started, and the spikes attached to my shoes began to bite into the ice as I trotted gently away from beneath the start banner.

The race started on a level section of the slippery gravel road and I settled down towards the rear of the field. I had just one goal for this adventure: to pass under the finish banner within the four-hour time limit, although my competitive inner self was a little more ambitious and I would be dancing for joy if I could break the three-hour barrier.

The early stages were all about assessing how much grip my footwear gave me. The faster runners, who were already speeding away from me, would be using lightweight spikes on their shoes to give them traction on the ice, but not at the expense of adding so much weight to their shoes that it slowed them down markedly. For me, as I had shown on that muddy Redditch field, stability on the ice was paramount; I just didn't need a heavy fall at my age.

The extra weight was noticeable, but I'd carried out a quick calculation on the proverbial 'back of a fag packet' and it revealed that the extra weight my legs would have to lift during the half-marathon amounted to almost 60 times my body weight. It was a price worth paying.

The day before the race we had been taken on to the polar ice-cap to test our footwear and, while others tumbled and slithered around me, my heavy-duty spikes glued me firmly to the polished surface.

After the initial mile or so the trail gradually turned into the long, steady and sometimes seriously steep climb towards the ice-cap. A runner some 200 yards in front of me, barely visible through a low-hanging mist, was suddenly launched into the air after stepping on to a lethal patch of ice. Within seconds he was being picked up and dusted down by his fellow runners. Yes, we were in a competitive race, but we were all going to look out for each other in this hostile Arctic environment.

The climb up to the ice-cap was relentless. On the steeper sections I was reduced to a brisk walk but I'd made a deal with myself that I would run as much of this route as possible, and the recent snowfall had actually made this easier as the cushioning effect of the layer of fresh snow provided extra traction on the slippery surface beneath.

Then the snowy gravel road ran out. We turned right on to a fearsomely steep icy ramp and began to follow a narrow rocky trail that led towards the polar ice. As we climbed, the mist was clearing, and a vivid blue sky was revealed, but the marked route was barely three feet wide and already the leading athletes were running downhill towards me after exiting their loop on the ice. No room to pass each other safely without tumbling into piles of loose rock, so I stood aside and yelled encouragement as each one passed. In time, the route opened out a little, and it was my turn to run on the polar ice.

It was a very emotional experience: at times I felt moved to tears. The route we had to follow was clearly marked with poles and red and white tape. To deviate from this would risk falling into a crevasse on this constantly moving mile-thick block of ice. Through the dusting of the snow on its surface, the ice appeared like black, shiny granite beneath my feet; only on closer inspection could I see it was translucent, and could see the rocks and tiny pebbles embedded within it.

A massive smile stretched across my face. Here I was, a 65-year-old granddad, and I was taking part in a running race on Arctic ice. For the umpteenth time in my life, I gave thanks that I had discovered running and the opportunity to experience parts of our world that so few people get to see. The euphoria triggered crazy thoughts that drifted through my mind as I almost floated across the polished surface – what would our government think if they could see me right now? Would they demand I return my free bus pass and winter fuel allowance? As far as the eye could see, and in every direction, gentle rolling undulations of ice stretched to every horizon, glistening, sparkling in the sunlight that now bathed the whole scene: just ice, just sunshine, nothing else.

There was a little more wind on the ice-cap and it was noticeably colder than it had been earlier, but personal discomfort was the last thing on my mind. A lone figure came into view; it was one of our doctors keeping a watchful and reassuring eye on everybody as they passed. I reached the six-kilometre marker flag, and then began the descent back off the ice. Running downhill might sound easier, and is of course easier in a normal environment, but running downhill on ice is a whole different story. As I returned to the gravel road, a small truck signalled the first of the aid stations, a chance to grab a mouthful of water and a welcome cup of a warm elderflower drink. This was no ordinary aid station – it was manned by Henrik Jorgensen, the winner of the 1988 London Marathon. This race was just becoming more and more extraordinary. 'Have a great run,' he called as I set off down the hill after the briefest of pauses.

With so few in the race, and with such a wide range of abilities, we were now well and truly spread out over this vast, barren landscape, so were running solo for much of the time. To be honest I find it hard to find the words that do justice to the beauty of the scenery that I was running through. At each brow of a hill, or turn of a corner on the icy trail, a new breathtaking landscape would come into view and the tiny camera that I carried in a pouch around my waist would come out again. This run was just too special for me not to pause and capture an image of what lay ahead of me.

Towering but crumbling glacier tongues marked the exit points from which the ice flowed from the main body of the glacier. Rock-strewn but frozen rivers held the water that had melted from the ice-cap during the previous summer. Now locked in place for the winter, this moraine debris would have to wait for another summer melt before it could continue its journey towards the fjord and eventually, the open sea. Massive frozen lakes decorated the horizon, and, high on the mountain slopes, small herds of reindeer and caribou playfully chased each other around.

We passed through areas of Arctic desert. Extraordinary. Flat, sandy plains and small dunes as you might expect in any desert, punctuated by the occasional thorny bush of Arctic willow, but instead of searing heat, pools of ice lay in the hollows.

And then there were areas of tundra – bare, rolling landscapes, patrolled by the occasional herd of musk ox, with virtually no vegetation at all. There are no large trees in Greenland; an attempt to plant a pine forest alongside the gravel road some 40 years ago now has just three trees surviving, the tallest an imposing four feet high!

There was another benefit to this extraordinary journey. So breathtaking were the views, it left little time for internal reflection on any personal pain and suffering and the kilometre markers just seemed to fly by. It had been my plan to remove the heavy spikes from my shoes once the going underfoot became less treacherous but, in fact, the recent snowfall ensured that this was never to happen. As I entered the final couple of miles, I began to experience severe cramps in both calves that inevitably slowed my progress. These were the type of cramps I might expect to get in the final stages of a full marathon, but were undoubtedly hitting me earlier here because of the extra weight I was carrying on my feet.

The Long Lake came into view, so named because it appears to stretch to infinity. I ran past two small wooden boats frozen into the ice, took a right turn and began one final steep climb towards the finish line banner that stretched across the road half a mile away. I so wanted to run all of this final long hill, but the cramps were agony, so it was more a case of run, stretch, walk; run, stretch, walk, but then I was there! I passed under the banner to the enthusiastic applause of the single timekeeper, who then placed a medal around my neck and managed to take a photograph with his frozen fingers to commemorate my achievement.

I glanced at my watch. I had finished the race in less than three hours and, in the words of a well-known television advertisement, I felt epic. Could I have gone on to finish the full marathon? With those cramps I very much doubt it; by sticking to my guns I had reached the right decision. It was another challenge confronted and overcome, and another encounter with Mother Nature that will leave indelible memories forever.

* * * * *

Where to next? Somewhat to my surprise, the anxiety persisted for several months after I returned from Greenland, so it probably wasn't related to the race in any case. What triggered it I have no idea, but I had defeated it in the past and would do so again, even if it took a few months of medication to help me on the way. Once on the road to recovery, there is no better medicine than the uplift I get from my running, whether on the roads and trails at home or in desert or icy landscapes abroad.

The clock continues to tick but I know there is still more to come. I am still making improvements to my personal best time at parkrun, and I have just received my first prize money cheque after over 30 years of running, coming third in my age category at a local half-marathon. See, there are benefits of running into your later years – fewer competitors in your age group.

For the first time in many years, I have run half-marathons in under two hours and, at the age of 66, I have recently completed my fastest ten-kilometre race for 12 years. Don't let age be a barrier that limits your ambitions.

Future adventure destinations? I have my eye on races in Myanmar, in Scandinavia, and I still have unfinished business in South America. A race in the Australian Outback is a definite draw, and I would love to visit and run in New Zealand and meet again the wonderful friends I made in Africa. Antarctica? That might need a lottery win but never say never.

It's an ambitious list and just how much of it I achieve will not only be down to me. One thing is for certain. Aside from my much-loved family and friends, running has enriched my time in this world more than anything else. If you place a small child into an empty, open space, they will start to run around. In that respect, I guess I have just never grown up.

Little did I realise when Chris had that childhood nightmare, and I vowed to go for a run the following morning, just where that journey would take me. Unforgettable experiences, fabulous friendships and confronting Mother Nature in all her extremes. And the journey hasn't ended yet!